MORALITY and LAW

in

CANADIAN POLITICS

THE ABORTION CONTROVERSY

by

Alphonse de Valk

PALM PUBLISHERS
1949, 55th AVENUE, DORVAL
1974

Palm Publishers
1949, 55th Avenue, Dorval
Montréal, P.Q., Canada

ISBN 0-919-366-36-8

Library of Congress Catalog Number 74-79210

Printed in Canada by Ateliers des Sourds (Mtl) Inc. 85 De Castelnau, St., West

Introduction

Throughout the sixties, countries belonging to the Western civilization have gone through a major social revolution which has centered around the morality and mores of marriage and sex. The term revolution, so often abused to describe one change or another, is here applied correctly, I believe, in view of the age-old traditions which have been attacked and overthrown in such a short period of time.

It is still too early to see the nature, the direction or the consequences of this revolution in detail. Some will argue that Western society has once again made a great leap forward; others that we are witnessing the decline and degeneration of our civilization. At any rate, at no time have more people been concerned and involved in the discussion of these complex issues than in the sixties. As a result legislative bodies throughout the Western hemisphere have been forced to confront and discuss these issues at length. Among these issues, the most prominent and controversial one has been abortion.

An investigation of the recent legal and political history of the abortion controversy in this country should not be looked upon as something of interest to professional historians only. Abortion is one of the rare examples of a legal reform which stirs up more controversy after the law has been amended than before. An examination of newspapers across the country will show that after the law was changed in 1969, few issues have been given more space and attention than abortion.[1] All this attention clearly points to the desirability for an account of its recent history, so that the present issue can be seen in the perspective of its own immediate past.

In Canada the abortion question involves two separate levels of government. As a question of law and as an item in the Criminal Code it comes under federal jurisdiction; as a question of medical technology and an item in the health departments it falls under the authority of the provinces. The application of the new legal permissiveness in the matter of abortions, therefore, rests firstly with local communities and hospitals and, secondly, with provincial governments.

---

1. For example, during the 8-month period of April 1 – Nov. 30, 1970, the Toronto *Globe and Mail* carried 45 articles and news-reports, six editorials, plus assorted letters to the editor, distributed over the entire period. In the non-typical week of Friday Jan. 28 – Friday Feb. 4, 1972 the same paper carried 10 news-reports, 1 editorial and half a dozen letters to the editor on the subject.

Whatever action these bodies deem necessary will hinge on what people think the law means or what they think the law is meant to accomplish. Furthermore, it will depend on what legal technicalities and the wording of the law will allow people to think and do, whether or not this conforms to the original intentions of the legislators. It is the author's belief that the new law has come to mean something quite different from what the government which introduced it, and the many public bodies and legislators who supported it, intended it to mean.

The object of this book is to explain how and why the law in Canada was changed. Chapter one recalls the background and the international influences at work upon the developments in Canada. Chapter two describes the attitude of the press, and the role of some Canadian professional associations in generating a consensus favourable to change. Chapter three describes the increased agitation for legal abortion and briefly recalls the events surrounding the issues of birth control and divorce whose political treatment immediately preceded that of abortion. Like abortion, both issues touched upon marital morality and both required changes in the Criminal Code. Chapters four to seven examine in detail the developments during 1967, especially the public pressure brought to bear by the *Globe and Mail*, the examination of the abortion issue by a Committee of the House of Commons and the introduction of revisions to the Criminal Code in December 1967. Chapter eight discusses developments within the Roman Catholic Church which had a direct bearing upon the issue. Chapter nine relates the debate in the House of Commons in the spring of 1969 and the final position of political parties and individuals before the vote. This chapter concludes the formal historical account of the controversy.

The author hopes that in chapters one to nine which deal exclusively with the *history* of the controversy, he has presented as fair and as neutral an account as may be made. Perhaps it is useful to note that this examination is restricted to the debate in the *public* forum. Opinion polls or studies which have remained unpublished or which failed to draw the attention of Canadians have not been taken into account. Radio and television programs, though belonging to the public forum, have not been examined either, but the author believes that abortion was rarely mentioned in those media until sometime in the early seventies when it became a fairly regular topic of discussion. Among the foremost opinion makers are editorials in magazines and newspapers. These have been used extensively even though it is impossible to trace the views expressed in any particular editorial to a particular number of people. The author believes that the role of the Toronto newspaper, the *Globe and Mail*, has been an important one. Not only is it the only Canadian paper which is read nationally, but it also seems to be the most determined among newspapers to influence national and provincial legislation through the nature and quality of its editorials and news-reports. On the other hand, no thorough examination of the French-Canadian press has been attempted, because of lack of resources. This is less serious than may first appear. The legalization of abortion has been first and foremost an issue in English-speaking Canada just as it became an issue in

England and the United States long before it arose as an issue in France or Western continental Europe.

Finally, the author himself takes position in chapter ten. Adding a few notes on what has happened since 1969 and briefly examining the issue which was basic to the entire controversy, namely the relationship of law and morality in a pluralistic society, this chapter is essentially interpretative. Some people will disagree with its interpretation. But it seemed rather inappropriate to examine and to relate the Canadian history of an issue which is more controversial than ever without presenting certain conclusions and opinions which were formed as a consequence of this study.

The author gratefully acknowledges the patience of those who have lent assistance in one way or another, especially his colleague Professor E. J. McCullough. He also extends his thanks to Dr. Margot King, Marlie Gleason, and Professor Margaret Dutli.

This book is published with the help of a grant from the Social Science of Research Council of Canada using fund provided by the Canada Council.

Contents

CHAPTER I

Origins and Background

The Canadian movement to widen the grounds for abortion had its primary ideological origins in Great Britain. While discussions at home and abroad may have had a variety of origins, there are several reasons why the developments in Canada have been influenced more by the events in Britain than by those from elsewhere. For one thing, English speaking Canada has traditionally closely reflected the British moral climate. For another, the ideology of British political parties is parent to much of the ideology of Canadian parties.[1]

Perhaps of most consequence in the question of British influence is the fact that Canada's legal system is derived directly from that of Great Britain. Not only did the British North America Act preserve existing common law, but when criminal law came to be codified in 1892 the (Canadian) Bill Respecting Criminal Law closely followed the earlier British Draft Code of 1880. The 1892 Code was further consolidated in 1906 and 1927, with the 1906 consolidation expressly preserving the criminal law of England insofar as this had not been altered by (Canadian) Statute.[2]

It is not surprising, therefore, that British judicial decisions and interpretations have had a profound influence upon Canadian law, or that British Royal Commissions and legislation have had considerable influence on Canadian legislation. As the president of the Canadian Bar Association, J.R. Weir, stated at the annual meeting of the Association in 1966: "we tend to make a change in our law only after England has done so."[3]

Britain

In Britain abortion was not codified into a statute until 1803. Previous to that date "ancient and persistent" common law traditions reaching back well into the Middle Ages, "traditionally treated abortion as a grave crime."[4] The 1803 codification merely made into a statute what

---

1. This is especially true for the British Labour Party and the Canadian NDP, whose members have been prominent in demanding changes in the Criminal Code.
2. See Alan Mewett, "The Criminal Law, 1867-1967," *The Canadian Bar Review*, Dec. 1967, pp. 726-740.
3. See Presidential Address, *Can. Bar Journal*, 1966, p. 341. He also added that as time passes the gap between British and Canadian law tends to widen.
4. Norman St. John-Stevas, "Abortion and the Law" in *The Dublin Review*, 1967, pp. 274-299.

2 MORALITY AND LAW IN CANADIAN POLITICS

had been considered a criminal offense by custom, although it may be noted that in England the law never equated abortion with murder. This term has been reserved exclusively for an attack upon life already born.[5]

The 1803 statute was changed several times until it was consolidated in 1861 in Section 58 of the Offences Against the Person Act. The significant clause of the 1861 Act reads as follows:

> Every woman, being with child, who, with intent to procure her own miscarriage, shall unlawfully administer to herself any poison or other noxious thing, or shall unlawfully use any instrument or other means whatsoever with the like intent, and whosoever, with intent to procure the miscarriage of any woman, whether she be or not with child, shall unlawfully administer to her or cause to be taken by her any poison or other noxious thing, or shall unlawfully use any instrument or other means whatsoever with the like intent, shall be guilty of felony, and being convicted thereof shall be liable... to be kept in penal servitude for life.[6]

The use of the term "unlawfully" left some uncertainty whether there were circumstances when abortion could be lawful. In fact the Commissioners who drew up the earlier Criminal Law report of 1846 had suggested a provision allowing abortion to save the life of the mother. But it is not at all certain that that suggestion was reflected in the use of the term "unlawfully" in 1861. The term may have been added accidentally.[7]

With the establishment of Confederation in 1867 Canada inherited this Act together with the rest of British civil and criminal legislation, insofar as it had not been abrogated by local colonial law. As noted above, the Canadian body of criminal law went through several consolidations including one in 1955 which was more a revision than a mere consolidation. Yet, the Canadian Code still faithfully reflected its British parent which now included a change introduced in 1929. In that year the British parliament finally took up the suggestion of the 1846 Commissioners and passed the Infant Life (Preservation) Act. This Act allowed that under its own provisions abortion could be lawful if done in good faith for the preservation of the life of the mother.[8] Section 58 of the Offenses Against the Person Act and Section 1 of the 1929 Act had parallel sections in the Canadian Code, namely Sections 237 and 289. There was only one difference. Perhaps because of faulty drafting, Section 237 of the 1955 revised Code did not contain the word "unlawfully" even though this term had appeared in the Canadian Code prior to 1955. Its absence and the consequent opinion of some interpretations that Canadian law, therefore, did not permit abortions for any reason whatever, not even to save the mother's life, may have played a role in changing the attitude of the Canadian

---

5. *Ibid.,* p. 276.
6. *Ibid.,* p. 274.
7. *Ibid.,* p. 276, footnote 1.
8. *Ibid.,*

Medical Association in favour of abortion law revision.[9]

Another important British development came in 1938 with the famous Bourne case. An English court upheld a gynecologist who pleaded not guilty to a charge of illegal abortion brought against him for terminating the pregnancy of a girl who had been criminally assaulted while under the age of fifteen. The judge held that 'preserving life' was not to be narrowly construed as 'preserving the woman from death', but also included the possibility of the woman becoming a "physical or mental wreck."

This decision represented a major departure. 'Preservation from death' is basically a scientific and medical decision even though absolute medical certainty can never be attained. Preservation from the possibility of becoming a physical or mental wreck, however, is something essentially different and based not on what medical evidence says *will* happen, but on what society believes *may* happen, not only for medical reasons, but also for social, economic or cultural reasons.[10]

The Bourne decision was undoubtedly a reflection of the shifting climate of opinion. By 1939 the movement for the changed legal status of abortions was well under way, primarily in association with the spreading knowledge of contraceptives and budding programs and promotions of birth control. At this time, too, some of the stock arguments in favour of legalized abortions were developing: that it

---

9. cf. Lederman, J.J. "The Doctor, Abortion and the Law, A Medicolegal Dilemma", *C.M.A.J.* (Can. Med. Assoc. Journal), Vol. 87, August 1962, pp. 216ff. Reprinted in *The Canadian Bar Journal*, Feb. 1963, pp. 136-147. Also Lederman, J.J. and Parker, G.E., "Therapeutic Abortion and the Canadian Criminal Code", *The Criminal Law Quarterly*, Vol. 6, June 1963, pp. 36-85.

L. held that Section 209, while under certain conditions allowing some mutilating procedure upon a viable child to preserve the life of the mother, did not refer to the procurement of abortions, *C.B.J.*, p. 139. To some extent the argument was one of semantics because the general opinion among medical men was that "abortion" to save the life of the mother was permitted. It remained that way even after the appearance of Dr. Lederman's articles.

Edson Haines, solicitor of the Ontario Medical Assoc., disagreed almost at once (*O.M.R.*, Sept. 1962, pp. 761ff.) Three years later the Therapeutic Abortion Committee of the OMA simply stated as authoritative that in Mr. Haines' opinion "it is lawful to terminate a pregnancy when the procedure is essential to preserve the physical or mental health of the mother." *Report to Council*, 1965, p. 5. At the abortion hearings of the Commons Committee of Health and Welfare, Dr. Aitken, assistant secretary of the CMA, answered the question 'In what cases can a doctor perform a legal abortion today?' with: 'The Criminal Code gives one indication only and that is where the life of the mother is threatened.' On further questioning he admitted that this did not appear to be an 'unquestioned right.' *Proceedings*, 1967, Oct. 31, pp. 107 + 108.

Mr. Lederman's arguments were quoted again in a 1966 *Chatelaine* article. Earl Damude, "The Medical Discovery that could legalize Abortion", Sept., 1966, pp. 35ff.

10. Leaving aside the problem of the term 'abortion' itself, J.J. Lederman, in the articles cited above, appears, in my opinion, to have misunderstood the significance of the Bourne case. Rather than forming "the foundation upon which rests the generally accepted legality of therapeutic abortion in England", as he claims, the Bourne case provided the foundation for a new interpretation of the phrase 'preserving life', namely one that included mental health, thereby allowing for a much broader range of 'therapeutic' abortions than what had been acceptable until then.

would reduce illegal abortions; that it would stop "discrimination" against the poor; that it would help the poor to limit their families.

The second world war called a temporary halt to the movement. When the war was over various members of the Conservative and Labour parties attempted to help the cause move forward by introducing private bills, but none met with success, though these efforts were undoubtedly helpful in keeping the issue alive. However, the agitation for legalizing abortion had two turning points, an intellectual and a political one, with the former the more important.

The intellectual turning point in the history of the abortion controversy and, perhaps, in that of modern criminal law in general came in 1957, the year of the *Report of the Committee on Homosexual Offences and Prostitution,* also known as the Wolfenden Report, after its chairman, Sir John Wolfenden. This Report had nothing whatever to do with abortion and it restricted itself to the narrow point of law under its scrutiny, namely homosexuality. Nevertheless, it laid down principles which could be applied to other areas of the Criminal Code. In answer to the question: 'What acts ought to be punished by the state?', the authors answered that the function of criminal law:

> is to preserve public order and decency, to protect the citizen from what is offensive or injurious, and to provide safeguards against exploitation and corruption of others, particularly those who are specially vulnerable because they are young, weak in body or mind, inexperienced, or in a state of special physical, official or economic dependence.

To this it added that:

> there must remain a realm of private morality and immorality which is... not the law's business...

The Report seemed to sum up what most people, rightly or wrongly, believed was appropriate for the state to do in matters which many regarded as belonging to the individual's private life. It coincided with, and was part of, the drive for individual rather than corporate responsibility in matters moral and religious, which was to become so characteristic of the sixties.[12]

The political turning point in Britain came in 1966 with the return to power of a Labour government. Rather than taking direct and open responsibility for the new venture, the government allowed a private member of another party, Mr. David Steel of the Liberals, to introduce the Bill which was to become law in little more than a year, namely in October 1967. Being the first 'reformed' abortion law in a major country of the West European and American civilization it was bound to have a considerable impact upon developments elsewhere.[13]

---

12. Para. 13 and 61, *The Wolfenden Report,* New York, 1963. For a further discussion of the report and its impact, see chapter ten.

13. The impact of Sweden's example, which legalized abortions before the second world war, is not to be minimized, but for many people Sweden seems to have remained a country from which one could expect anything in the area of sexual morality without imitation being necessary or desirable.

The new British law leaves abortion as a residual crime, but provides four categories where it becomes legal and justifiable:[14]
- where there is 'serious risk to the life or grave injury to the health, whether physical or mental' of the pregnant woman, 'before at or after the birth of a child'.
- where 'there is a substantial risk that if the child were born it would suffer from such physical or mental abnormalities as to be seriously handicapped'.
- where 'the pregnant woman's capacity as a mother' would be 'severely overstrained by the care of the child or of another child as the case may be'.
- where the woman becomes pregnant while 'under the age of sixteen' or as the result of rape.

The first category covers life and health, the second provides eugenic grounds, the third concerns social reasons and the fourth covers criminal assault. Together they provide for practically all possibilities with the sole restriction that the provisions of the Infant Life (Preservation) Act are to be preserved, thus protecting unborn babies after the age of twenty-eight weeks.

United States

While Britain led the way in radically widening the legal grounds for abortion, matters did not remain at a standstill in the United States. In 1954 Dr. H. Rosen published a number of papers under the title *Therapeutic Abortion*. In 1955 the Planned Parenthood Federation of America sponsored a conference on abortion. In 1956 the English jurist, Glanville Williams, made a plea for permissive legislation while delivering the Carpentier lectures at the School of Law of Columbia University.[15] These lectures were published the following year as *The Sanctity of Life and the Criminal Law*. In 1958 two more books appeared, Calderone, *Abortion in the United States* and Gebhard et al, *Pregnancy, Birth and Abortions*.[16]

While the movement was gaining strength, it also gained respectability. In 1959 the American Law Institute proposed a radical liberalizing of abortions in its first presentation of a reform of criminal law, the Model Penal Code. Three years later, in the official draft of 1962, this code proposed that abortions be legal if a licensed physician

> believes there is substantial risk that continuance of the pregnancy would gravely impair the physical or mental health of the mother or that the child would be born with grave physical or mental defect, or that the pregnancy resulted from rape, incest, or other felonious intercourse.[17]

---

14. As described in St. John-Stevas, *op. cit.*, p. 278.
15. Robert M. Byrn, "The Future in America", in Abortion issue of *America*, December 9, 1967, p. 710. Professor Williams became president of the Abortion Law Reform Association which handled much of the publicity in Britain until its purpose was achieved with the 1968 Bill. *Illus. London News*, April 27, 1968, p. 16.
16. R.M. Byrn, "The Abortion Question: A Nonsectarian Approach", in *The Catholic Lawyer*, Autumn, 1965, p. 316.
17. *Ibid.*, p. 316.

A first indication of how deeply and rapidly the moral consensus of the middle class establishment and the dominant elite in Western societies was changing, came with the celebrated Van de Put case in Liège, Belgium, in 1962. This case aroused interest throughout the world. Having given birth to a baby girl without arms as a result of taking the thalidomide drug, the mother agreed with her husband, her sister, her mother and the family doctor one week later to give the newborn baby barbiturates in a mixture of honey. Subsequently all five were charged with murder. There was much popular sentiment favouring the defendants and a demand for acquittal. The defense was based on the assertion that the five defendants felt pity for a "hopelessly condemned and wretched human thing who faced a prospective existence without a glimmer of human existence."[18] In his summation the defense attorney stated:

> If you tell the accused that they are not guilty you will have found the human conclusion to this trial. If these people chose a solution which may be erroneous they have only to account to their own conscience. God, perhaps, has already forgiven them. You may disapprove of the stand they took, but you cannot condemn them.[19]

The all male jury found the defendants not guilty.

The early sixties were also the years of the birth control debate and the controversy about the pill. Frequently enough, though not always, those who favoured most strongly the free circulation of birth control information and the public availability of contraceptive devices, were also inclined to favour abortion. Certainly those who actively promoted abortion always came from their ranks and they often considered abortion part and parcel of one and the same movement. The first president of the Association for the Study of Abortion, Dr. Robert Hall wrote in the *Columbia University Forum,* Winter 1963: "Birth control in its broadest sense includes contraception, sterilization and abortion, none of which will suffice alone." In the following issue of the *Forum* he wrote: "The birth control cause extends from sex education to contraception to sterilization to abortion."[20] Other promoters of the movement made similar statements.[21] Mr. Lawrence Lader, in advocating a more liberal law stated:

> ...though abortion is surely no substitute for conventional birth control, liberal laws might even offer poor mothers with large families an opportunity to limit the number of off-spring.[22]

---

18. *Boston Globe,* Nov. 13, 1962, as quoted in Harrington, "Abortion-Part VI", *Linacre Quarterly,* August 1967, p. 250.
19. *Ibid.,* The Toronto *Globe and Mail* carried front page reports on Nov. 6 and 12, 1962, and on page two on November 9, 1962.
20. *America,* "The Birth Control Cause", June 5, 1965, pp. 818-19.
21. R.M. Byrn, "The Future in America," *op. cit.,* p. 710
22. *New York Times* magazine, April 25, 1965, quoted by P.V. Harrington, "Abortion", in *Linacre Quarterly,* Feb., 1966, p. 81.

The International Planned Parenthood group actively promoted abortion at international gatherings such as the 1965 World Population Conference at Belgrade.[23]

By the mid-sixties an increasing number of commentaries had begun to appear, first in the more serious periodicals, then in the more popular magazines, most of them calling for radical changes. In 1964 the *American Bar Association Journal*, for example, published an article in which a lawyer and a doctor urged modification of the law in conformity with what they considered modern medical practice.[24] By 1965 the popular press began to find the abortion controversy an attractive subject providing the magazines with the opportunity to be at once progressive and popular. Abortions, of course, fitted both the increasingly dominant trend towards greater sexual freedom and the revolt against traditional authority of any kind, whether political, social, moral, legal or religious.

Pageant, the *Saturday Evening Post*, *Parents Magazine*, the *Atlantic Monthly*, *Redbook*, *New York Times Magazine*, *Look* and other magazines all pleaded for liberalized abortion laws. The subject was usually dealt with in a standard version, opening with a series of horror stories of bungled back-street abortions, followed by statements of indignation at the absence of safe legal ways, and proceeding with quotes from eminent doctors in favour of abortions. The article would then move on to a consideration of proposed law reforms and conclude with an illustration of a particular bill going through a state legislature. From the illustration it would become clear that members of only one Church opposed the new legislation, and that the attitude of this Church compared unfavourably with that of more 'broadminded' and 'progressive' religious bodies. Indeed, its attitude could be explained only as an unacceptable attempt to impose the views of a minority upon the majority.[25]

By 1966 the promoters of revised abortion laws seemed to have almost won their battle. In January of that year a nationwide Gallup poll indicated that there was a growing public consensus in favour of legal abortions. Of the people interviewed, 77 per cent favoured laws permitting abortion where pregnancy placed the mother's *health* (rather than her *life*) in danger. Fifty-four per cent would legally permit abortion if the child might be born deformed. Only a minority, 18 per cent, approved of abortion as a means of preventing the birth of a child that the family would not be able to support.[26] Four years later fourteen states had changed their abortion laws, including New York which had removed practically all restrictions.

---

23. *Ibid.*, p. 83.
24. Leavy and Kummer, "Criminal Abortion: A Failure of Law," *A.B.A.J.*, 52 (1964), cf. *Catholic Lawyer*, Spring 1964, p. 161.
25. See the analysis of an article in *Look*, Oct. 19, 1965, as typical of this genre, by F. Canavan, "History Repeats Itself," *America*, May 21, 1966, p. 738. The church in question was, of course, the Roman Catholic Church.
26. Editorial, *America*, Feb. 12, 1966, p. 219.

CHAPTER II

Abortion in Canada 1960 – 1965

In view of the developments in Britain and the United States, it would have been surprising if Canadian history had taken a different road. Influenced by one country in matters of legal theory and legal precedents, and subjected by another country's popular mass media to the latest trend in social behaviour, public opinion in Canada, especially in English Canada, was simply swept along. Nevertheless, the Canadian development is not without distinctive characteristics, as is its final product, the new abortion law itself.

PHASE ONE:

The Press in Canada

Abortions were first openly advocated in Canada in the late fifties. In August 1959 *Chatelaine*, the Canadian women's magazine, published what was probably the first article in a popular Canadian periodical to call for legalized abortions.[1] Though the article's headline ended in a question mark the author left no doubt that Canada's abortion law should be amended. She called the law "the world's harshest," and claimed that it forced "desperate women to seek help from a vicious back-room racket that often deals in death." As support for future change she pointed to the discussions in Britain and the proposal of the American Law Institute. While events had not yet advanced that quickly in Canada, she could point to a recent symposium on the meaning of 'therapeutic abortion' by the *University of Toronto Medical Journal* in which several doctors had expressed their preference for a different law.

In favouring a revision of the Criminal Code clause on abortion, *Chatelaine* was to remain alone among popular magazines for half a dozen years. Canada's national magazine, *Maclean's*, published by the same Toronto company as *Chatelaine*, did not broach the subject until 1967, although, like practically every other public organ in the country, *MacLean's* had earlier attacked the birth control clause of the Criminal Code.[2] However, *Chatelaine* did receive support from

---

1. Joan Finnigan, "Should Canada change its Abortion Law?", *Chatelaine,* August, 1959, pp. 17, 103ff.
2. There were two descriptive articles in the French language edition of *Maclean's* before this date: "Le Drame de l'avortement," March 1963 and Constantineau, G., "Une séance chez l'avorteur numéro 1 de Montréal", November 1966. The birth control clause was attacked in "Hypocrisy in the Criminal Code: 'preventing conception' is an offense", Editorial, *Maclean's,* March 21, 1964, p. 4.

two other important publications, the United Church *Observer* and the Toronto *Globe and Mail.*

In its 19th General Council of 1960 the United Church had already approved the legality of therapeutic abortions for physical or mental reasons. At that time this Church still disapproved of abortion either as a means of family planning or as relief to the unmarried mother.[3] But from then on the thinking of many ministers and official bodies in this Canadian Church was to go through a rapid evolution.[4]

A United Church minister of Vancouver, the Reverend Ray Goodall, published an article in favour of permitting abortion in the March 1963 *Chatelaine.* He charged that the Canadian abortion law was not only wrong but cruel and "grossly immoral". "There is no human life in an embryo; it is simply living tissue", he stated, and "human life begins with birth and therefore abortion can never be the destruction of human life."[5] The same author had earlier made a strong plea for world-wide scientific birth control in a 1961 issue of the United Church *Observer,* claiming, among other things, that "abstinence and continence are fine for saints and celibates; the majority of men and women are neither."[6]

In a May 1963 issue of the *Observer,* the Rev. Goodall repeated his *Chatelaine* plea in a somewhat more subdued tone.[7] It was the counterpart to a lead article by the Rev. Gerald Paul who in the March issue of the same magazine argued that abortion was wrong.[8] That article in turn, was a reply to an earlier *Globe and Mail* editorial calling for a change in the law. Four years later the same Rev. Paul published in *Chatelaine* a laudation on the exciting and liberating new morality ("New Moralists insist that charity... not chastity, is the chief virtue". The New Morality insists that persons are more important than principles. The New Morality is not anti-Christ; rather, it is the church catching up to Christianity").[9] As one illustration among many of how quickly a man changes his mind, the minister, campus chaplain by then, mentioned that once he, too, had taken

3. "Christian conscience cannot approve abortion, either as a means of limiting or spacing one's family, or as relief to the unmarried mother, because it involves the destruction of human life. However, if in the judgment of reputable medical authorities the continuation of pregnancy seriously endangers the physical or mental health of the mother, therapeutic abortion may be necessary."

4. By 1971 the Council had come to accept abortion as a private matter between a woman and her doctor, morally justifiable not only in medical but also in certain social and economic circumstances, and to be freely available on request.

5. Rev. Ray Goodall, "Is Abortion ever right?" *Chatelaine,* March 1963, pp. 40 & 48. *Chatelaine* did not mention abortion again until 1966: Earl Damude, "The Medical Discovery that could legalize Abortion", Sept. 1966, pp. 35ff. Also see editorial August 1967. *Chatelaine* opposed the 1969 legislation and has favoured its repeal and abortion on demand since.

6. R.M. Goodall, "Our crowded world needs Scientific Birth Control", U.C. *Observer,* Feb. 15, 1961.

7. Ray Goodall, "A Case for Induced Abortion," May, 1963, U.C. *Observer,* pp. 15-16.

8. "Abortion is Wrong," United Church *Observer,* March 15, 1963, pp. 16-17.

9. Rev. Gerald W. Paul, "The New Morality," *Chatelaine,* June 1967, pp. 29, 95-96.

a strong stand against abortion.[10]

While *Chatelaine* espoused legalized abortion openly among its women readers, and the *Observer* raised both pros and cons in a more balanced context among members of the United Church, the Toronto *Globe and Mail* had become the most formidable protagonist of the legalization of abortion among the general public. It supported the movement from the beginning and, indeed, has been primarily responsible for systematically drawing the attention of the wider public to the issue.

Among the first reports on opinions in Canada, a Canadian Press story published in the *Globe and Mail* at the end of August 1961 set off a chain reaction of lasting consequence. A top official of the British Columbia division of the Canadian Medical Association, Dr. E.C. McCoy, had called for modification of the law to allow legal abortions for broad physical or mental reasons. The report stated that members of Parliament for the Vancouver area, NDPers as well as Conservatives, favoured a thorough investigation of the matter by the federal government. Another doctor, P.L. McGeer, professor at the University of British Columbia, was also quoted as forecasting that abortion would eventually become a scientific question rather than the moral one it was now. Furthermore, the report gave the opinion of Professor Michael Wheeler at the UBC School of Social Work that induced abortion was "no more suitable a subject for the Criminal Code than suicide, contraception or voluntary sterilization." "But", said the professor "the chances of getting agreement on this in Canada are about as good as for those for the re-unification of Germany."[11]

The very next day the *Globe* made a first attempt to prove Mr. Wheeler's forecast wrong. In an editorial entitled "The Abortion Issue", the *Globe* recapitulated the information of the previous day, adding that in the opinion of Professor Douglas Cannell, head of the obstetrics department at the University of Toronto, "the general feeling was that the laws do need revision." Referring to illegal abortions and to the fact that many women were obviously following a moral code of their own, the editorial somewhat cautiously queried whether "such women should be permitted to make their own moral decision." This is a question, it said,

> which is beginning to be asked seriously not only in Canada, but in the United States, Britain, and a number of European countries. The churches have a right to present their view of the moral issue to their adherents; but is this perhaps where their right should stop and that of the individual begin? A law which is rejected by the public is seldom a sound law...[12]

Having drawn attention to the issue of abortion for the first time, the paper then invited seven representatives of the professions and

---

10. *Op. cit.,* p. 96. As another illustration he hinted at his changed feelings about euthanasia.

11. "Relaxation of Federal Abortion Law is asked by B.C. Doctor", *Globe and Mail,* August 31, 1961, p. 1.

12. *Globe and Mail,* Sept. 1, 1961, p. 6.

the churches to express their views in a series of articles. In October 1961, under the title 'Murder or Mercy', the *Globe* presented the views of Norman Borins, Q.C.; the Rt. Rev. F.H. Wilkinson, Anglican Bishop of Toronto; Gordon George, Superior of the Jesuit province of Upper Canada; Dr. B. Schlesinger, lecturer in the School of Social Work, University of Toronto; Dr. Abraham Feinberg, rabbi emeritus of Holy Blossom Temple, Toronto; Dr. L. Harkins, obstetrician-gynecologist for the Toronto Academy of Medicine; and G.P. Gilmour, former president of McMaster University.[13]

Mr. Borins favoured an extension of the law permitting abortion, first, to save the life of the mother, secondly, to prevent serious physical or mental injuries, and finally, in the case of sexual assault. "The effect of the law in its present state", he said, "is not to eliminate abortion but to compel secrecy and abortions by unqualified abortionists." The Anglican bishop found it difficult to regard an unborn life and a mature personality as of equal merit. He supported Dr. Fletcher's opinion expressed in the book, *Morals in Medicine*, that "to refuse to interrupt or prevent a pregnancy from rape would be an obvious injustice." Father Gordon George rejected abortion absolutely on the grounds that an evil means may never be used, not even to procure some presumed good.

Dr. Schlesinger attempted to show that reasonable people had accepted abortion throughout history and that the opposition to it was only the result of the Church's attempt to make the sexual act as difficult as possible. Quoting from Rattray Taylor's book, *Sex in History*, he traced the whole opposition to abortion to a mistranslation of Exodus 21,22 by the church father Tertullian.[14] Professor Schlesinger recommended amending the law to allow abortions for medical, eugenic and humanitarian reasons as well as for mental health. Rabbi Feinberg accepted much the same reasons but with much graver caution and concern for moral values. He reiterated the principle that one life may not be sacrificed to save the life of someone else, but explained that the Talmudic approval of abortion to rescue the mother did not contradict this principle because the embryo was not considered to be really alive and possessed of a soul until extrusion and the completion of the birth-process.

Dr. Harkins explained that some therapeutic abortions were actually being carried out in hospitals for both medical and mental reasons. He welcomed clarification of the law in that respect and forecast that most doctors would be reluctant to request widening of grounds for abortion. Finally, Dr. Gilmour rejected the 'No, even

---

13. *Globe and Mail,* Oct. 2-10, p. 7.

14. Rev. Ray Goodall repeated the same story in his *Observer* article of May 1963 (see above). In reality, approval of abortion has been the exception and opposition to it has been constant throughout history with the earliest references going back to the Sumerian Empire and the Code of Hammurabi, 2000 and 1800 B.C. respectively. Christianity also opposed abortion from its beginning. For a detailed account, see P.V. Harrington, "Abortion – Part VIII', *Linacre Quarterly,* Feb. 1968, pp. 43-60, summarizing the doctoral dissertation, *The Crime of Abortion in Canon Law,* by R.J. Huser, 1942, Cath. Univ. of America. See Appendix nine.

though...' attitude of "certain authoritarian" churches in favour of the "Yes, but..." answer. He approved abortion whenever beneficial, while expressing hesitation and reserve because of the complexity of the problem. Thus, of the seven participants only the representative of the Catholic Church opposed abortion outright.

Except for a half dozen letters to the editors immediately following the series 'Murder or Mercy', the *Globe* did not bring up abortion again until 1963. The Toronto paper, and presumably most Canadian papers, did give extensive coverage to the thalidomide tragedy and to such events as the Van de Put trial in Belgium in November 1962 and the earlier case of Mrs. Finkbine of Arizona.[15] While the thalidomide crisis was short-lived it was, nevertheless, of great and lasting importance. First, it suddenly revealed that many people were quite prepared to allow and accept abortion. Secondly, it became clear that they were prepared to do so on the mere *possibility* of a baby being born seriously deformed.

The next occasion for comment came in December 1962, when Judge Ken Langdon of Oakville publicly recommended that abortion be made legal for unmarried girls under 16 and for victims of rape and, also, that voluntary sterilization be made available for parents of large families. On January 2, 1963, the *Globe* congratulated the judge for his forthrightness. Without direct mention but with clear reference to the August 1961 news report and to its own series of articles in October of that year, the editorial continued:

> Pressure for reform of the laws governing abortion has been growing in recent years at many levels of Canadian society. Highly placed members of the legal, medical and university professions have urged the extension of legal abortion. The National Council of Women presented a brief to the Royal Commission on Health Services which disclosed that illegal abortion is the commonest cause of maternal mortality in Canada. Leading clergymen of major Protestant communions and of the Jewish faith have endorsed extension of legal abortion. Members of Parliament representing all four political parties have also gone on record as favoring extension.

The *Globe* further declared that a law which no longer conformed to the practices of society could bring all law into contempt and that Canada's law had attained this status "because it was fashioned to meet a particular moral code which is no longer embraced by the majority of Canadians." It concluded by recommending that abortion be legalized as proposed by Mr. Borins and Judge Langdon.[16]

---

15. For Van de Put trial, see Chapter one. The Finkbine case occured in August, 1962. Mrs. Finkbine, a Phoenix housewife and local television performer, believed her baby might be deformed. Upon being denied an abortion in Arizona, the then 30-year old mother of four flew to Sweden for an abortion. The foetus was reported deformed. Her case was mentioned again, for instance, by Joan Hollobon in an April 1967 *Globe and Mail* article reporting on a few abortions being done in Canadian hospitals for the same reasons. *Globe and Mail*, April 11, 1967, p. 1.

16. "Two Problems to be Faced", Editorial, *Globe and Mail*, Jan. 2, 1963.

PHASE TWO:

The Professions

The *Globe* editorial of January 1963 may be taken as the beginning of the second, more public and organized phase of the movement for the legalization of abortion in Canada. Although any such division remains arbitrary, the January editorial is useful as a dividing line, because it does mark the beginning of a period of activity by a greater variety of organizations and publicity media. As noted above, both *Chatelaine* and the United Church *Observer* were to run articles strongly in favour of abortion, the former in March, the latter in May 1963. More important, perhaps, the year 1963 also marked the beginning of stirrings among the professional bodies, including the Canadian Medical Association and the Canadian Bar Association.

It must not be supposed that the more public phase of the movement for widening the abortion law was managed or controlled by a central organization. It started rather with spontaneous actions of unrelated semi-public bodies, often as a consequence of developments in what many people considered related areas, such as birth control, contraceptives, divorce and homosexuality. Perhaps the most that may be assumed is that those who took the initiative in proposing changes shared similar views on the place of morality in society.

Canadian Bar Association

An important moment of the second phase came at the time of the annual meeting of the Canadian Bar Association at Banff in September 1963. As in other countries, it was the legal profession which first introduced the question in a systematic form in Canada, under the umbrella of its own large, respected, and influential organization.

A resolution for the amendment of the Criminal Code to legalize abortion was proposed at the meeting of the Association's Section on Criminal Justice. It was sponsored by the British Columbia Subsection of the same name under chairmanship of A. Stewart McMorran. The proposed resolution suggested a Termination Board and offered three grounds for legal abortions: a) danger to the mother's life or health; b) unwanted pregnancy due to rape or a similar unlawful act; c) danger of a mentally or physically defective child.[17] It did not include, therefore, the socio-economic grounds recommended in Britain. There was considerable opposition to the whole idea from the start, but especially to the introduction of the third and last category, that of abortion in case of danger of a defective child. According to the chairman this had been added because of the horror expressed for deformations such as found in the thalidomide babies.[18]

---

17. *Proceedings* of the Canadian Bar Association, Forty-Seventh Annual Meeting, 1965, p. 90. The Proceedings of 1963 and 1964 do not give the text but apparently the 1965 resolution was little different from the original 1963 proposal.

18. *Op. cit.,* pp. 92-93.

The British Columbia Sub-section had also submitted a brief of the B.C. Catholic Lawyers' Guild opposing the motion on the grounds that the "direct taking of an innocent life... is an act clearly forbidden by the laws of God and of our country." This was strongly opposed by Mr. George L. Murray of Vancouver who claimed that, in his opinion, "mixing our religious views with our views as lawyers is a terrible mistake." According to him, "it was once said that Christianity is not a part of the law of Canada."[19] Whether Mr. Murray believed himself to be summing up the state of affairs as it was or as he would like it to have been, was not clear; in any case Mr. John Scollin of Winnipeg declared it was nonsense to say that law had no relation to the Judeo-Christian spirit. Whereupon Mr. Arthur Dawe of Mission, B.C., describing himself as a non-Christian, objected to Christians speaking for all the people of the country. For good measure he added that "only an inhuman person could oppose this progressive step."[20] It was soon clear to everyone that the matter was highly controversial and would require further study.[21] It was decided that the provincial Sub-sections on Criminal Justice would require time for such study and consequently the proposed resolution was held over till the following year.[22]

The postponement incurred the ire of the Toronto *Globe and Mail* which declared the step "regrettable" and a less than courageous "stalling for time." The editorial attacked as "pointless" the position of the spokesman for the B.C. Catholic Lawyers' Guild, Mr. Bruce Emerson, when he said that the abortion issue should not be taken up, because "apart from legal implications, it has religious, social, moral and sociological implications, and in my opinion, the least of these is the legal one." The law of Canada "already permits abortion when it is performed to save the life of the mother," declared the *Globe*, going on to say that the resolution was "a mild one" in view of the necessity to "prevent needless deaths" resulting from illegal abortions. The *Globe* saw the key point of the issue as follows:

> ...what he (Mr. Emerson) is really saying is that the law should not permit some individuals to abide by their own standards of morality, even when society as a whole is not affected.

The *Globe* concluded:

> This raises the whole difficult problem of how far the law should be based on a code of morals, or ethics, which is in turn based on religious belief not shared by many people subject to the law.[23]

At the 1964 annual meeting in Montreal the 1963 abortion resolution of the CBA was deferred for a year once more. The chairman

---

19. Ralph Hyman, "Canadian Bar Stalls B.C. Bid to Have Abortion Laws Relaxed," *Globe and Mail*, Sept. 3, 1963, p. 3. Quote from Catholic Guild's *Brief on Proposed Changes of the Law on Abortions*, September 1963, p. 2.

20. *Ibid.*

21. *Proceedings*, CBA, 1965, pp. 92 & 93.

22. *Proceedings*, CBA, 1963, p. 177.

23. "The Moral Issue," *Globe and Mail*, September 7, 1963.

of the Criminal Justice section could report no more than that the provincial Sub-sections had done "insufficient work."[24] In fact, when the Bar Association met at Toronto in September 1965, that is, two years after the original introduction of the resolution, the chairman of the Criminal Justice Section had to admit again that no written reports had been received from other provincial Sub-sections.[25] This time, however, on his assurances that abortions had definitely been discussed by the Sub-sections even though no written reports had been sent in, the resolution was brought forward for consideration after the Section itself had voted approval first.

On September 3, the *Canadian Press* could report that "legalizing of abortions was urged Thursday by the criminal justice section of the Canadian Bar Association." But *CP* also reported that it appeared doubtful whether the proposal would get the backing of the full association this time.[26] And indeed, once again the resolution did not come to a vote. There was too little time left and there were too few people still at the Conference to pass a resolution on such a controversial issue. Instead, it was decided that all members of the Association be sent a copy of the resolution and that the matter be definitely placed on the agenda for the annual meeting in 1966. It was further suggested that contact be made with the medical profession to ascertain the views of the doctors.[27]

Canadian Medical Association

Like the legal profession, the Canadian Medical Association, too, had begun to discuss the question of therapeutic abortion in 1963. In spite of the fact that British Columbia doctors had first raised the issue in 1961 and had sparked the interest of the *Globe and Mail* at that time, it was Ontario which took the lead in the medical association. On the initiative of the Executive of the Section on Obstetrics and Gynecology, the Ontario Medical Association authorized a special committee for the study of sterilization and therapeutic abortions in its Council meeting of May 1963. The terms of reference required a review of therapeutic abortion (and sterilization) from the standpoint of:

I "The medical indications for procedures of therapeutic abortion and sterilization."

II "Proper hospital machinery for the assessment of such cases."

III "Legal aspects involved in the carrying out of these procedures."[28]

The Board realized that a study of abortion should be conducted "under the premise that the medical aspects, legal requirements, and

---

24. *Proceedings,* CBA, 1964, p. 194.
25. *Proceedings,* CBA, 1965, p. 98.
26. "Legalizing abortions urged," Saskatoon *Star-Phoenix,* Sept. 3, 1965, p. 2.
27. *Proceedings,* CBA, 1968, pp. 92 & 93.
28. Number 96 in "Transactions of Council", May 10, 11 — 1963, O.M.R. *(Ontario Medical Review),* July 1963, p. 418.

religious implications are three distinct areas which must be taken into account." However, it obviously felt competent to study only the medical and technical side of the problem.

Some light on the thinking of the Board at this time is provided by the aims of the study which, in addition to a report on "the modern aspect of this problem" are stated as "Recommendations either for changes in the (Ontario) Public Hospitals Act or for new legislation."[29] The Board apparently did not envisage the possibility that the law might remain unchanged. Another indication of the trend of thought was the fact that therapeutic abortion was to be studied together with sterilization as if there were no qualitative difference between the two subjects.

As for the choice of personnel, the Board was advised "that a senior and highly respected member of the Section (on Obstetrics and Gynaecology) had volunteered to chair the committee." This proved to be Dr. D.M. Low.[30] He was invited to head the section and was subsequently joined by Dr. D.E. Cannell, representing the Maternal Welfare Committee, and Dr. K.G. Gray, both of whom had already indicated that they desired a revision of the law.[31] Together with Dr. M.G. Tompkins of Halifax, these men were to remain the key medical men on the abortion question. Dr. Low and Dr. Cannell presented the Ontario report to the CMA; Dr. Low and Dr. Tompkins, chairman of the CMA Maternal Welfare Committee were the CMA representatives who met with the representatives of the Canadian Bar Association; and all four men, together with Dr. Aitken, the assistant-secretary of the CMA, presented the CMA case at the hearings of the Commons committee considering legislation to legalize abortion in the fall of 1967. At that time Gerald Waring, in his 'Report from Ottawa', wrote as follows in the medical journal:

> Dr. Aitken acted as spokesman for the CMA delegation, which also included Dr. Gregg Tompkins of Halifax and Dr. Douglas Cannell and Dr. Donald Low of Toronto, three distinguished practitioners and teachers of obstetrics and gynecology, and Dr. Kenneth Gray of the Clarke Institute of Psychiatry.
> Dr. Lewis Brand (PC, Saskatoon) referred to them as "distinguished lawbreakers" and Robert Stanbury (L, York-Scarborough) as "the biggest gathering of criminal abortionists ever held in Canada"—a bantering reaction to Dr. Cannell's admission that "I and my colleagues have been breaking the law now for a long time", both in performing therapeutic abortions and in advising patients on methods of contraception.[32]

In short, all four men had long since been convinced of the need for change in the abortion law and were now committed to help bring

---

29. *Op. cit.,* Numbers 95 and 97.

30. *Ibid.*

31. "Transactions of Council, May 25, 26 – 1964", *O.M.R.,* August 1964, p. 606.

32. *C.M.A.J.,* Vol. 97, November 11, 1967, p. 1233. See also Standing Committee on Health and Welfare, *Minutes of Proceedings and Evidence.* (re abortion), No. 4, Oct. 31, 1967, p. 104. (Hereafter referred to as *Proceedings – Abortion*)

it about. Dr. Low, moreover, was also to play an important part in shaping the official views of the United Church, in virtue of being its chief medical advisor on the question of abortion.[33]

The Sterilization and Therapeutic Abortion Committee reported to the Council of the Ontario Medical Association in May 1965, two years from the date of its inception. It recommended that operations terminating a pregnancy be lawful if performed "to preserve the life or physical or the mental health" of the mother, and if they were done in a properly qualified place and manner, after consultation with an abortion committee.[34] The Committee wanted it understood that it had not considered it their function "to encourage 'wide' liberalization" of abortion procedures but "rather to make them legal and to provide... better precautionary standards for the protection of both the public and the profession."[35]

Although the committee had suggested further consultations with other medical sections, Council decided to approve the recommendations without delay. Within a week the *Globe and Mail* could print an editorial congratulating the OMA for having joined the "growing chorus of responsible voices" calling for abortion reforms. Repeating its statement of September 1963, that the existing law permitted abortions even though only to save the life of the mother, the paper called it "a hard and cruel law" which "is so vague, so completely dependent on interpretation, that few lawyers, let alone doctors, profess to know what it means." Declaring once again that the problem had its roots in religious controversy, it concluded with the demand that "this law... be amended to save the health as well as the lives of mothers and to enable doctors to perform their duties according to their conscience and their calling."[36] The *Ontario Medical Review* reprinted the 1965 editorial in its regular feature "Clipper's Corner," just as two years earlier it had reprinted the September 1963 editorial.[37]

After adoption by the Ontario Council, the recommendations were presented to the parent body, the Canadian Medical Association, and its appropriate sub-section, the Committee on Maternal Welfare. The latter met in November 1965, having in the meantime received the proposed resolution of the Criminal Justice Section of the Canadian Bar Association. After studying the lawyers' resolution the committee formulated a proposal which was basically the Ontario model with slight modifications in wording.[38]

---

33. *Proceedings — Abortion,* 1968, No. 18. Feb. 6, 1968, p. 599.
34. "Transactions of Council," May 10, 11 — 1965, *O.M.R.,* July 1965, pp. 505-6.
35. *Report* of the Special Committee on Therapeutic Abortions and Sterilizations, p. 1.
36. "Free the Doctor," *Globe and Mail,* May 18, 1965.
37. *O.M.R.,* June 1965, p. 461.
38. For text, see 'Transactions,' Report on the Committee on Maternal Welfare, *C.M.A.J.* (Can. Med. Assoc. Journal) Vol. 95, Sept. 3, 1966, p. 487.

CHAPTER III

Agitation

The second and preparatory phase of the movement for legal abortions may be said to have drawn to a close at the end of 1965; from the beginning of 1966 the movement was marked by a rapid growth of interest on the part of the general public. During the third phase those who favoured legalization became more impatient; those who opposed it began to take more serious notice of it. Also, important professional and national organizations went on record in favour of a revision of the law. And while in Britain abortion moved into its last legislative phase under international attention, in Canada abortion entered its first legislative phase by being referred to a Standing Committee of the House of Commons.

Yet, while these events were significant steps in the political and legislative evolution of the abortion issue, both public and parliament were, for the time being, more occupied with two other issues: birth control and divorce. Like abortion, both issues touched upon marital morality and, like abortion, both required changes in the Criminal Code. Thus their treatment in parliament provided not only an indication of what might happen to the abortion issue, but, in fact, prepared the way for similar treatment.

Religion

In Great Britain the abortion debate had assumed sharp religious overtones early in 1966 after the Board for Social Responsibility of the Church of England issued an abortion report on December 31, 1965.[1] By the standards of committed abortion reformers, the Anglican Committee ranked almost as reactionary. It rejected abortion on demand, or terminating life for the prevention of possible deformed babies, or abortion for rape. Yet when it came to proposing legislation, it recommended such vague wording as to make the grounds very broad indeed, justifying abortion not only when the mothers's life was threatened, but also when her health or the well-being of her family were endangered. It suggested making "serious injury to the mother's physical or mental well-being" an indication for legal abortion, authorizing doctors to "take into account the patient's total environment, actual or reasonably forseeable."[2]

---

1. *Abortion: An Ethical Discussion,* Westminster, Church House, 1965.
2. Letitia Fairfield "Abortion and the Law" An Anglican Committee's Views. *The Tablet* (London) Jan. 15, 1966, p. 69.

The Roman Catholic primate, John Cardinal Heenan, replied to this statement in his diocesan journal. "Until recently," he wrote, "the accepted view of Christians and, so far as I know, of all believers, has been that direct killing of the child-to-be is immoral." He went on to say that

> It is only because of what is called the liberalizing of the law against abortion that the Catholic attitude has begun to appear eccentric — as if abstaining from killing the fetus in the womb were a Catholic foible like abstaining from meat on Friday...[3]

The Cardinal charged that the Committee deliberately rejected the Christian tradition of viewing the killing of the foetus as a form of homicide by declaring this tradition to be too simple a principle to fit the complexities of the case. "If it is justifiable," he wrote,

> to kill the foetus which may be born deformed because, for example, the pregnant mother has contracted German measles, it is hard to see why children who manage to be born deaf, blind or otherwise handicapped should not be... put to death.[4]

Hardly were Cardinal Heenan's words in print before the bill came up again in the House of Lords and the Anglican Bishop of Exeter, the Right Rev. Robert Cecil Mortimer, walked out of the debate in protest against attacks upon the unborn child.

While Canadian Catholic weeklies passed on to their readers the words of the British Cardinal Heenan, the national monthly of the Anglican Church in Canada, the *Canadian Churchman*, reviewed favourably the report of its British Sister Church.[5] Indeed, this report eventually provided the basis for the policy formulation of the Canadian Anglican Church in its submission to the House of Commons in the fall of 1967. The Anglican brief recommended the report to the Commons Committee.[6]

In Canada, too, the issue began to be explained more and more in terms of religion and Church membership, following the direction indicated by the *Globe and Mail*. Often, appearances seemed to confirm that only Roman Catholics opposed the legalization of abortion. Dr. D.M. Low, speaking at the annual meeting of the United Church of Canada's Board of Evangelism and Social Service held in February of that year, reported that out of 177 active treatment hospitals in Ontario only the 40 Roman Catholic-administered hospitals totally disapproved of abortion. Furthermore, out of 187 obstetricians and

---

3. *Westminister Cathedral Chronicles*, February issue, as quoted in *Western Catholic Reporter*, Edmonton, Feb. 24, 1966, p. 3.
4. *Ibid.*, See also *Prairie Messenger*, Saskatchewan's Catholic weekly, Feb. 16, 1966, p. 2.
5. "Some abortions may be justified", *Canadian Churchman*, March 1966, pp. 12 & 19.
6. *Proceedings — Abortion*, 1967, December 15, Appendix "B B", p. 474.

gynecologists surveyed in Ontario, 169 approved widening the grounds
for therapeutic abortions. The remainder were, presumably, once again
Roman Catholics.[7]

The notion that only Catholics opposed abortion found further
credence when the largest Protestant Church, the United Church of
Canada, appeared ready to accept wider grounds for legal abortions.
At the above-mentioned February meeting of the Board of Evangelism,
the secretary of the Board, Rev. R.J. Hord, blamed the law for
consigning thousands of women annually to "illegal back-room abortionists."[8] A resolution was passed in favour of legal abortions, not
just when a mother's life was endangered, but also when her mental
or physical health was threatened. While in 1960 the General Council
had started its statement on abortion with the clause that the
"Christian conscience cannot approve abortion," in February 1966 the
Board of Evangelism made no mention of this. Instead, it declared
that the sections on abortion in the Criminal Code were "conflicting,
leaving the impression that abortion is wrong and even murderous
in all circumstances." It also denounced "the air of secrecy and guilt
surrounding abortions." The Board's decision was duly publicized
before it was sent on to the General Council.[9]

When the General Council met for its 22nd annual meeting six
months later, in September 1966, a resolution based on the proposal
of the Board of Evangelism was readily adopted. It justified abortion
"when the life of the foetus threatens the life or health of the mother."[10]
None of the 400 clerical and lay delegates stood to oppose it. Rev.
A.R. Huband of Toronto was quoted as saying that "Every child has
a right to be well born, and in some cases this means the right not
to be born at all."[11] Favouring birth control and favouring abortion,
he said, involved "a reverence for a quality of life rather than for
life itself."[12]

National Organizations

While some Churches gradually changed their position, other organizations, too, took a stand. Some were small, like the Planned Parenthood Group in Edmonton, which in April voted in favour of widening
the abortion laws.[13] Others were of medium size, such as the 45,000
member Central Ontario Women's Institute which called abortion laws
archaic and futile.[14] One group, the National Council of Women of
Canada, was very large. A federation of approximately 1800 organiza-

7. "Pressure to ease Abortion laws...," *Western Catholic Reporter,* Feb. 24, 1966,
   p. 3.
8. *Ibid.*
9. "Churchmen urge wider ground for legal abortion," *Globe and Mail,* February
   16, 1966, p. 3.
10. *Proceedings — Abortion,* 1968, Feb 6, Appendix "L L," p. 627.
11. "United Church backs therapeutic abortion," *Globe and Mail,* Sept. 13, 1966.
12. *Ibid.*
13. *Western Catholic Reporter,* April 21, 1966, p. 1.
14. Canadian Press report, "High abortion rate..." Saskatoon *Star Phoenix,* No-
    vember 6, 1965.

tions with 800,000 members, this body was the first national organization to go on record in favour of legal abortions. It adopted a resolution as early as June 1964, during its annual meeting in Hamilton. Subsequently, the resolution was presented to the government twice, on January 21, 1965 and again on January 31, 1966. Although it urged the government to establish a Royal Commission to provide "an objective and non-partisan basis for amending the law," it also called the existing law "confused, conflicting, outdated, and in certain instances, cruel and unjust," thus leaving no doubt about its own attitude. The reason given for this resolution was the need "to bring these laws into conformity with the realities of Canadian life."[15] Among the various national bodies only one organization defied the trend. At its 46th national convention in Hamilton in September 1966 the Catholic Women's League, representing 160,000 women mainly in English speaking Canada, urged the government to reject broader abortion laws.[16]

Also during 1966 the Canadian Medical Association and the Canadian Bar Association completed the internal process of consultation Before presenting their proposal to the general meeting of the Canadian Medical Association, the Committee on Maternal Welfare, which was in charge of the abortion resolution, desired to seek further consultation with the CBA. As a result of the initiative of the Committee on Medical Aspects of Traffic Accidents, the CMA had already adopted a motion at its annual meeting in June of 1965 to investigate the possibility for a Medical-Legal Liaison Committee in conjunction with the CBA.[17] The initiative was put to good use and the Chairman of the Maternal Welfare Committee, Dr. M.G. Tompkins, together with Dr. Low, discussed the abortion resolutions with representatives of the CBA in Ottawa on two Saturdays in April 1966.[18] In these meetings the doctors strongly disagreed with the lawyers' proposed Termination Board and they questioned the CBA's third ground for legal abortions, the possibility of a defective child.[19]

Unable to agree, the medical men went ahead with their own recommendation. In a May issue, the Association's medical journal could report that the Executive Committee meeting on April 29 and 30th had received reports from 24 Standing Committes for submission to the annual meeting in Edmonton, including a recommendation of the Maternal Welfare Committee that "sterilization and therapeutic abortion should be made lawful when performed under certain circumstances."[20] Two months later newspapers reported that the CMA in its annual meeting at Edmonton had officially approved the legislation

15. For Text of 1964 resolution, see *Proceedings — Abortion*, 1967 Dec. 8, p. 396. The press stressed the Royal Commission more than the abortion aspect. The *Globe* report of June 1964 refers only to the Royal Commission. Its January 1965 report mentions only birth control.

16. *Globe and Mail*, Sept. 1, 1966, *Prairie Messenger*, Sept. 7, 1966, pp. 1 & 16.

17. "Association News" in *C.M.A.J.*, Vol. 94, Jan. 15, 1966, p. 149.

18. April 2nd and April 23rd, 1966, "Administrative Reports 1965-6", *Can. Bar Journal*, Oct. 1966, p. 381.

19. *C.M.A.J.*, Vol. 95, p. 487.

20. "Association News, *C.M.A.J.*, Vol. 95, May 21, 1966, p. 1137.

of abortion. A motion to add to the medical resolution the indications for legal abortions proposed by the CBA had been defeated and the approved resolution was still essentially the same as the one proposed a year earlier by the Ontario Medical Association.[21]

Again the *Globe and Mail* had cause to cheer. Under the title "A Long Overdue Reform", it called the CMA's decision "a landmark." "More important perhaps than the recommendation itself" the paper wrote, "was the rationale behind it. Dr. M.G. Tompkins, chairman of the association's committee on maternal welfare, put it rather well when he said that an amendment to the Criminal Code to permit therapeutic abortions would only 'legalize what has been done and is being done'." The *Globe* interpreted this statement to mean that in the opinion of the CMA, legalization would nullify the need for illegal back-street abortions which the paper estimated "at between 20,000 and 120,000 annually."[22] Dr. Tompkins, however, was probably referring to the small number of therapeutic abortions already being carried out in hospitals. One year later, at the hearings of the abortion Committee of the House of Commons, he and his colleagues refused to commit themselves to the view that legal abortions would necessarily reduce the illegal ones. Their answers ranged from 'I don't know', to 'It is possible, but not very likely'.[23]

Canadian Bar Association

In spite of the disagreement with the medical men the Canadian Bar Association, too, proceeded with its own, slightly revised, resolution. By this time its proposal included a lengthy second part dealing with provincial Termination Boards which were supposed to judge the necessity of an abortion in cases of criminal assault. A copy of this resolution was sent to all members of the association in June 1966 in preparation for discussion and a vote at the Bar Association's annual meeting in Winnipeg in the following August.[24]

The CBA debate at the end of that month was lively and at times emotional. It lasted three hours and illustrated two things. First of all, it showed that the climate of opinion among the population had shifted so much that approval of the resolution was a foregone conclusion. Secondly and more significantly, it indicated the almost totally diverse roads by which proponents and opponents of the resolution had arrived at their respective positions.

The arguments for and against never met on common ground. The division between pros and cons was not one between those who found different answers to the same question; rather it was a division between people who had answers to different questions. Insisting that their own questions were the more important and legitimate ones,

---

21. *C.M.A.J.*, Vol. 95, Sept. 3, 1966, p. 487.
22. *Globe and Mail*, June 18, 1966. The editorial was reprinted in the *Ontario Medical Review*, (*O.M.R.*, July 1966, p. 545).
23. See *Proceedings — Abortion*, 1967, No. 4, pp. 98ff.
24. "Administrative Reports, 1965-6", *C.B.J.*, Oct. 1966, p. 381. Records of the debate appear in *Proceedings* of the Canadian Bar Association, Vol. 49, 1966, pp. 74-120.

overriding consideration of any others, they found themselves in opposing positions. Those who favoured the resolution were interested only in asking: What is to be done about illegal abortions here and now? On the other hand, those who opposed the resolution wanted first an answer to the question: Is abortion moral or immoral? Is it good or bad for society? Proponents of wider grounds for abortion had no patience with these questions, while opponents of abortion revision were maddened by the suggestion that something could be presented as a solution when no one had examined its principles or consequences. In this sense, then, the division was basically one between pragmatists and idealists, between those who stressed the importance of practical solutions and "getting on" with it without bothering much about "religious or philosophical niceties," and those who believed these same "niceties" to be essential in upholding ideals and, therefore, fundamental for a sane society.[25]

By design rather than by accident, those who wanted an answer first to the more general question proved to be mostly "conservative" or "fundamentalist" in religion. Accustomed to consider matters in the light of basic (religious) principles, they refused to discuss *illegal* abortions separate from the question of abortion as such. Meanwhile, their opponents succeeded in making them look like men who not only dragged their heels and who were unwilling to come to grips with "reality", but also as men who were so preoccupied with principle and dogma that they ignored compassion and charity.

The resolution was introduced by the Chairman of the Criminal Justice section, Stewart McMorran of Vancouver, who explained the details of its two parts, but did not state the reasons for this bill other than that "there is nothing being forced on anyone" and that England which was pretty good at things done in the realm of law, had just passed an abortion law in the House of Lords.[26] The seconder of the original motion in 1963, Anthony C. Bazos of Toronto, stated the issue more clearly and more directly. According to him, the sole purpose of the resolution was to protect the pregnant female seeking an abortion. "You are not being asked, any of you people," he said to his colleagues, "to say that you are legalizing abortions... you're aiming to protect the pregnant female."[27]

Mr. Bazos' view was supported by Donald Diplock, one of the three Bar representatives who had met with the medical men in Ottawa. Mr. Diplock explained that a major concern of their meetings had been the question of how to stop illegal abortions. "It would suffice" he said, "to eliminate illegal abortions if the medical profession were allowed to operate, say, within the first sixteen weeks of pregnancy"; after that period, he suggested, it should be done for the

25. This division is not to be taken as applying under all circumstances. The 1963 debate of the CBA clearly indicates that some of those who favoured removal of abortion from the Criminal Code did so precisely on philosophical grounds, insisting that Christianity cease to be the dominant morality. See above, chapter 2.
26. *Proceedings,* Can. Bar Association, Vol. 49, 1966, pp. 81 & 83. The reference was to Lord Silkin's bill.
27. *Op. cit.,* p. 109.

purpose of saving the mother's life. Although he himself recognized the question as basically one of *moral* attitude, not of medical or social facts, he said that he failed to understand these moral objections because, when a spontaneous abortion occurs "no one thinks that a human being has died, only that a potential child has failed to be born."[28]

Except for the passing reference to it by Mr. Diplock, not one of those who favoured legalizing abortion or widening the grounds for abortion seemed interested in discussing the issue of human life. Undoubtedly this reflected the widespread unwillingness of the public in general at this time to examine this aspect. Some people believed or assumed without further reflection that human life was not involved at all, thinking, perhaps, like the American Professor of Psychiatry, Thomas Szasz, that an abortion should be available in the same way as an operation for the beautification of the nose.[29] At the Winnipeg convention the issue of human life was mentioned, however, and no one was allowed to go home without hearing something about it as well as about other philosophical and practical objections to the CBA resolutions. These were presented by Alex Sarchuk, Crown prosecutor in Winnipeg.

Mr. Sarchuk, quoting extensively from religious and medical sources, argued that life was bestowed by God, not by man; that one could not justify destruction of innocent human life; that everyone agreed that the child is human just before birth; that since it is impossible to demonstrate the precise time when the unborn becomes human, it leaves the moment of conception as the only rational choice; that except for emergencies to save the mother's life, churches such as the United Church and the Anglican Church had opposed abortion as recently as 1960 and 1958; that there was much dispute whether or not therapeutic abortions were good medicine; that medical indications for therapeutic abortions were minimal; that some psychiatrists held that there were no real psychiatric grounds for termination of pregnancy either; and that in the early months of pregnancy doctors could not state whether a child would be born defective. "I submit," he concluded, "that if abortion is made readily available, responsibility will not be encouraged, legal and illegal abortions will increase, and the indications for abortion will become more liberal as women demand readier access to this solution."[30]

Following the speech of Mr. Sarchuk, Saul Froomkin, speaking for the Manitoba Criminal Justice Subsection, quickly announced that, notwithstanding Mr. Sarchuk's remarks, the majority of the Manitoba Subsection favoured the resolution. When other lawyers, too, spoke against the resolution, they made just as little impact as Mr. Sarchuk. Among them was Sydney Paikin, speaking for himself

28. *Op. cit.,* p. 114. During the 1968 hearings of the House of Commons Committee on Abortion it was pointed out that in Catholic hospitals a foetus is traditionally baptized and buried in a cemetery whenever possible. *Proceedings — Abortion* — 1968, #19, Feb. 8, p. 642.

29. Thomas Szasz, "The Ethics of Abortion," *Humanist,* Sept./Oct. 1966, p. 148.

30. *Proceedings,* CBA, 1966, p. 91.

and for his Hamilton partner, John White. Mr. Paikin argued that
there was no doubt that therapeutic abortions were legal the only
time they counted, namely, when necessary to save the mother's life.
In rejecting a widening of grounds he again stressed the rights of the
unborn child, quoting the presumably impeccable authority of the
United Nations' 1959 Declaration on Human Rights. This Declaration
stated that:

> The child by reason of its physical and mental immaturity
> needs special safeguards and care, including appropriate legal
> protection *before* as well as after birth.

It was all to no avail. The majority of lawyers were not to be
budged. The general mood was summed up by Mr. David Bowman
of Winnipeg. Classifying the objections as religious and moral, and
dismissing them, therefore, as purely private opinions of no real
concern to the rest of society ("Lord knows we have heard, on so
many questions over the years, this kind of argument") he exclaimed
under applause: "And surely we, who do not have these moral objections, have the right to say to the moral objectors, "Let us, let us,
too, have our rights."[31] Without explaining whose rights or what rights
he meant and not satisfied with merely brushing arguments and
opponents aside, he presented his own views on morality: "And surely,
further, Mr. Chairman, there can be nothing more immoral, nothing
more irreligious than turning medical practitioners and decent people
into criminals in the way which our present legislation does."[32] After
having thus implied that people become criminals because of some
law and not because they perform acts harmful to society, presumably
no one was surprised when Mr. Bowman concluded by ridiculing "all
the exaggerated fears of what will happen if this thing is adopted."
He placed these fears in the same classification as the fears of British
Lords a hundred and thirty years ago when these august gentlemen
supposedly expected a national revolution after pickpocketing had
been removed from the list of capital crimes.

The vote crowned with success the three year campaign led by
the B.C. Bar, and the CBA endorsement of legalized abortions was
hailed by a number of persons across Canada. Stephen Lewis of the
Ontario NDP, whose bill for liberalized abortion laws had died on
the order paper at the Ontario Legislature in the spring, said that
all Canada should applaud the stand. His father, David Lewis, federal
NDP member for Scarborough West declared: "There is a desperate
need in Canada for such a change in the laws." Dr. R.F. Stackhouse,
professor of religion at Wycliffe College in Toronto, columnist for the
Toronto Telegram and member of the Anglican delegation to the House
of Commons hearings in December 1967, recommended all possible
support for the association's stand.[33]

---

31. *Proceedings*, CBA, 1966, p. 102. See also *Globe and Mail*, August 31, 1966, p. 1.
32. *Proceedings*, CBA, 1966, p. 102.
33. News report, *Toronto Telegram,* August 31, 1966. Report was reprinted in *O.M.R.*,
    Sept. 1966, p. 702.

Progress

Progress for the revision of abortion laws at the beginning of 1967 can best be summed up by the confident words of Mr. Ian Wahn, Liberal MP for Toronto-St. Paul, in January: "Reform is under way!" Commenting on these words, Mr. Gerald Waring, in his regular column in the *Canadian Medical Association Journal,* reported that "in a few days it will be a full year since this reform-minded lawyer-MP introduced a bill in the Commons to relieve medical practitioners of the risk of criminal liability... This session the abortion bill is scheduled to get a commission hearing.[34] If he had written two weeks later, he could have said not only that the government in Ottawa had decided to give the abortion question an airing in a House of Commons' Committee — a decision made in the spring of 1966 — but also that the Prime Minister, Mr. Pearson, had now hinted that abortion reform might actually be included in a proposed revision of the Criminal Code.

The Prime Minister and his cabinet were no doubt influenced by the authority of the CMA and the CBA resolutions, as well as the pressure from other organizations. A hint of possible legislative action came at a reception of a delegation of the National Council of Women of Canada on Monday, January 30th. Calling Canadian abortion laws "unjust", the President Mrs. H.H. Steen of Vancouver submitted the Association's brief for a third year in a row and asked again for a royal commission to investigate the matter. Mr. Pearson replied that he was not sure a royal commission was needed or even desirable and that the question might be considered later in the current session of Parliament.[35]

There can be little doubt that the government would not have seriously contemplated new abortion legislation at this time, if it had not been for the fact that other issues involving marriage, morality, and law, had preceded the abortion issue and were receiving a sympathetic hearing from the general public. One of these issues was the legalization of contraceptives; another was the widening of grounds for divorce. To many people it seemed natural that the removal of contraceptives from the Code would be followed by the legalization of sterilization and abortion. That was the way the *Globe and Mail* saw it. "Abortion and birth control are closely related subjects," an editorial following the Prime Minister's announcement stated, and it would not be unreasonable, if one of them is to be dealt with, to expect that consideration of the other will come soon."[36] Edmonton's *Western Catholic Reporter* protested the editorial. "We submit", the weekly warned, "that it is unreasonable to talk of contraception and abortion in the same breath.... The government of Canada will make a great mistake if it ever forgets the difference between contraception and abortion."[37] The fact of the matter was that a great many people

---

34. "Report from Ottawa", *C.M.A.J.,* Vol. 96, Jan. 21, 1967.
35. *Globe and Mail,* Jan. 31, 1967, p. 8.
36. Editorial, "A distant hope flickers," *Globe and Mail,* Feb. 4, 1967.
37. *Western Catholic Reporter,* Editorial, Feb. 9, 1967.

were doing just that, including Ian Wahn in his already mentioned bill.

Mr. Wahn's bill consisted of two parts, part one on abortion; part two on contraception. Together with three other private bills which dealt with contraception only, it was referred by the House of Commons to its standing Committee on Health and Welfare on February 21,1966. In his statement of purpose at the Committee's first hearing it became clear that Mr. Wahn did not distinguish between the two issues.[38]

In explaining that the Committee would deal first with the contraception issue only, the chairman, Dr. Harry Harley (L, Halton), pointed out that the two issues differed in principle, "one being the prevention of conception and the other being the destruction of conception." However, the chairman assured Mr. Wahn that the Committee considered abortion part of the mandate given to it by the Commons and that the issue would not be shelved but considered later.[39] Thus, consideration of abortion was ensured a full year before the hearings on this subject actually started.

In the same spring session of 1966, after it had referred the four bills on contraception to the Committee on Health and Welfare, the Commons also sent the Committee on Justice and Legal Affairs seven private bills on divorce. In the past, private bills on both these subjects had either been "talked out" or let die on the order paper without any debate. The move to refer them to committee indicated a new approach to these issues and was no doubt the result of growing pressure on the government to deal with them. As the Minister of Justice, Lucien Cardin, declared in the House: "These two subjects are no longer taboo. Previous governments have been hesitant in dealing with them — I think properly so — but we cannot close our eyes to them. We have had a number of briefs from interested organizations which were very well argued and they are being studied."[40] The key question was, of course, how parliament and the government intended to treat these very touchy and controversial issues.

Birth Control

All four private bills on contraception proposed to change Section 150 of the Criminal Code which prohibited selling, distributing or advertising "any means, instructions, medicine, drug or article intended or represented as a method of preventing conception or causing abortion or miscarriage." Robert Stanbury (L, York-Scarborough) and Ronald Basford (L, Vancouver Centre) desired that the provisions of the Code on contraception should not apply to authorized agents

---

38. Dr. Brand (PC, Saskatoon) remarked: "I think he is using the words 'birth control' to include therapeutic abortions." Standing Committee on Health and Welfare. *Minutes of Proceedings and Evidence. (hereafter referred to as Proceedings, Birth Control).* No. 2. March 3, 1966, p. 35.

39. *Op. cit.,* p. 34.

40. "Commons committees study divorce, birth control bills", *Prairie Messenger,* March 9, 1966, p. 16.

such as doctors, nurses, family planning agents, etc. Robert Prittie (NDP, Burnaby Richmond) and Ian Wahn wanted to eliminate contraception from the Criminal Code altogether.

In questioning the position of MP's Prittie and Wahn, Robert Stanbury came at once to the key question when he noted that their position "perhaps suggests that no element of this field is worthy of treatment in criminal law." He himself thought that there were aspects of public health and safety, and public morality "which still have a place in criminal law in this matter of birth control."[41] His view was similar to the view of the Canadian Bar Association which in its brief later in the year also wanted sales of contraceptives legalized but still thought restrictions on advertising desirable. On the other hand, the Canadian Medical Association sided with Messrs. Prittie and Wahn and favoured the direct elimination of all references to contraceptives from the Code.[42]

Possible explosive religious overtones of the contraception issue were defused fairly early in the hearings — insofar as they needed defusing at all — when Jean Paul Matte (L, Champlain) read a letter from two priest professors into the Committee's record, explaining that in their view Catholics would not do morally wrong if they favoured proposed changes in the Criminal Code.[43] Accepting a suggestion made two years earlier by the *Globe*, the principal author declared that in his opinion existing Canadian law held illegal even the Church's marriage preparation courses, insofar as these mentioned (Church approved) birth control methods. The two theologians then referred to the explanatory notes of Mr. Wahn's Bill.[44] They simply agreed with him, stating that the 'function of law is not exactly that of morality and that human law is not meant to forbid or punish all evil actions.' A spokesman for the Voice of Women pointed out to the Committee that in the book, *Brief to the Bishops*, Toronto Catholic lawyer John O'Driscoll had taken a position "exactly as set out here" by Father Vezina.[45]

41. Bernard Daly, "MP's may draft 'most forward' family planning law," *Prairie Messenger,* March 16, 1966, p. 8. See also *Proceedings,* Birth Control, 1966, p. 42.

42. Bernard Daly, "Briefs heard on contraception," *Prairie Messenger,* March 30, 1966, p. 3. The CBA resolution went back to Sept. 7, 1963, and the CMA resolution also to 1963. *Proceedings, Birth Control,* 1966, pp. 55 & 58.

43. The priests were Rev. Louis P. Vezina, O.M.I., superior of the Oblates Fathers' centre for ecclesiastical studies in Ottawa and Director of the Institute of Pastoral Studies, St. Paul's University; and Jean Guy Lemarier, O.M.I., moral theologian. See "Vote favoring changes in Code on birth control not immoral" *Prairie Messenger,* March 30, 1966, p. 1. Also *Proceedings, Birth Control,* March 22, 1966, p. 84.

44. Mr. Wahn's explanation of his Bill C-40 reads as follows: "The purpose of this bill is to exclude criminal liability, in circumstances where there is no serious danger to the public interest, in respect of acts of birth control which more properly should be left to the individual conscience and to ecclesiastical and moral laws and not made the subject of criminal legislation."

45. *Ibid.* It may be noted that the spring hearings of the Health and Welfare Committee on Birth Control were very poorly reported in the daily newspapers. The country was pre-occupied with the Gerda Munsinger affair and the capital punishment debate in the house. The meeting of March 22nd was not reported

Authoritative confirmation of these views came when the Catholic Bishops of Canada responded to an invitation of the Committee and submitted a brief in October 1966. The Bishops declared that they would not oppose changes in the legislation on contraceptives if 'safeguards against irresponsible sales and advertising... were provided' and if personal freedom was protected.[46] They gave as their reason that, in their opinion, legislation on contraceptives was an example where it does "not serve the common good to translate moral laws into civil laws." In order to turn a wrongful act into a statutory crime punishable by law at least four conditions should be fulfilled, the bishops said:

1 – It should first of all be clear that the wrongful act notably injures the common good;

2 – The law forbidding the wrongful act should be capable of enforcement, because it is not in the interest of the common good to pass a law which cannot be enforced;

3 – The law should be equitable in its incidence – i.e., its burden should not fall on one group in society alone;

4 – It should not give rise to evils greater than those it was designed to suppress.[47]

The Bishops considered the existing law inadequate and deficient under all four conditions "independently of the morality or immorality of various methods of birth prevention." They added, however, that they wanted "to make it absolutely clear that the modification of Civil Law in no way implies the modification of God's moral law." They also warned that the application of these principles would be quite different in regard to that part of the Code which had to do with abortion.[48]

The Committee on Health and Welfare sent its final report to the Commons on December 5, 1966. It recommended that birth control be removed from the Criminal Code, declaring that the dissemination of family planning information should be free from any fear of illegality. Family planning, the committee stated, is a personal affair and "the state should not interfere with action or laws in any way to influence such a personal decision." While the Committee expressed gratitude for the views of the Churches and others, it did not respond with much vigour to their fears of blatant advertising and uncontrolled

at all in five papers examined. (*Halifax Herald, Montreal Gazette, Ottawa Journal*, Toronto *Globe and Mail, Winnipeg Free Press*). The book in question was Harris, Paul T., edit., *Brief to the Bishops, Canadian Catholic Laymen speak their minds.* Toronto, Longmans, 1965.

46. See: *Contraception, Divorce, Abortion:* Three statements by Canadian Catholic Conference, Ottawa, 1968, pp. 64. See also *Prairie Messenger*, Oct. 19, 1966, p. 1; *West. Cath. Reporter*, Oct. 13, 1966, pp. 1, 5, 15; *Proceedings, Birth Control*, Oct. 11, 1966, pp. 466ff. "RC bishops won't fight legislation making contraceptive sales legal", *Globe and Mail*, Oct. 12, 1966, p. 12.

47. *Contraception, Divorce, Abortion*, p. 17. See also Editorial "Recipe for workable laws", *Globe and Mail*, October 14, 1966.

48. *Op. cit.*, p. 18.

sales to minors. The parliamentary body merely suggested that "necessary regulations on the distribution and advertising of contraceptives" be placed under the Food and Drugs Act.[49] This suggestion was accepted by the government later on and while undoubtedly it had some effect on the quality of contraceptives, it was to prove entirely ineffective in restricting their distribution.

Divorce

The Special Joint Committee of the Commons and Senate on Divorce, announced on March 15, 1966, began its hearings in the fall of 1966. Nine private bills were referred to it, eight from the House of Commons and one sponsored by Senator Roebuck.[50] Here, as in the matter of contraception, the climate of opinion favoured liberalization. All nine bills proposed to add to the hitherto sole ground for divorce, adultery, others such as desertion, cruelty and incurable insanity. Some bills even suggested drunkenness, drug addiction, frequent criminal convictions, or non-support.[51]

Like birth control, divorce again, was an international issue. For example, in April 1966, New York state changed its divorce law for the first time since its enactment 179 years earlier. The new law included homosexuality, sodomy, cruel and inhuman treatment, abandonment for two years, imprisonment for three consecutive years, and living apart for two years following either a separation agreement or a formal court decree of separation. New York Catholics had opposed an even more liberal bill, charging that it was not meant to 'reform' but simply intended to make divorces easier, thus undermining the family structure by introducing divorce by consent.[52]

In Canada the United Church was among the first religious bodies to submit a brief to the Divorce Committee, presenting a lengthy study which included a 100 page brief by the Pastoral Institute of the United Church in Calgary on the concept of "marriage breakdown." The church suggested a "totally new" divorce law, making "marriage breakdown" rather than "marital offences" the basis for granting divorces. As an intrinsic part of its proposal it also requested new marital court procedures to deal with distressed marriages and help with the preservation of marriage and family life.[53]

---

49. Third Report to the House, *Proceedings, Birth Control,* 1966, pp. 590-1. Also "Commons hears report on contraceptives", *Prairie Messenger,* Dec. 14, 1966, p. 2. Birth Control Report Tabled in Commons, *Globe and Mail,* December 6, 1966.

50. *Proceedings of the Special Joint Committee of the Senate and House of Commons on Divorce,* Oct. 18, 1966, no. 1, p. 3. Hereafter referred to as *Proceedings — Divorce.*

51. cf. B. Daly, "Bills on Divorce Under Study", *Prairie Messenger,* March 23, 1966, p. 3.

52. *Western Catholic Reporter,* May 5, 1966, p. 2. Britain was to introduce a Matrimonial Causes bill early in 1967.

53. "United Church submits brief on "divorce", *Prairie Messenger,* Dec. 7, 1966, p. 8. *Proceedings — Divorce,* 1966, p. 374. Even though the United Church believed that marriage should be a life-long union, the brief said, the Church had presented its submission on divorce because it wanted to acknowledge that

Like the United Church brief which was supported by the Anglicans, other submissions also suggested that marriage ought to be protected by positive measures. Among the strongest expression of these views was the brief of the Roman Catholic Bishops submitted in April, 1967. While leaving the "details about grounds for divorce that would be acceptable or not" to the "well-informed conscience" of legislators, they stated that "we cannot overemphasize that an indiscriminate broadening of the grounds for divorce is not the solution to the problem of unhappy marriages." Instead they suggested an extensive rethinking of the entire body of legislation dealing with marriage and the family as a part of a revision of the divorce law, including important changes in the procedures of divorce courts.[54]

The joint Committee of the Senate and House of Commons concluded its hearings in the late spring of 1967. It submitted its report and draft bill to the government in the middle of June. Although empowered to report on both the divorce law itself and on "the social and legal problems relating thereto", the report and the bill it proposed dealt with the law only, under the title "Divorce (Extension of Grounds) Act." In fact, the Committee had ignored the bulk of the testimony. It simply declared the other matters to have been outside the scope of its investigations.[55] The suggested divorce courts, judges and trained investigators, the report said, might cause delays and "far from making divorces simpler and cheaper, might well have the opposite effect."[56]

Observers of the parliamentary scene detected two other reasons why the proposal for positive government action had been rejected. First of all, the fear that it might cost money and secondly, a refusal to accept marriage reconciliation as a proper government task. At least that was the way the Churches saw it as expressed in their joint statement of protest which was formulated after the publication of the Committee's recommendations. Signed by representatives of the Anglican, Catholic, Lutheran, Mennonite, Presbyterian and United Church communities, the statement expressed the deep disappointment of the Churches. Their own study of the 1600 pages of proceedings, they stated, clearly indicated three areas in which there had been general agreement among those who had submitted briefs. These principles were that the federal government should take a creative lead in programs fostering successful marriages; secondly, that the social requirements for successful marriages would not be attained by a single legislative act; and thirdly, that federal divorce law should not merely play the purely negative role of facilitating the burial of

---

Christian partners do fail in marriage. As explanation for making a presentation to a parliamentary Committee, the brief gave compassion for all members of society, not just its own members, as reason. *Proceedings — Divorce,* 1966, p. 376.

54. "Bishops express views on divorce", *Prairie Messenger,* April 12, 1967; Text: April 19, p. 8. "Catholic Bishops end opposition to reform of divorce legislation," *Globe and Mail,* April 7, 1967, p. 11.

55. See B. Daly, "New Divorce Proposals: Reconciliation Measures Weak", *Western Catholic Reporter,* July 6, 1967, p. 1.

56. *Ibid.*

some dead marriages.[57] The joint statement was submitted to Justice Minister Trudeau on November 8, 1967, filed away, and not heard from again.

By the end of 1967, then, the attitude of both parliament and government was clear. On the one hand they were willing, even anxious, to remove matters such as contraception and divorce from the supervision of the law; on the other hand, they proved unwilling to assume responsibility for positive action. That this attitude was fully approved in some quarters, was made clear by an editorial in the *Winnipeg Free Press* following the third and final reading of the new Divorce Bill in the House of Commons.[58]

The editorial noted that "fortunately" nothing came of the efforts of some members to introduce the "marriage-breakdown" concept as the sole evidence for divorce. The danger of that proposal was, the paper pointed out, that the state would have to set up "a moral and social inquisitorial system:

> It is evident from some of the things that Justice Minister Trudeau has said that he wishes our courts to remain legal, and not become moral, institutions. Whether some of the advocates of marriage-breakdown as the sole ground are or are not aware of it, the principle of marriage-breakdown would hand over to the courts whole areas of our lives that are not the business of the courts. The present adversary principle leaves the courts with a theoretically simple decision to make: Is there a legal case for the ending of a given marriage? The marriage-breakdown principle, as the sole ground, would involve the courts in something quite different and something utterly abhorrent to our traditions.

Summary

By the close of 1966 strong voices had been raised in Canada in favour of the revision of the Criminal Code. These voices probably represented a considerable section of public opinion, especially in English-speaking Canada.

Canadian public opinion had been influenced by three developments: the introduction of a bill for the legalization of abortion in Britain, a country which had traditionally influenced Canada in matters of legal theory and legal precedents; the discussions of abortions in the popular mass media of the United States; and the occurrence of the 'thalidomide crisis', which revealed that the horror of cruelly deformed babies was such that many people almost instinctively preferred abortion. Public opinion had been shaped from within the country by the Toronto *Globe and Mail*, supported by *Chatelaine* and the United Church *Observer*.

By the end of 1966 a number of national organizations had

---

57. "Joint Church Statement on Divorce", Nov. 1967, reprinted in *Contraception, Divorce and Abortion, op. cit.,* pp. 50-54. Text also in *Prairie Messenger,* Nov. 22, pp. 3, 15, "Revive a dead marriage, don't bury it." See also "Measures to prevent broken marriages not included, churches complain," *Globe and Mail,* Nov. 9, 1969, p. 2.

58. "Grounds for Divorce," *Winnipeg Free Press,* December 20, 1967.

indicated support for the amendment of the abortion clauses in the Criminal Code. These groups included the principal representative bodies of the legal and medical professions as well as the largest Protestant church, the United Church of Canada. Their motives and solutions differed in detail, but their overall thrust was identical: they agreed on the need to prevent the evil effects of illegal abortions and on permitting abortions for the sake of the mother's 'health'. They disagreed as to what the word 'health' should mean, and what other 'grounds' or 'indications' should be permitted.

Articulate opposition to abortion law revision, meanwhile, had been almost non-existent. Aside from the unsuccessful efforts of a handful of individuals, no efforts had been made to stop or even analyze the sudden trend in favour of extending the grounds for abortions. Inarticulate opposition, however, was widespread but rested mainly on traditional religious and moral authority. While by the end of 1966 the largest Church in the country, the Roman Catholic Church, together with its affiliated organizations and press, had indicated opposition to revision of the law, as yet, this Church had done little to explain its stand either to its own members or to the country at large. Moreover, its position as well as that of traditional religious authority in Canada in general had been weakened by two factors. First, the largest Protestant Church, the United Church of Canada, together with the Anglican Church in Great Britain, denied that there were insuperable theological objections to abortion. Secondly, the Canadian Catholic Church itself had accepted revision of the Criminal Code in two other areas of marital morality which it had hitherto opposed: birth control and divorce. On the grounds that civil law must serve the common good, it had reluctantly withdrawn its opposition to revision of the law after acknowledging that this common good appeared more harmed than served by the existing legislation. Many people now thought that the common good would also be served by 'legalizing' abortions.

The abortion controversy had also given renewed emphasis to another development promoted in Canada principally by the *Globe and Mail*: separation of law and morality. The *Globe*, chief advocate of abortion law revision among the general public, had observed in 1963 that abortion "raised the whole difficult problem" of the relationship between law and morality. By the close of 1966 the paper had repeatedly asserted that abortion was a question of private morality and that law, therefore, should not be concerned with it. As an explanation as to why the law had made abortion its concern in the past, the paper had offered religious beliefs, which it now declared to be both outmoded and representative only of a minority.

From the beginning of 1967 on, the struggle between pro and anti-revisionists was to increase in intensity. In the spring of 1967 the *Globe* felt it necessary to challenge the renewed refusal of the Catholic hierarchy to accept abortion. At the same time the paper was to attack the Pearson government for refusing to commit itself to revision of the law, hoping to force the government's hand by revealing that some abortions were being done in hospitals for reasons other than saving the life of the mother.

CHAPTER **IV**

More Agitation

The Globe and the Government

From the time of Mr. Pearson's intimation at the January reception of the National Council of Women that a Royal Commission might not be needed to study the abortion issue, the Toronto *Globe* kept a close watch for any signs of legislative action. It welcomed the Prime Minister's "faintest of hints" as the "first major crack in the façade of governmental indifference toward the need for humane and intelligent adjustments to our legislation." It felt greatly encouraged, not having suspected that "we might even be close to change."[1] Before the month of February was out the Toronto journal could report further news. In addressing a fund-raising dinner for the Liberal party, Mr. Pearson had announced a new package of government legislation. We must deal, the Prime Minister had said, with such things as divorce reform, elimination of air and water pollution, changes in the Criminal Code dealing with birth control and abortion, consumer protection against fraud and greed, etc. He went on to list other items. The next day most papers stressed such things as divorce but the *Globe's* front page headline read: "Laws outlawing abortion, birth control to be changed, Pearson says."[2]

While encouraging the ranks of the reformers, the *Globe* kept an eye on the opponents of legal abortions, especially Roman Catholics. It made a point not only of covering activities emanating from that quarter, but of identifying opposition to legalized abortion with the Catholic Church. This was not difficult to do because, by and large, Catholics appeared to be the ones willing to speak out. As an *AP* news report printed in Canadian newspapers put it, "Doctors, sociologists and the Planned Parenthood Organization are in the forefront of moves seeking liberalization... The Roman Catholic Church is the leading opponent..."[3]

In covering the events in Britain and the United States, the *Globe* had already reported under such headings as, "Move to change abortion laws under fire by R.C. MP's in Britain," and "New York R.C.'s

1. Editorial, "A distant hope flickers," Feb. 4, 1967.
2. *Globe and Mail,* February 24, 1967. *Ottawa Journal,* "PM hopes for Action on Divorce Reform this Year," Feb. 24, 1967, p. 25. *Winnipeg Free Press,* "Pearson Wants Action," p. 1.
3. Printed, for instance, in the Saskatoon *Star-Phoenix,* March 25, 1967, p. 9, "Abortion law changes face opposition."

urged to fight abortion bill."[4] Early in April the *Globe* found similar news in Canada with a report on the spring meeting of the Canadian Catholic Conference of Bishops in Ottawa. Reporter Martin O'Malley observed that the new Minister of Justice, Pierre Trudeau, had indicated on his appointment earlier that week that he had strong views on laws governing divorce, birth control and abortion and that he favoured 'liberalization.' Now, Mr. O'Malley reported, a letter was being sent by the Bishops to the federal government asking for a delay in legislation. The letter, he said, informed the Government that the Bishops were preparing a detailed report, to be finished late this year. In the meantime, the Church was giving up opposition to divorce reform on the same grounds that it had abandoned opposition to the legalization of birth control. But the line was to be drawn at abortion, and the Bishops did not like the Government to include it in the same breath with divorce and birth control.[5] The article was placed on the front page under the heading "Delay in Reforms urged — R.C. bishops preparing fight on abortion." It made a further point in noting that the campaign against abortion had been generally confined to Roman Catholic publications where it had been gaining momentum. A recent editorial in the *Canadian Register* entitled "A License to Kill" was quoted in evidence.[6]

Within three days of the O'Malley report the *Globe* was ready with an editorial.[7] Starting with a somewhat sarcastic observation about the "remarkable ability of Roman Catholic bishops to make clear distinctions," it focussed in on the fact that the Bishops had seen fit to treat the legalization of contraceptives and the broadening of the grounds for divorce differently from abortion. But the writer did not analyze the Bishops' "distinctions." Instead, quoting Archbishop Pocock of Toronto as saying that "in a society such as ours, the state may take steps to lessen the evil that exists at the present time," he wanted to know why the Archbishop was unable to apply the same rule to the evil of the "more than 100,000 — perhaps as many as 300,000" illegal abortions. "Are these not cases where the law is brought into disrespect, where the state should 'take steps to lessen the evil that exists?' he asked. The editorial pointed out that the Anglican Archbishop of Canterbury and the British House of Commons also favoured legal abortions and that "a recent" opinion poll in Britain showed "that a substantial majority of Catholics" favoured legal abortions in cases of rape or a deformed child, and "that 44 per cent supported social abortions."[8]

---

4. *Globe and Mail,* February 1, 1967, p. 1; *Globe and Mail,* February 13, 1967, p. 10. Actually, the petition for a Royal Commission asked for by opponents to the British bill was initiated and organized by a Conservative MP, Mrs. Jill Knight, who was not a Roman Catholic at all. See *The Tablet,* March 18, 1967, pp. 285-6.

5. *Globe and Mail,* April 7, 1967, p. 1. See also *Western Catholic Reporter,* April 13, 1967, p. 1. *Prairie Messenger,* April 19, 1967, p. 1.

6. *Op. cit.,* p. 2. The article on divorce: "Catholic bishops end opposition to reform of divorce legislation," *Globe & Mail,* April 7, p. 11.

7. "Steps to lessen the evil," *Globe and Mail,* April 10, 1967.

8. The editorial could not have been referring to the March 1967 Gallup poll, held

Archbishop Pocock felt obliged to make a prepared statement to the press in response to the editorial. This he did the next day.[9] After protesting that "we cannot allow ourselves to be guided by the findings of Gallup polls," the Archbishop stated the Church might relax its opposition to proposed changes *if* research indicated change would be for the common good. "The bishops had taken no absolute stand on the problem," he added, "they will try to make an honest and thorough study of the facts." He asked Canadians to join his church in getting the facts before the laws governing abortion were changed, and to study, for example, the number of illegal abortions in Canada or the effects of liberalized abortions in such countries as Japan and Sweden. The onus of proof rests on those who recommend the broadening of the grounds of abortion, he said. It would be rash indeed to adopt legislation increasing the grounds for destroying human life unless it can be proved "that by increasing the grounds we can decrease the incidence." "Rather than engaging in polemics," he concluded, "we should unite our efforts in seeking exactly what is in the best interest of society."

While most of this was subsequently reported by the *Globe*, the paper devoted a single sentence to the Archbishop's explicit rejection of the argument that there was no difference between what was applicable to contraception or divorce and what applied to abortion. No such conclusion could be drawn, the Bishop had said, because in considering abortion, a new factor, the matter of human life, had to be taken into account:

> We must assure ourselves that we are not succumbing to specious arguments. We must all approach the problem with deep human concern not only for the welfare of mothers and the children who are born with equal human concern for the right of life of innocent unborn children who are unable to speak on their own behalf...[10]

The Archbishop's reply indicated that the Canadian Catholic bishops were not clear in their own minds how to treat the question of abortion. If, as yet, they had taken "no absolute stand," it could only be because they themselves had had no time to study it, and that like everybody else, they, too, were torn between the traditional abhorrence and condemnation of abortion on the one hand and the powerful public pressure and temptation to find a quick solution to the problem of illegal abortions on the other. It was the question of illegal abortions which raised the problem of what steps were required to serve the common good, thus putting abortion in the same position as the issues of birth control and divorce. The editors of the *Globe* were not alone with their difficulty in understanding why the

---

on behalf of the *Sunday Telegraph*, the first and only poll ever taken among British Catholics. That poll showed that while 39% of Catholics approved abortion in case of a deformed child (with 43% disapproving), only 6% supported 'social abortions) ("where mother wants it") with 78% disapproving. Full details printed in *The Tablet,* April 1, 1967, p. 361, by permission of the *Sunday Telegraph.*

9. Ian Porter, "Archbishop calls for study on laws," *Globe and Mail,* April 11, 1967, p. 2.

10. "Stand on Abortion clarified," *Prairie Messenger,* April 26, 1967, p. 3.

Bishops treated abortion differently from divorce and birth control. This confusion would continue as long as the Bishops failed to point out clearly that their opposition was based on the defense of innocent human life, and that this defense of innocent human life was not a religious foible, as the British Cardinal Heenan had said, but based on a defense of the common good, But as long as they left the impression that they, too, believed the common good to be primarily tied up with the possibility of reducing illegal abortions, they would do nothing to diminish the confusion about their position, including confusion among Catholics.[10a]

Meanwhile, the difficulty with getting the facts was that detailed research and studies were simply not available. At no time did anybody provide reliable statistics to replace the customary wild guesses of illegal abortions in Canada. These estimates had started with figures of 25,000 to 75,000 in 1963, had grown to 100,000 to 300,000 in 1967, and would even reach the figure of half a million by 1969.[11] Again, little attention was paid to information from Sweden which indicated that legalization of abortion might not substantially affect the number of illegal abortions. This data had made medical men careful not to claim such grounds as reason for *their* stand in favour of widening the grounds for abortion.[12] The problem was that the situation there was sufficiently different to make comparisons unreliable. And in Japan, sociological studies seemed too difficult because of the lack of processed statistical data.[13]

The Globe and Mr. Pearson

During the remainder of the spring of 1967, the *Globe and Mail* did not waste time and vigorously pursued a campaign of public pressure similar in nature to its birth control crusade three years earlier. At that time the paper had gathered evidence to show that the law was being broken without anyone making efforts to punish the "criminals." This had provided the paper with the opportunity to indignantly castigate the government for refusing to reform the law.[14] The approach had been effective, because when Mr. Wahn, Liberal member for Toronto-St. Paul, introduced his birth control bill at the House of Commons Committee hearings two years later, he claimed that apart from all *other* considerations the law should be repealed because

---

10a. Among those who did not think the Bishops were consistent in treating abortion differently from birth control and divorce was Mr. Mark MacGuigan, professor of law. See his "Unity in the secular city" in *One Church, Two Nations* (ed. Leblanc and Edinborough), Longmans, 1968, p. 154.

11. For the last figure see, for instance, MP Peters (NDP, Timiskaming) in House of Commons, *Hansard,* Feb. 11, 1969, p. 5413.

12. Almost the only place where this question was touched upon in Canada was an article in the *Canadian Medical Association Journal,* Vol. 95, Aug. 20, 1966, pp. 360-366. Dr. Harrison noted that only "some fragmentary reports" were available, which were "to say the least, discouraging."

13. "Japan Abortion Picture is too Fogged to Study," *Canadian Register,* Feb. 3, 1968, p. 3.

14. See the reference to this campaign in the editorial of April 12, 1967, mentioned below.

of its wholesale violation. Whereupon Mr. Stanley Knowles (NDP, Winnipeg North Centre), who favoured the removal of birth control from the Code, had remarked that "if we act on that principle, we would wipe out the Criminal Code and the Ten Commandments in the process."[15]

On April 11, the day of Archbishop Pocock's statement, the paper scored its first success. It gave front page treatment to the disclosure by one of its regular contributors that Toronto's Women's College Hospital had performed twelve abortions during 1966.[16] The article pointed out that only one of these twelve abortions could have been legal under the Criminal Code because the others had been done for psychiatric reasons or to prevent the possibility of the birth of a deformed baby. Having thus established that respected people were doing abortions illegally, the article struck home with a variety of observations: even the one abortion might have been illegal because of the law's "ambiguous phrasing"; according to the views of "a Vancouver group" abortions were forbidden in Canada "for any reason whatever"; doctors, therefore, were in search of legal protection; a Vancouver obstetrician who had aborted a number of women, whose babies "stood a high risk of being born blind, deaf or malformed," looked back on several of these cases as "among the most valuable things he had done in his life"; and the CMA general council which in 1966 had rejected deformity as grounds for abortion, would be asked in June to recommend just that.

Naturally, the *Globe* would not forego this opportunity to return to the subject of abortion. An editorial appeared the next day, the second one in three days, the third one on abortion in as many months. It compared the Prime Minister to a ship's captain who cries, "Cast off!" when his vessel is already 40 miles at sea. "Mr. Pearson is long out of date," the paper said. "First he is out of date with his birth control legislation which he now says he is anxious to see passed though it is three years since the *Globe and Mail* drew the attention of then Justice Minister Favreau that the birth control section of the Criminal Code was being breached..." He is almost as late with broadening the grounds for legal abortions, continued the *Globe*, when medical and legal bodies have long since expressed a desire for change, and evidence has been brought once more that a law is being broken by respectable persons and bodies. Concluded the paper:

> the will of the public and the practice of conscientious citizens are well ahead of Government thinking. The ship is already out of port, and Mr. Pearson should delay no longer in revising the law to admit that it is, and rightly so.[17]

One day later the *Globe* reported that in 1966 six Toronto hospitals had performed a total of 50 abortions and that several others had

15. *Proceedings, Birth Control*, No. 2, March 3, 1966, pp. 36 and 38 respectively.
16. Joan Hollobon, "Psychiatric, health reasons get hospital abortions," *Globe and Mail*, April 11, 1967, pp. 1 &2.
17. Editorial, "Mr. Pearson's laggard law," *Globe and Mail*, April 12, 1967.

probably done an equal number.[18]

In spite of Mr. Pearson's earlier announcement to deal with abortion, the government just did not move fast enough in the eyes of the *Globe*. Two weeks after the throne speech of May 8 promised legislation on divorce but made no explicit mention of abortion, the paper published a prominent four column article under the heading "Abortion: A Matter of Conscience."[19] At the beginning of the article the author, Jean Howarth, inquired whether Prime Minister Pearson was "developing cold feet about introducing abortion legislation." She knew who was responsible for this delay:

> At least one reason for timidity has surfaced. The Roman Catholic Church, after conceding that it will no longer try to impose its views of divorce and birth control on a pluralistic society, has drawn the line at abortion...

At the end of her article she parted with the hint that the Pearson government might be "tempted to bargain" divorce and birth control legislation for a stand-pat attitude on abortion. Such "control of the majority by the minority," the author suggested, would really be beyond comprehension. After all, "a broadening of grounds... would compel no woman to have an abortion whose conscience forbade it; it would merely make legal abortions possible for women whose consciences command them."

In the remainder of the article Miss Howarth approached the future revision of the law from her own angle. While on April 11 Joan Hollobon had suggested that revision of existing Canadian law was considered necessary because it was so "ambiguously phrased" that no one knew with certainty whether or not abortions were permissible, Miss Howarth observed that while Catholics might consider the direct interruption of pregnancy the killing of human beings, the legal view in Canada was that abortions were permitted already, namely to save the life of the mother. What was under discussion, then, she said, was not whether abortions could be done, but whether they should be done for reasons other than saving the life of the mother.[20] In passing she also noted that "even the killing of a newborn child by the mother is not murder but infanticide, punishable by not more than five years in prison."

This argumentation, however, together with the quoting of the views of the United Church of Canada, the Archbishop of Canterbury and the usual opinion polls from Britain and the United States, proved secondary to her real reason for rejecting existing Canadian law: the right of women to decide their own destiny.

> The present law of Canada treats women where abortion is concerned... as though their bodies were state property. If

---

18. Joan Hollobon, "Six hospitals report 50 abortions...," *Globe and Mail*, April 13, 1967, p. w2.

19. Jean Howarth, "Abortion: A Matter of Conscience," *Globe and Mail*, May 25, 1967, p. 7.

20. Roman Catholics generally accepted that attempts to save the mother's life were permissible.

the rights of the individual were given absolute recognition, the decision of whether or not to have an abortion would reside wholly with the woman.

This demand for the "absolute recognition" of the rights of the individual was the first inkling in the *Globe* of the individualism soon to be propagated throughout the country by a section of the Women's Liberation movement. Those who disagreed with their views were accused of disagreeing simply because they were male. Birth control, wrote Mrs. G.W. Cadbury, President of Planned Parenthood of Toronto in congratulating Jean Howarth on her "splendidly written article," appears to the Roman Catholic hierarchy as "contrary to the will of God" because they are "enforced celibates."[21] "I am," wrote Anne Davidson in congratulating Jean Howarth, "one of those Catholics who do not feel that they owe their Catholicity to the say-so of the hierarchy, particularly an exclusively male and exclusively celibate hierarchy." It was, she further remarked in support of her belief that a woman's right to have an abortion should be absolute, only recently that Catholics were no longer exhorted "to produce as many little Catholics as possible, for the greater glory of (a male) God."[22]

Summary

By spring 1967 the drive for new abortion laws had run into its first major obstacle. Almost a year after a number of important national and professional organizations had taken official positions in favour of revising the law on abortions, and several years after the abortion agitation had broken out in full force, the Roman Catholic Bishops of Canada had announced that they were preparing a study for publication later that year. In the meantime they let it be known that they were opposed to revision of the law as proposed by various organizations. They requested the Government not to proceed with legislation without further study.

Challenged by the Toronto *Globe and Mail*, the Bishops' rejection of abortion proved not without ambiguity. It appeared to be founded more on an almost instinctive reliance on the traditional theological condemnation of abortion and on the fear "of succumbing to specious arguments" than on clarity of principle and strength of reasoned argument. Consequently, the Bishops were unable to provide those who opposed amendment of the Criminal Code with effective leadership. On the other hand, the Toronto *Globe and Mail* had firmly established the major lines of its strategy to be used until "reform" had been passed: laws which were not observed should be removed; the law should not represent 'religious morality'; opposition to a revision of the law came only from Roman Catholics; this minority was attempting to impose its views upon the nation; and, reform of the law would compel no one to do anything. The paper had also hinted at a future development of its position, namely that women

---

21. Letter to the editor, *Globe and Mail*, May 29, 1967.
22. Letter to the editor, *Globe and Mail*, May 30, 1967.

should have the absolute right to decide whether or not to have an abortion.

The abortion controversy finally was to reach parliament in the fall of 1967. The official start of the legislative phase was marked by a series of special hearings by means of which Government intended to 'take the pulse' of the nation and then take action. What action and when, of course, remained to be seen.

CHAPTER V

House of Commons Committee Hearings

With the recess of parliament during the summer of 1967 the newspaper agitation for more open abortion laws slowed down though it was not as if the issue no longer made news. On the contrary, those who favoured a change in the law were greatly encouraged both by events in Canada and in Great Britain.

In Canada, the general council of the Canadian Medical Association adopted in early June what it had turned down the year before: it accepted deformity and sexual offenses as grounds for terminating a pregnancy. The resolution was hotly debated. Dr. George Gibson of Chilliwack, B.C., described it "as the most noble resolution" presented to the council for many years. Reform of the law, he said, is long overdue and "rather than being contrary to the evolution of society, this reform is in keeping with it." In his view, the medical profession had a heavy responsibility to lead in this reform, because it was motivated by a deep concern for human rights and the right of the mother to avert tragedy and unhappiness. Dr. Tallon of Cornwall, on the other hand, made an impassioned plea to reject the resolution. He said it showed no respect for human life or the life of the individual at all.[1]

In Great Britain the House of Commons appeared to have come almost to the final stage of its new legislation. At the beginning of July it first removed homosexuality between consenting adults from its Criminal Code.[2] Shortly after, the House of Lords gave second reading to Mr. David Steel's private abortion bill, entitled Medical Termination of Pregnancy Bill, which was interpreted as virtually assuring it approval in principle. This British bill was considered so "liberal" that even some of those who favoured a changed law such as the Anglican Archbishop of Canterbury, Michael Ramsay, actually refused to support it.[3] A number of opponents were convinced the bill introduced abortion on request.[4]

1. Joan Hollobon, "CMA urges 2 new legal abortion grounds," *Globe and Mail*, June 10, 1967. See also "Transactions," Report on the Committee on Maternal Welfare, #278, *C.M.A.J.*, Sept. 9, 1967, Vol. 97, pp. 677 & 8.
2. See "Homosexual reform bill passed by British MP's," *Globe and Mail*, July 5, 1967, p. 4.
3. John Greaves, "Britain's abortion bill approved," *Prairie Messenger*, August 2, 1967, p. 11.
4. "Abortion on Request," *The Tablet*, July 22, 1967, p. 79.

Aside from the summer heat, the other reason for the diminished activity around the abortion issue in Canada was that the government seemed to have determined its course of action. As forecast by its Chairman a year earlier, the Standing Committee on Health and Welfare was given the green light to take up the study of abortion when the House of Commons referred to it three private bills including Ian Wahn's two-part bill of the previous year, just before parliament went on recess. This ensured hearings later in the fall after parliament resumed its activities.[5]

The Committee began its hearings on October 3, 1967, first taking up the bills of the three Members of Parliament, then sitting regularly on Tuesdays or Thursdays to receive submissions and briefs from a variety of organizations and individuals who had either been invited to do so, or who had applied for permission to appear before the group of parliamentarians. The Committee sat from the beginning of October until the Christmas recess, and then again from the end of January until the beginning of March. Its proceedings ran to 850 pages.[6]

Mrs. Grace MacInnis

The hearings opened with a consideration of the bill of Grace MacInnis, the only woman in the House of Commons and herself a member of the Committee. The NDP member for Vancouver-Kingsway favoured the British model, but feared that this might never get through the Canadian parliament. Thus she restricted herself to the recommendations of the Bar and Medical Associations, that is: widening the grounds for abortion to include not only life, but also health, as well as criminal assault and the possibility of a defective child. Half a loaf is better than no loaf at all, she said.

In her presentation Mrs. MacInnis stated four reasons why the law should be changed: Canada should face up to the situation as it had finally faced up to the birth control situation, especially because "nobody would be forcing abortion procedures on anybody else"; Canadian laws were a century old and, therefore, obviously out of date; other progressive countries were moving forward and Canada should not fall behind; and last, but not least, the country was ready for a change: the Gallup Poll showed that 71 per cent of Canadians favoured legalization of abortions.[7] It is not a choice today between having abortions in Canada and not having abortions, she said; "the question is whether we have legal abortions or whether we go on closing our eyes to backstreet bungling and butchery."

---

5. Bill c-122. Sponsor Grace MacInnis (NDP, Vancouver-Kingsway) (Abortion)
   Bill c-123. Sponsor Ian Wahn (L, St. Paul's) (Birth Control)
   Bill c-136. Sponsor H.W. Herridge (NDP, Kootenay West) (An Act concerning the Termination of Pregnancy by Registered Medical Practitioners.)

6. House of Commons, the Standing Committee on Health and Welfare, *Minutes of Proceedings*, 2 Vols. (Hereafter referred to as *Proceedings — Abortion*).

7. *Proceedings — Abortion*, 1967, No. 1, October 3, p. 3. See also: "Mrs. MacInnis startles colleagues with quality-control population," Ottawa Bureau, *Globe and Mail*, Oct. 4, 1967, p. 10.

As if aware that her four 'reasons' could be taken as little more than an exhortation to change for the sake of changing, the British Columbia representative reformulated them. In doing so she created headlines. The reasons for revising the law she said on the second time around, were first, that abortions should be up to the individual conscience; second, that an end should be put to a bad law; third, that backstreet operations should be ended; and

> Fourthly — and this is the positive side — I think it is time that we began to work toward quality population in this country. We are beginning to hear about the need for improving population, and certainly to have children born into a country as a result of rape or incest is not going to be too helpful... Also... if conditions like those of thalidomide babies or congenital diseases are known ahead of time, I do not think it is a good thing for Canada to allow those beings to come into the world... women ought to have far more control over what happens to them when monstrosities are born....[8]

It was the 'quality population' statement which not only startled her colleagues on the committee but which received attention in the press.[9]

Ralph Cowan (L, York-Humber), a Presbyterian who turned out to be the most consistent and the most caustic critic of the submissions by the pro-revisionists, wanted to know whether Mrs. MacInnis had seen the picture of Queen Victoria in the Senate foyer, showing one arm shorter than the other. "Do you think she should have been born?" he asked. Whereupon the startled Mrs. MacInnis retorted: "What was all right in 1861 is not all right in 1967." As he proceeded Mr. Cowan grew increasingly sarcastic. "Why not let the child be born and if it is defective, kill it?" he asked. "Do you favor that... Why kill it three months before birth when you can wait till birth?" As reported by the *Globe*, Mrs. MacInnis grew increasingly flustered as Mr. Cowan pressed the attack; among other things he asked if she would have ordered President Franklin Roosevelt shot when he became paralyzed.[10] The tone of the hearing was somewhat less acrimonious with other hostile committee members, though Mr. Joseph O'Keefe (L, St. John's East) made the remark that quality population control had already been tried by Hitler. Even those who favoured wider grounds for abortion were disturbed at the idea. Said Mr. Stanbury: "I am a bit shocked by this, frankly."[11] Mrs. MacInnis explained she did not want MP's going into homes and ruling which families should have children, and which should not. She considered defective children

8. *Proceedings — Abortion*, 1967, October 3, p. 4.

9. Among papers examined, see *Globe*, op. cit.; *CP* report as printed, for instance, in Saskatoon *Star Phoenix*, Oct. 1967, p. 16, "Fiery debate on abortion legislation erupts." Other references to the statement may be found in the Halifax *Chronicle-Herald*, Oct. 4, 1967, p. 17 and the *Ottawa Citizen*, p. 7. The *Winnipeg Free Press*, the *Ottawa Journal* and the *Montreal Gazette* carried no reports of the hearing.

10. *Globe and Mail*, op. cit. See also *Proceedings — Abortion*, Oct. 3, 1967, pp. 4ff.

11. *Ibid.*

a tragedy: "I have seen those vegetables in our hospitals, our mental hospitals, and I know they have no chance for a normal life."

The Committee soon moved on to the ever present pre-occupation of doing something about illegal abortions. Mr. Wahn claimed that that was the purpose of his bill, saying that we ought to clear up once and for all whether or not therapeutic abortions are legal and we ought to provide medical safeguards to see that they are carried out properly.[12] After a brief discussion of Mr. Wahn's proposal, the Committee concluded its first hearing with the private bill of Mr. Herridge who quoted the figure of 100,000 - 300,000 illegal abortions in Canada. Mr. Herridge believed it necessary that the new law should permit abortions wherever there was a risk to "the future well-being of the mother and her children," taking into account "the patient's total environment." He denied that this would "open the gates" to abortion on request.[13]

At this point the *Globe* felt it necessary to publicly comment on the proceedings, apparently disturbed by the thought that Mr. Wahn's explanation might be taken as indicating a desire for no more than a clarification of the existing statute and no more than the legalization of what doctors were already doing in legitimate hospitals. On October 6th the paper published the first of three editorials during that month.[14] This first editorial suspected 'timidity' on the part of the "elected representatives of the Canadian people." In the face of the fact that "it has been estimated that as many as 300,000 illegal abortions are performed in Canada every year," it demanded "real reform." Abortions should be legal in all cases "where a failure to permit it would be an infringement of a pregnant woman's right to ordinary justice," the writer said, continuing almost in the same breath with the advice that the decision whether or not an abortion should be performed "should legally reside with the medical profession which alone is adequate to judge what are medical questions." If the Government failed to present the proper legislation, he warned, or if Parliament failed to pass it:

> then our elected representatives are simply submitting to intimidation from what they know is not the majority of the Canadian people.

During the following week the *Globe's* Ottawa bureau reported that the Government had just lifted abortion from its fall legislative program pending completion of the Committee hearings. Abortion was not included in the Omnibus bill, Government House Leader Allan MacEachen declared, because it would probably be dealt with separately after the committee had reported.[15]

As its first group the Committee received the representatives of the Canadian Bar Association. Their brief consisted mainly of the

12. *Proceedings — Abortion,* Oct. 3, 1967, pp. 15ff.
13. *Op. cit.,* pp. 19ff.
14. "The Reform must be real," *Globe and Mail,* October 6, 1967.
15. "Abortion change dropped from House priority list," *Globe and Mail,* October 11, 1967, p. 1.

resolution which had been approved at their 1966 Winnipeg convention, including the cumbersome part which dealt with the proposed Termination Board in cases of indecent assault. Especially because of the latter, CBA President Gordon Cooper of Halifax and CBA Secretary Ronald Merriam of Ottawa ran into fire from both pro- and anti-revisionists. The two men gave the main purpose for the CBA stand as 'doing away with illegal abortions' and 'clarifying the law for therapeutic abortions.'[16] Health, they felt, ought to include both physical and mental health. After they admitted that the CBA had consulted no one but the Canadian Medical Association, Mr. Forrestall (PC, Dartmouth-Halifax East) noted that this proposal, then, was "divorced entirely from any moral considerations," and that the problem had been approached from a purely legalistic or professional point of view only.[17] In reply to a remark by Mr. O'Keefe that legal abortion would inevitably lead to the devaluation of human life, Mr. Cooper said he did not believe human life was involved.[18]

While undoubtedly the CBA men had expected opposition from Committee members hostile to revision of the law, they probably had not expected to be so severely taken to task by the pro-amendment people. The latter revealed the proposed Termination Board as complicated and poorly drafted, forcing the CBA men to admit that their scheme needed more thought and rewriting. As the *Toronto Daily Star* pointed out, the Bar Association had unnecessarily complicated matters and if abortions to end pregnancies resulting from sexual crime be approved, it might be handled more simply by an ordinary abortion panel.[19]

The whole affair infuriated the *Globe*. Perhaps it feared that the cause of abortion might be discredited if this continued, or that the country would discover just how deeply divided it was on the subject which, even at this preliminary stage, began to reveal itself as far more complicated than its proponents had suggested. Be that as it may, the *Globe* attacked.[20] The Committee had "no notion at all of its proper function," it charged. Thoughtful and reasonable men had been "verbally pounded and pummelled, asked loaded questions, sneered at and accused of professional incompetence." They had "their motives challenged and their moral attitudes questioned"; they had been treated with "the ultimate in disrespect and discourtesy." Committee members were "without objectivity," having "brought all their prejudices into the committee room with them," nay, having been "selected only for their bias either for or against liberalization of the abortion law." This "group of bullies, tearing strips off the citizens," exclaimed the *Globe*, ought to be disbanded and replaced by those who "know that an investigation is not a witchhunt."

Fortunately for the *Globe*, the weekly sessions which followed were almost all favourable to amending the law. On Thursday, October

16. *Proceedings — Abortion,* Oct. 12, 1967, pp. 36 and 49.
17. *Ibid.,* p. 41.
18. *Ibid.* See also the report in *Globe and Mail,* October 13, 1967, p. 11.
19. "Who decides if Abortion Needed," Editorial, *Toronto Daily Star,* Oct. 21, 1967.
20. Editorial, "A parliamentary bearpit," *Globe and Mail,* October 14, 1967.

19, Dr. Morgenthaler, representing the Humanist Fellowships of Montreal, Toronto, and Victoria, held the spotlight. Rather than relying on the supernatural, he said, the philosophy of naturalistic humanism believes that "scientific methods decide what is fact and what is fiction." "Abortions and unwanted pregnancies must be viewed as accidents," he observed. Convinced that "it is woman's inalienable right to have mastery of her own body," Dr. Morgenthaler recommended abortion on request for the first three months of pregnancy.[21] While Liberals O'Keefe and Isabelle strongly demurred at the idea of abortion on demand, New Democratic Party MP's Stanley Knowles and Grace MacInnis were quite receptive to it.

Hearings resumed two weeks later with the appearance of the Canadian Medical Association representatives, Doctors Aitken, Cannell, Low, Gray and Tompkins. These men presented the CMA resolution which since June of that year also included the genetic and criminal assault clauses. The doctors stressed the importance of passing concomitant birth control and sterilization legislation, presumably on the understanding that this would reduce the need for abortions. They further expressed a strong aversion to compulsion in the use of abortion. As for illegal abortion, Dr. Aitken said that they had "no way of knowing what effect" legalization would have on illegal abortions, while Dr. Tompkins gave as his impression that it might not cut down illegal abortions.[22]

In answer to a question how abortions on grounds of possible deformity would affect the number of babies born with genetic defects, Dr. Tompkins referred to a recent study published by the University of Michigan Medical School. This study indicated that "a liberal attitude towards therapeutic abortion on genetic grounds" would result in no more than "a fractional decrease in the frequency of congenital effects."[23] When the doctors were asked by Mr. Robert Stanbury whether, then, "the main purpose of your resolution is to try to clarify the fact that it is permissible for doctors to do what they have been doing?", Dr. Cannell answered: "I would say that is correct".[24] A little later it was repeated that the doctors' principal interest in legalization was that of making certain that the (small) number of abortions already being done in hospitals were definitely legal by Canadian law and "to end our life as lawbreakers."[25]

Great Britain

While the Commons Committee faced four more months of hearings, Canadian newspapers reported the end of the struggle in Great Britain. The British abortion bill completed its stormy passage through Parliament on Wednesday, October 25. On Thursday night it received approval of the House of Lords. On Friday the Queen gave royal assent,

21. *Proceedings — Abortion*, Oct. 9, 1967.
22. *Proceedings — Abortion*, Tuesday, October 31, 1967, p. 101.
23. *Op. cit.*, p. 108.
24. *Op. cit.*, p. 102.
25. *Op. cit.*, p. 108.

making abortions legal six months later.[26] The British bill not only adopted the legal grounds of danger to life or health, criminal assault and a threat of deformity, but it also accepted "socio-economic" reasons as legitimate. For a few days it had looked as if the Lords would balk at the vaguely worded bill. But in a sudden about-turn that left many peers bewildered, the House of Lords reversed an earlier decision to send back to the Commons two amendments which would almost certainly have meant the death of the bill. Some claimed that the collapse of resistance in the Upper House was brought about when Labour MP's began to organize a campaign to cut the power of the Lords.[27] Others claimed it was due more to the fact that some people changed their minds at the eleventh hour than to any threat of bringing about a constitutional crisis.

There were some spectacular changes of mind, especially those of the Bishop of Durham and the Archbishop of Canterbury.[28] While the Anglican hierarchy had been divided from the beginning, Archbishop Ramsey had favoured revision of the law all along. Earlier, at the second reading in July, however, he had drawn the line at including the well-being of the mother's family in addition to the life and health of the mother herself, and had voted against the bill. Now both he and the Bishop of Durham claimed that they had been converted by the arguments, though according to one report, no one else could see anything new in any of these. "An extraordinary spectacle," snorted one opponent, according to the same report "even his own bench of bishops had their heads in their hands."[29] In a subsequent letter to *The Times*, the Bishop of Durham argued that the wording of the Bill was not important: what counted was the spirit in which it was carried out. Britain, he said, stood not at the end of the reform but at its beginning.[30] But that of course was exactly what some opponents said they feared, fully expecting the floodgates to be opened despite the fact that proponents of the Bill had always stoutly maintained that the Bill did *not* mean abortion on demand.[31]

The passage of the bill in Britain was described by some as a social revolution. The Canadian Press story on the events in Britain opened with the line: "After months of sound and fury, a social revolution on behalf of British women has taken place almost overnight."[32] While printing the article, the *Globe* omitted that part which noted that the man whose 1938 trial started the reformers on their way — Dr. Aleck Bourne, then 81 years old — had denounced the socio-economic provisions as "rubbish" and the bill as "bad." It also

26. "U.K. passes abortion bill" (Reuters), Saskatoon *Star Phoenix*, "Abortion bill gains assent," (Reuters), *Op. cit.,* Oct. 27, 1967.

27. For instance, the *Globe and Mail.* See editorial, Oct. 27, 1967.

28. The Anglican Church is the officially recognized and "established" Church of England. Its bishops have seats in the House of Lords.

29. Canadian Press report, *Globe and Mail,* Nov. 8, 1967, p. 13.

30. *The Tablet,* (London) November 4, 1967, p. 1143.

31. *Ibid.*

32. "Social Revolution expected with new law," (CP) *Globe and Mail,* November 8, 1967, p. 13. Compare same CP report in Saskatoon *Star-Phoenix,* November 8, 1967.

omitted the part that questioned whether British hospitals would be able to cope with this social revolution.

One would have expected the *Globe* to have been pleased. But evidently still worried about the slow progress of the abortion cause in this country, the paper offered only a few stern notes in an editorial headed: "Reform is here — for the Rich." Canada follows the British lead sooner or later, it observed, but unfortunately at this moment the "British action in this field underlines the extreme caution of the reforms being considered here." If Canada "extends the grounds for abortion so slightly that the social need is not met," the paper warned, "the people who will be denied relief will be the poor, who need it most."[33]

November Hearings

On November 2nd the Commons Committee on Health and Welfare heard AMCAL, Association for the Modernization of Canadian Abortion Laws, a group of 300 members founded by Mrs. Lore Perron in Ottawa a year earlier. While AMCAL itself did not endorse abortion on demand according to Mrs. Perron, she herself, in a news interview a week earlier, had indicated that abortions ought to be permitted because every "mature, intelligent woman should have the right to decide when she wants to have a child."[34] At the hearing she advised that women should not seek abortions too hastily. Those who regard abortion as murder, she said, do not have the right to impose their views on others.[35] Mr. Ralph Cowan who earlier had been admonished by the Committee Chairman, Dr. Harley (L, Halton), for commenting on the fact that Mrs. Perron had immigrated to Canada 10 years earlier in spite of Canada's abortion laws, wanted to know whether she would "deny St. Paul" on the need for temperance and self-control in all things. Mrs. Perron did not answer that question but replied that sexual intercourse was not just for procreation but was also an act of love.[36]

The opponents of abortion had their turn on November 7th with the appearance of the Emergency Organization for the Defense of Unborn Children, a five week old group. NPD'ers Stanley Knowles and Grace MacInnis, together with Dr. Lewis Brand (PC, Saskatoon) failed to get the group to acknowledge the need for abortions. Dr. Brand angrily clashed with Mr. Philip Cooper of Ottawa over a statement in a so-called fact-sheet submitted by the group. It quoted *Time* magazine as saying that aborted babies had cried for hours before dying. "It's a lie, that's what it is" Dr. Brand said angrily... "I don't think this sort of nonsense should be brought before the committee

---

33. Editorial, *Globe and Mail*, Oct. 27, 1967, p. 6.

34. "Forecasts abortions allowed on demand," *Globe and Mail*, Oct. 24, 1967.

35. *Proceedings — Abortion*, Nov. 2, 1967, pp. 117ff. See also Lewis Seale, "Abort after birth control fails, brief asks Ottawa committee," *Globe and Mail*, Nov. 3, 1967, p. 11.

36. See "Abortion backers urge nation-wide plebiscite," *CP* Report in Saskatoon *Star Phoenix*, Nov. 3, 1967.

unless you have the facts to prove it... I think it's disgraceful this sort of material should be introduced." Mr. Cooper retorted that the group had been told by a doctor that a baby could cry after abortion.[37]

The brief of this group stated that legalization would cause Canada to step backward in time:

> We would enter a second Dark Ages where human life counted for little... When we find ourselves killing off our unwanted babies, why not our old people, our crippled, our blind and our sick? Why not all inmates of prisons and mental institutions?...
>
> All abortion, in fact, is human sacrifice. If not to appease our anger, it is the sacrifice of an innocent life to our own comfort and convenience, our social and economic position or perhaps a woman's peace of mind or physical well-being... To legalize abortion is to give official sanction to it and therefore encourage it — not only in some special circumstances, but whenever someone thinks it convenient...[38]

Under questioning by Mr. Knowles, whether he really thought that "we who favor the modernization of our abortion laws are ready to go on killing off our unwanted old people, our crippled, our blind, our sick and the inmates of prisons and mental institutions," Mr. Cooper answered that the response was, obviously, no. "Nevertheless," he said, "we are laying the framework for other people who come after us... when we blaze a trail, we do not know how far other people are going along that trail..."[39]

During the remainder of November and early December other groups and individuals appeared before the committee without shedding much new light on the issue. The Unitarians who favoured abortions were represented on November 14th. Dr. Paul Adams and Dr. Kevin Ford, representing the Catholic Physicians Guild of Manitoba, accompanied by Dr. Tallon from Cornwall, spoke against abortions on November 16. Dr. F. Clarke Fraser of Montreal spoke in favour of a revised law on November 21st. He was succeeded by Mr. David Dehler of Ottawa who was opposed to amending the law. The positions of the pro- and anti-revisionists remained hopelessly irreconcilable. Those members of the Committee who favoured a new law were intent on forcing an acknowledgment from opponents that at some time or other, abortions, however few or limited in number, might be necessary. They hoped, thereby, to establish the fact that the need for abortion was recognized in principle by all and that the difference between

---

37. *Proceedings — Abortion*, Nov. 7, 1967, pp. 160ff. See also "MP's arguments fail with anti-abortion group," *Globe and Mail*, Nov. 8, 1967. Several years later some denounced as untrue the case of a crying foetus being taken to the incinerator in Glasgow, Scotland, though it had been reported in newspapers throughout Great Britain and the world, and had been verified by the British Medical Association.

38. *Proceedings — Abortion*, Appendix "F," pp. 168ff. Also in *Globe and Mail*, November 8, 1967.

39. *Proceedings — Abortion*, Nov. 8, 1967, p. 164.

proponents and opponents was merely a difference of degree.[40] On the other hand, those members of the Committee who opposed legalization attempted to show that 'hard cases make poor laws,' and that sad case histories of genetic deformities or criminal assaults did not suffice for approving the removal of laws which, in their opinion, safeguarded the rights of millions.

Meanwhile, the popular trend continued to favour legalization. On November 14th the Union of American Hebrew Congregations, meeting in Montreal and representing the majority of Reform Jews in North America, voted by a strong majority to approve legalization. The resolution included the socio-economic grounds and typically referred to proponents as "forward-looking" citizens, thus, by implication, tagging opponents such as their Orthodox co-religionists, as 'backward-looking'.[41] On November 18th the socio-economic grounds for abortion were accepted by the National Council of the New Democratic Party as party of official party policy. The Social Credit Party of Ontario, however, voted against relaxation of the abortion law when it met in Kitchener that fall.[42]

The Presbyterian Church was the first of the Churches to submit a brief to the Standing Committee. It advocated legal abortions not just when the mother's life was endangered but also when her health was threatened. Rejecting abortion as a general practice, the Church insisted on stressing *serious* impairment of health. This it recognized as the only reason for therapeutic abortions; neither the expediency of reducing illegal abortions, nor abortion as a measure of population control carried her approval. "Abortion terminates life," the brief said, and it "involves a decision fraught with serious moral and spiritual implications."[43]

A week later it was the turn of the National Council of Women. In presenting their four year old resolution, the Council repeated the customary estimate of illegal abortions ("from 30,000 to 300,000").[44] It defined abortion as the premature expulsion of the "mammalian" foetus, adding that abortion was not spelled "a-b-h-o-r-etc." It also presented an historical survey which included the statement that "even the history of the Roman Catholic Church indicates that attitudes against abortion were expressed only in the last few centuries." A month earlier the Unitarians had submitted a survey which, although far from complete, at least showed that the opposition of the Church was not of recent origin but dated from the beginning of Christianity.[45]

40. Compare, for instance, Knowles to Cooper: "If you have the right to qualify it in one instance (the rare case of saving the mother's life) have not others the right to qualify it for some other reason? *Ibid.,* p. 162.

41. "Liberalize abortion laws, Reform Jews recommend," *Globe and Mail,* November 14, 1967, p. 31.

42. "Social clause a part of NDP policy," and "Socreds against relaxation of abortion law," *Globe and Mail,* Nov. 20, 1967, p. 14.

43. *Proceedings — Abortion,* Dec. 5, 1967, Appendix "X," p. 391.

44. *Ibid.,* No. 13, Dec. 8 and Dec. 12, Appendix "Y," pp. 433-434.

45. *Ibid.,* No. 7, November 14, 1967, Appendix "J," pp. 211ff.

On December 14 the Anglican delegation appeared before the Committee. Part of the hearing was spent in an attempt to discover the exact meaning of the Church's brief and position.[46] The brief noted the Church's "responsibility both to uphold and to interpret the long-standing Christian tradition in opposition to abortion."

But the authors claimed change was needed in view of "the impact of medical science," "an increase in biological knowledge" and the "recognition of the place of women." Their dilemma was summed up by clause 11 of the brief which rejected as "indefensible positions" both abortion on demand and the absolute prohibition of all abortion.[47]

The difficulty came with the description of the actual changes the delegation proposed. Clause 9 of the brief stated that "abortion should not be used to solve those social problems which should be dealth with by social and economic measures..." Clause 10 asserted "the general inviolability of the foetus." Clause 12 requested that due consideration be given to the sacredness of human life. But Clause 13 recommended that termination of pregnancy be permissible whenever life or health was threatened, with health understood, the brief pointed out, "in its broadest sense," including "the relationship of the expectant mother to her total environment and her ability to cope with the problems within it." Participants in the hearing indicated this definition as the key line of the brief.[48] Thus it became evident that in line with the most free-thinking wing of the Church in Britain, the members of this delegation would support abortion for any serious reason.

Summary

During the last six months of 1967 Britain had finally completed its new legislation which permitted abortions for four reasons, including socio-economic reasons.

During the same period the legislative process for revision of the law had finally been initiated in Canada with the start of special hearings on abortion before the Standing Committee on Health and Welfare of the House of Commons. In general these hearings had revealed that, except for very small groups, there was no approval of abortion on demand. It was also apparent, however, that many people were ready to accept abortion whenever the life and health of the mother was endangered, as well as in cases of criminal assault and possible deformity. Some people desired the new British legislation as a model for Canada but the majority seemed reluctant to go that far.

The contribution of Mrs. Grace MacInnis probably drew the most attention of any of the fall hearings, especially because of her inference that the country was ready to embark on a policy of ensuring "quality

---

46. *Proceedings — Abortion*, December 14, 1967, Appendix "BB," pp. 473-475.
47. The brief claimed that the absolute rejection of abortion could in certain circumstances "condemn both the mother and the unborn child to death."
48. It was indicated as such by Dr. Paul Christie, member of the delegation. *Proceedings — Abortion*, Dec. 14, 1967, p. 449.

life." The *Globe* vigorously pursued its policy of maintaining public pressure upon Government and parliament in favour of as broad a law as possible with no less than three editorials on the subject during the month of October. The paper now proposed a law which at once would allow every woman to have an abortion as a matter of right, yet leave the decision in the hands of the medical profession.

In early December the attitude of the Government was still obscure. Within a matter of weeks, however, the Standing Committee conducting the abortion hearings was to publish a surprising Interim Report, followed immediately by the introduction into parliament of new legislation. The approach of the government would leave opponents of broader abortion laws angry and dissatisfied.

CHAPTER VI

Criminal Code Reforms

While the House of Commons Committee meetings progressed steadily, winter set in and the country prepared for Christmas and the conclusion of Canada's Centennial year. Whether out of indifference, or because it appeared out of season, few daily papers in the country carried reports on the weekly abortion hearings, and if they did, the news was buried in the back pages. Only the Toronto *Globe and Mail* reported faithfully and in detail.

The meeting with the Anglican delegates on December 14 proved to be the last public hearing for 1967, although this had not been the original intention. At the beginning, one more session had been programmed for Tuesday, December 19, namely to receive the delegation of the Canadian Catholic Conference of Bishops. But by December 5 this hearing had been cancelled, the Bishops had been asked to accept a date in January of the following year, and the Chairman had announced that the December 19 meeting, instead, would be devoted to an "in camera" meeting of the Committee itself. Therefore, it came as a complete surprise when the press was informed, after this December 19 meeting was over, that the Committee had presented the Government with an Interim Report advising a revision of the law. This decision surprised, perhaps, even the Committee's own members: only eleven of the twenty-four were present that day. Despite the fact that, as yet, their own work was only half done, these eleven members passed the recommendation to proceed with legislation by a vote of 9 to 2. The two dissenting votes were cast by George Chatterton (PC, Esquimalt — Saanich) and Ralph Cowan (L, York-Humber).[1]

The Interim Report declared that the existing law was 'ambiguous' and that Sections 209 and 237 were contradictory. It proposed that the Standing Committee continue with further research and make studies relevant to other countries. But on "the understanding that the Government may wish to introduce some legislative changes", it recommended that, in the meantime, the Criminal Code be amended to "allow therapeutic abortion under appropriate medical safeguards where a pregnancy will seriously endanger the life or the health of the mother."[2] As if to forestall recriminations from the pro-revisionists, Dr. Harley emphasized that it was only an interim report and that

---

1. *The Calgary Herald*, Wednesday, December 20, 1967, p. 2.
2. "Report to the House," *Proceedings — Abortion*, December 19, 1967, pp. 14-3, 14-4.

the Committee might well recommend broader liberalizing amendments later.[3]

The next morning few papers carried the news at all, except for *The Globe* which gave it prompt and prominent display on the front-page with the heading: "Trudeau gets green light for easing abortion law."[4] Yet an even bigger surprise was in store on the day following. While previously Dr. Harley had stated that the Government would not bring forward a bill while the matter was before the Committee, someone, evidently, had changed the plans.[5] On Wednesday, December 20, it became known that the Government did actually intend to put on the order paper legislation which also covered abortion. And indeed, on Thursday, December 21, two days after the Interim Report of the Standing Committee, the Government deposited in the House of Commons a 72 page, 104 clause, Omnibus bill which covered a great many revisions in the Criminal Code, including the legalization of abortion. That same day, within hours of adjournment for the Christmas holiday, the bill was given first reading by the Commons.

The Government's move came so quickly that even the *Globe* could barely keep up. The paper came out with an editorial on Thursday morning. Although the editorial writer noted that legislation was to be brought before the House that very day, his article was based on the Tuesday report. In it he expressed his dislike for the Committee's "minimum position" of allowing abortions only for serious threats to life and health. According to him, "Such changes... would do no more than legalize what is already being done by reputable doctors in reputable hospitals."[6] He suggested that it would be much better if the Government followed the example of Great Britain which now permitted abortions for social reasons. "Reform has been bitterly opposed by those whose religious beliefs preclude abortion," he concluded, "chiefly, that is, by Roman Catholics." Nevertheless:

> ... this Government has decided, in the similar cases of birth control and divorce, that where religious moralities conflict, the State should support none, but leave the choice to individual conscience. It is a policy that should also be followed with abortion.

The following Saturday, the *Globe* published a second editorial indicating just how strongly the editors felt about this matter. Once again the paper devoted more editorial space to the abortion issue than all other major newspapers in Canada combined.[7] Referring to

---

3. *The Calgary Herald,* Wednesday, December 20, 1967, p. 2.

4. *Globe and Mail,* December 20, p. 1. To my knowledge no other paper carried this news on the front page with the exception of *The Calgary Herald* which included it in small print with the primary news that the Commons had given third reading to the Divorce Bill.

5. On November 30, see Committee witness John Hackett in Letter to editor, *Canadian Register,* January 13, 1968.

6. "Now the job is to be done, let it be done right," *Globe and Mail* December 21, 1967.

7. "A Bold New program that Touches us All," *Globe and Mail,* Saturday, December 23, 1967. To my knowledge, after examining newspapers from coast

the bill as "a bold new program," it noted this time that while the proposed abortion changes:

> may not satisfy many of those in the vanguard of the abortion reform movement... it does open the door to far more humane practices. What constitutes health — physical, emotional and mental — is left to qualified practitioners, as it should be.

The Press

As of December 21, 1967, the proposed legislative change on abortion lay sandwiched among the many proposed changes of the Criminal Code. That, apparently, had been the deliberate intention of Mr. Trudeau. A day before the introduction of the Omnibus bill, *The Calgary Herald* reported that the Justice Minister felt that "these amendments would have a better chance of passing if they were included in a bigger, diverse bill with its obvious advantages of psychological inertia."[14] It was certainly done with foresight as was the presentation of the Bill just before the Christmas holidays near the close of Canada's Centennial year.

The Omnibus bill included over one hundred items, ranging from drunken driving to jury trials, from bail reform to marijuana, from firearms, lotteries and harrassing phone calls, to homosexuality, cruelty to animals and Canadian passports. It was while discussing homosexuality that Justice Minister Pierre Trudeau explained to newsmen that "the state has no business in the bedrooms of the nation," a statement which would soon come to be indiscriminately applied to abortion as well. Mr. Trudeau also informed reporters that he saw no reason to allow a free vote on any part of the bill.[15] As for the actual wording of the proposed abortion legislation, it was almost identical to the suggestion in the Committee's Interim Report. The only difference was that the government proposal read "endanger the life and health of the mother" rather than "*seriously* endanger"... as proposed in the Interim Report.

The news of the proposed Criminal Code reform made the headlines and the front pages of practically every paper in the country. For the first time, really, the country took note of the Minister of Justice, Pierre Elliot Trudeau, who had been appointed to the Department only eight months earlier. Still, no one would have guessed then, that within another four months the same man would be leader of the Liberal Party and Prime-Minister designate of Canada.

While most newspapers carried front page headlines such as "Criminal Code Overhaul Asked" or "Sweeping Changes for Criminal Code," many were satisfied with simply printing a list of the proposed changes. In some cases, usually a day or two later, the papers carried a more detailed description of four or five of the more important items

---

to coast, no other daily newspaper carried an editorial on abortion; several papers referred to abortions in general editorial comments on the proposed Code reforms.

14. *The Calgary Herald*, "Senate gets Divorce Bill" — Abortion Study Tabled," Wednesday Dec. 20, 1967, p. 2.

15. *Globe and Mail*, December 22, 1967, p. 1.

in the Bill. Many, but by no means all papers, eventually carried a general editorial on the proposed Criminal Code reform. These editorials ranged from outright approval to approval with reservations.

Among the newspapers, *The Chronical Herald* of Halifax approved the proposed reform, but reserved editorial comments on specific items for a later date.[17] The *Ottawa Journal* entitled its editorial, "Amending the Code to suit the Times." It discussed various items and observed that Justice Minister Trudeau had shown courage. The laws on abortion and homosexuality would involve conscience and instinctive resistance... "But modern knowledge supports him in proposing changes and the reception given his revisions shows the country generally has not been shocked by them..."[18]

The Montreal *Gazette*, apparently pre-occupied with problems of how the province of Quebec should raise money, devoted its appraisal of the Criminal Law reforms to: "Would Government Lotteries Help?"[19] *The Winnipeg Free Press* carried no editorial comment at all, at least not before the end of the year. *The Calgary Herald* headlined the news of the Omnibus bill as "Drinking Drivers Face New Attack." Commenting on various items in an editorial the following week, it noted that "clarification of the abortion law and its extension to cover the physical and mental health of the mother is commendable. Its effectiveness, however, depends on the manner in which hospitals and the medical profession exercise their judgment..."[20] The *Edmonton Journal* announced the original news under the heading, "Homosexual Law Change Backed."[21] Its editorial comments of the following week were very short, indicating general approval of the Bill, "though individual parts of it may be criticized."

Finally, the *Ottawa Citizen* fully approved. "Sweeping new look for Criminal Code," it announced on Friday, December 22nd. Its editorial of the same day discussed the 'updating' of the law and noted that "...the new reforms underline Mr. Trudeau's confident belief that Parliament is now ready to deal favourably with progressive legislation." The paper's regular columnist, Charles Lynch, headed his contribution: A retreat from hypocrisy. "The idea has been to tailor our laws to our times," Mr. Lynch wrote, "and this is shown vividly in the way the new amendments deal with matters of public morality." According to him, the proposed new measures reflected "the new tolerance that marks our 1967 society."

The Government's sponsorship of new abortion legislation also led to a flurry of articles in the periodical press. Of course, some groups and individuals had expressed their views already. A somewhat cautious opinion in the United Church *Observer* two months earlier had insisted on quick action, for fear that further delays would increase the number of illegal abortions and encourage the increasingly "loud and irresponsible voices" which "would make abortion a substitute

---

17. Tuesday, December 26, 1967. No comments appeared before the end of the year.
18. Wednesday, December 27, 1967.
19. Editorial, Tuesday, December 26, 1967.
20. Tuesday, December 26, 1967.
21. Thursday, December 21, 1967.

for birth control."[22] The Anglican monthly, the *Canadian Churchman*, devoted its entire January edition to the issue, naturally reflecting the position of its own Church in favour of legalization, though allowing a Roman Catholic columnist to write in opposition to it. Among smaller periodicals, the professional magazine for Social Workers, *Canadian Welfare*, approved of the Government's action, while a monthly from Saskatchewan, *Our Family*, had already devoted an entire issue to a symposium of a Presbyterian, a Lutheran, an Anglican, and Roman Catholics, in opposition to legalization.[23] *Weekend Magazine*, Saturday supplement to a number of daily papers across Canada, reviewed the Omnibus bill and the hearings of the Commons Committee in a January issue. It presented both sides, but its own view was implicitly indicated in the opening line which read: "She was 33 and she was dead... The verdict: An abortion that went wrong."[24]

French Canada

The most outspoken criticism of the abortion clause in the Omnibus bill came from the Catholic press, especially from English language weeklies. French Canada, Catholic almost by definition, could hardly be expected to cheer, but the situation there was different from that of English Canada where Catholics and their hospitals now felt themselves a beleaguered minority in all the provinces.[25] A year later, in 1968, the parliamentary opposition to abortion would come almost entirely from a Quebec group, the Créditistes, while English speaking Catholic politicians, many of them Liberals, would maintain a discreet silence. But in early 1968 the situation was nearly the reverse, though it concerned the press rather than the politicians. Preoccupied with the consequences of General de Gaulle's visit, as well as internal, constitutional, federal-provincial and language problems, Quebec tended to shrug its shoulders at the whole Omnibus bill and its supposed social revolution. The submissions of French language organizations to the Committee hearings were certainly minimal — two out of twenty-four; and of the witnesses, no more than half a dozen of the ninety-nine were French Canadians.[26]

Among the French language dailies, *Le Droit* of Ottawa saw no reason for alarm since it concerned only a projected law which could be changed easily in second or third reading. *L'Action* of Quebec did object to the Omnibus bill which, it said, "contained odious articles which surpassed the understanding of decent citizens." An editorial writer of Montreal's *Le Devoir*, Vincent Prince, indulged in a long

22. "Legalize abortion, but...," Editorial, U.C. *Observer*, Oct. 15, 1967.

23. P. Playfair, "Parliament faces up," *Canadian Welfare*, Vol. 44, Jan.-Feb., 1968, pp. 4-7. *Our family*, October, 1967.

24. Robert McKeown, "If you had to vote...," *Weekend Magazine*, No. 3, January, 1968.

25. Because of lack of resources the author has not examined the Quebec press in any depth.

26. The hearings were conducted, of course, almost exclusively in English, although translation services were available.

philosophical reflection about the need to protect life, promising to return to the subject later on. For the time being, he preferred the course of prudence and called for further study.[27]

The political and religiously radical Catholic monthly, *Maintenant*, gave the issue a four page long editorial: "Abortion From Solomon to P.E. Trudeau."[28] In all countries, the authors said, abortion is promoted in the name of pluralism and social utility. As they could not see what religious pluralism had to do with unborn human life and, as they rejected social utilitarianism, their answer to legalized abortion was no.

The more conservative intellectual monthly, *Relations*, had already spoken out against the legalization of abortion a year earlier[29]. Beginning in February, it started a series of articles on the subject by its expert on law and morality questions, Marcel Marcotte.[30] The way things are going, wrote Jesuit Father Marcotte in his opening paragraph, we will end up thinking that Canada is definitely an Anglo-Saxon country with her umbilical cord still not cut. No sooner does Britain provide herself with new laws on divorce, homosexuality and even abortion, then the Canadian government follows hot on her heels, copying her slavishly. Are the ashes of political colonialism surreptitiously giving rebirth to a new, judicial colonialism, he asked. Observing that the proposed abortion amendment was not merely one more step on a well-trodden path, but a complete and radical reversal of a long existing tradition, he wondered at the end of the article, what purposes the Minister of Justice could have had in mind by burying abortion among all the other items of the Omnibus bill. He noted as ominous that the Catholic Bishops had now refused to appear before the Commons Committee.

In Quebec, as elsewhere, those whose profession confronted them with the effects of illegal abortions were more inclined to seek immediate solutions. The director of the Montreal police, Jean-Paul Gilbert, preferred to see abortion removed from the criminal jurisdiction to that of medicine, on the grounds that the bigger hospitals in Montreal, Toronto and Vancouver had to treat the ill results of illegal abortions almost daily.[31] His colleagues in Toronto and Vancouver, however, refused to express an opinion.[32]

The difference between French and English speaking Catholics at this stage was perhaps best illustrated by the attitude of the respective hospital associations. While the predominantly English Association of Catholic Hospitals vowed to fight the bill, the president

---

27. "Reactions diverses au projet de loi sur l'avortement," *La Liberté et le Patriote*, 11 janvier, 1968, p. 142. (See also *Relations*, février, 1968, p. 52). Later on *Le Devoir* came out against the abortion amendments.

28. Vincent Harvey and Hélène Pelletier-Baillargeon, "L'avortement: de Salomon à P.-E. Trudeau," *Maintenant*, #73, 15 janvier, p. 3-6.

29. "L'avortement est un meurtre," *Relations*, avril 1966, pp. 106-107.

30. "L'avortement, la Morale et la Loi," *Relations*, février, 1968, pp. 30-36.

31. *La Liberté et le Patriote*, février 8, 1968, p. 1.

32. "Abortion not police affair, Montreal chief says," *Globe and Mail*, January 26, 1968, p. 12.

of l'Association des Hôpitaux du Québec, Dr. André Pothier, representing denominational as well as non-denominational hospitals, declared that the Association would not oppose it on the grounds that doctors and hospitals would be left to follow their own consciences and their own policies.[33] Evidently, Dr. Pothier did not expect that in Quebec Catholic hospitals could be forced to conform to Anglo-Saxon thinking.

English Canadian Catholics

Whatever the feelings among French Canadians, a number of English-speaking Catholics were upset. Already four weeks before the introduction of the Omnibus bill, in November 1967, there had been suspicion among some that the government might not comply with the requests for further study and might even by-pass its own Standing Committee.[34] Perhaps because of this apprehension, Toronto's Coadjutor Archbishop Philip Pocock, still Chairman of the ad hoc Committee of the Canadian Catholic Conference, announced that the Bishops had been invited to present their views on Tuesday, December 19, and that this date had been confirmed by the Standing Committee.[35] That, of course, was the meeting which had been cancelled again by December 5.

As there had been no further clarifications of the Bishops' position since the press statement in answer to the April 10 editorial in the *Globe* six months earlier, the Archbishop also took this opportunity to explain that the C.C.C. Committee was involved in drafting a position paper and in consulting "dozens of individuals and groups." After stating that "it would be premature to disclose policy now," he said that the C.C.C. did not intend this time to present two statements, one for Catholics and one for the general public as it had done on the birth control and divorce issues. "We will speak to the Parliamentary Committee, as Catholics and as citizens," he said, "as Catholics on spiritual and moral aspects and as citizens on law as it affects inalienable rights and the common good." He added:

> We are making every effort to express a consensus but in the field of law and the promotion of the common good any concerned citizen of any faith, or any of no faith, may feel that a more rigid or a more liberal position is preferable and is free to express it.[36]

The events of December 19th and 21st certainly seemed to vindicate the suspicions of those who had feared all along that the Minister of Justice was quietly preparing to go ahead with his legislative plans without waiting for the completion of the hearings by the Standing Committee. Following the publication of the Interim Report on

---

33. *La Liberté et le Patriote, op. cit.*
34. "Major Research Needed before Abortion Change," *Western Catholic Reporter,* December 7, 1967, p. 1.
35. *Ibid.*
36. *Ibid.*

Tuesday, December 19th, Archbishop Pocock felt obliged to express his disappointment. Amendments to the Criminal Code dealing with abortion, he said on Thursday before he had heard of the Omnibus bill, should be confined to eliminating ambiguity without "venturing into a hazardous, uncharted broadening of the law." He went on to say that the Bishops were deeply concerned regarding the interpretation of the word, "health." "Indeed we do not see how responsible limits can be set out in law," he said, "without additional knowledge from the research the committee itself recommends. A loose interpretation could bring widespread social and personal misfortune to our country."[37]

While the Toronto Archbishop still found something positive to say, (pleased with the decision of the Commons Committee that there should be more study), after the announcement of the Omnibus bill other Catholic spokesmen were less charitable. Rev. John Mole, information officer for the Catholic Hospital Association of Canada — with a membership of 300 hospitals offering 35 per cent of Canada's health services — protested strongly. Convinced that the very scope of the Criminal Code reforms obscured the nature and significance of the proposed legislation on abortion, he stated that the Association wanted a Royal Commission to examine "this complex and grave subject." He charged that the legislation would divide the country at a time when Canadians needed unity. He accused Justice Minister Trudeau of having "abused his office" by throwing the weight of his position behind the pro-abortion lobby. It was "a sheer act of contempt" on Mr. Trudeau's part to have introduced the legislation without hearing from either the Canadian bishops or the Catholic Hospital Association, he said. Turning to the Catholic Conference, he claimed that their brief would come too late and "that the Bishops should have made their position loud and clear in October."[38]

Following the Omnibus bill, the English Canadian Catholic weeklies also took up or renewed editorial positions.[39] The *Western Catholic Reporter* of Edmonton headed its editorial: "Abortion Law: A Blow at Life."[40] It recognized that much of the recent social legislation was good. But the proposed abortion amendment, it claimed, indicated a néed to slow down the government's haste in completing the social revolution, before the country was "sent down into deep and treacherous waters." As for the propriety of recent political events, it asked:

37. *Western Catholic Reporter,* January 4, 1968, p. 9. See also "Catholic Conference Chief Seeks Clarification of Abortion Laws," *Globe and Mail,* December 21, *Ottawa Journal,* December 21, p. 4.

38. "Catholic Hospital Assoc. Strikes at Abortion; Raps Trudeau for 'Contempt,' " *Western Catholic Reporter,* January 4, 1967, pp. 1 & 9: See also editorial in *The Canadian Register,* Jan. 6, 1968. Fr. Mole's protest apparently appeared in newspapers in Toronto and on television though I have been unable to find the evidence.

39. Of the six Catholic weeklies in existence in 1967 I have used the *Canadian Register* (Ontario), the *Western Catholic Reporter* (Alberta) and the *Prairie Messenger* (Saskatchewan) as representative. Not examined: the *B.C. Catholic,* the *Casket* (Nova Scotia) and the *New Freeman* (New Brunswick).

40. *Western Catholic Reporter,* January 4, 1968. Editor: Douglas Roche.

Is this a responsible way for the government of Canada to treat the bishops of a denomination making up nearly half the country's population? Or is this an accurate reflection of the present stage we have entered: that the government does not really care what the Church says even in the most fundamental matters of morality, and is just going through the motions in allowing the bishops to be heard?

The paper noticed 'in retrospect' that apparently the bishops had been too gentlemanly in waiting this long to make their stand public. It expressed the regret that it had been impossible to establish a united Christian front in opposition to abortion, which it blamed on the fact that "the Anglicans and United have not examined the matter carefully enough." A few weeks later, a United Church minister took the paper to task for that remark, quoting extensively from the Proceedings of the United Church General Council meeting at Waterloo in September, 1966.[41]

The Catholic weekly of Toronto, the *Canadian Register*, in its issue of January 6th, denounced the way things had been handled. The editorial writer "questioned Mr. Trudeau's qualifications for the high office" he held because of the manner he had "lumped" abortion with other items into an Omnibus bill. "He stands in the position of a man," the writer observed, "who seeks to pass off as shepherd's pie a concoction containing ten per cent pigeon and ninety per cent horse." He further observed that contrary to the government's thinking, doctors did *not* want the sole responsibility for deciding abortions and that it would be much better if abortion were removed from the Omnibus bill and treated separately.[42]

The following week the *Register* published a second editorial on the subject of conscience and a free vote.[43] The only conceivable justification for easing the existing law against abortion would be the drastic cutting down of the number of illegal abortions, it said. But this claim does not appear to stand up in view of the experience of other countries, it continued. Moreover, under the present law, "no woman whose health is seriously threatened by pregnancy is left without recourse." It noted that "conscience" does not derive from social or environmental influences and certainly not from the discipline of any political party. It concluded:

> We do not know the number of Catholics in the ranks of Liberal members of the House, because we do not keep tabs on such things. But if these men cannot persuade their caucus to permit a free vote on such an important matter, we hope they will have the courage and the sense of duty needed to stand up for their deepest convictions...

41. Rev. A.J. Griffin, Edmonton, Letter to the editor, *Western Catholic Reporter*, February 15, 1968.
42. "Mr. Trudeau's Composite Pill," *Canadian Register*, Jan. 6, 1968. P.A.G. McKay was listed as Editor and Manager. Associate editors: Rt. Rev. J.G. Hanley and Rev. R. Durocher, omi.
43. "A Duty to Follow Conscience," *Canadian Register*, Jan. 13, 1968.

Early in February the *Register* published a third editorial against abortion. This time it quoted from a lecture by a United Church pastor and lecturer at the Toronto School of Graduate Studies, the Rev. Graham Scott, noting especially that the great Protestant theologian, Karl Barth, had written: "...deliberate abortion is irrefutably seen to be sin, murder and transgression."[44]

The *Prairie Messenger*, Saskatchewan's Catholic weekly, published a very different editorial.[45] In "Abortion's unanswered questions," it remarked that most Catholics "favor restrictive abortions regulations." It observed that:

A healthy modicum of order and the preservation of much rich heritage and truth result frequently from the rather rigid observance of laws. But somehow the laws prescribed by men's limited understanding should cede to better laws arising from man's greater understanding.

The author expressed appreciation for the desire to stop illegal abortions and for the objection to a law favouring "the rights of the potential or hypothetical human being, the embryo, over the actual human being, the mother."[46] He sympathized with the case of the Vancouver doctor who, after refusing to perform an abortion, was faced with two suicides, that of the pregnant woman, and a few weeks later, that of her father. "What are they (doctors) to do in such cases?" he asked. He charged that "during the years of challenging and lambasting antiquated laws" researchers had not done their homework, leaving a host of unanswered questions: What are the effects of abortion on women? Do abortions cause sterility or complicate later pregnancies? Will legalization reduce illegal abortions? When is an unborn fetus a human being? He concluded:

It is doubtful whether the Canadian Churches can keep on arguing from the grounds of little scientific knowledge and moralistic attitudes. We must accept the principle of the sacredness of life but must also rely on scientific research.

The three weeklies probably reflected the spectrum of views among Catholics fairly accurately with the exception of those who already had accepted abortion outright. Judging by the editorials, Catholics were not of one mind, nor had they remained impervious to the barrage of arguments and emotional appeals of those who favoured legalization. Only the Edmonton weekly rejected abortion absolutely. It did so on the ground that the unborn fetus was human and that nothing, certainly not science, would change that fact. As evidence it printed on the front page of its January 4 edition, photos of a human fetus at five different stages.[47] The *Canadian Register* remained opposed

44. "Protestants on Abortion", *Canadian Register*, February 3, 1968.
45. *Prairie Messenger*, January 24, 1967. Editorial was signed: MMP. (Michael Pomedli).
46. The wording is identical to that used in the brief submitted by the United Church to the Commons Committee. See *Proceedings – Abortion*, Feb. 6, 1968, p. 605.
47. B. Lyons, "Abortion's Crucial Question: When does human life begin?" *Western Catholic Reporter*, pp. 1 & 5. Photos on Page 1 from *Extension*.

to abortion, but took its stand on the grounds that legalization would not reduce illegal abortions, thereby implicitly admitting that if the opposite could be proven it might accept legal abortions as the lesser of two evils. In fact, one month later it would take this stand openly, thinking that it reflected the views of the bishops.[48] Finally, the *Prairie Messenger* appeared to indicate an acceptance of the premise that science would probably modify such laws as were now presumably based on 'religious' principles. Though unwilling to come to a definite position, the writer had really conceded his case by the use of such terms as "antiquated laws" and "moralistic attitudes."

Pastoral Letter

The events before Christmas and the subsequent protests and comments led the Catholic Bishops to change their minds. On December 27th they confirmed their presentation before the Committee set for January the 23rd, but on January the 15th they cancelled it. The President of the Canadian Catholic Conference, Bishop Alexander Carter, informed the Commons Committee that the Conference could not present a document which was written "with a view to co-operating in an on-going study," when such a study was made obsolete by the Committee's recommendation and the Government's decision to go ahead with legislation. Instead, he said, the Bishops would set their general point of view before the Canadian people in a pastoral statement to be issued forthwith.[49]

The Bishops' cancellation was followed by further protests against the government's decision to go ahead without having completed the hearings, first from the Catholic Women's league of Ontario, then from the C.W.L.'s national body.[50] Early in February, Emmett Carter, Bishop of London and brother of Alexander Carter, Bishop of Sault Ste. Marie, urged Catholics to send protests to the government.[51] But no other group or organization in the country saw anything distasteful in the behaviour of the government, nor considered the incident worthy of protest.

The Pastoral Letter appeared at the beginning of February.[52] The Bishops rejected the abortion legislation presently before Parliament as "a too simple solution to a serious and complex problem." They suggested "a completely different approach" to resolving the problems that caused the demand for abortion. They mentioned education fostering respect for human life at all stages of development; research

---

48. Editorial, "Facing Abortion Together," *Canadian Register*, March 16, 1968.
49. Text of Bishop Carter's letter to Dr Harley in *Proceedings — Abortion*, January 25th, 1968, p. 479. Also in Catholic weeklies of Jan. 18-27.
50. "CWL protests decision on abortion legislation," CP report, for instance, in Saskatoon *Star Phoenix*, Jan. 22, 1968. Also reports in Catholic weeklies.
51. "Bishop urges R.C.'s to oppose easier abortion," *Globe and Mail*, Feb. 12, p. 13.
52. Complete texts of Pastoral Letter in *Western Catholic Reporter*, Feb. 8; *Canadian Register*, Feb. 10; *Prairie Messenger*, Feb. 14; *La Liberté et le Patriote*, Feb. 15. Also, CP report in *Globe and Mail*, Feb. 8, w3. ("Abortion an unspeakable crime, RC's say in opposing changes"). For text, see appendix V.

on the frequency of illicit abortions; medical and psychiatric care for mothers in distress; help for unwed mothers; better care for the mentally ill; and more adequate social and family policies to be developed by the state.

The Bishops repeated the Vatican Council statement that "from the moment of its conception, life must be guarded with the greatest care, while abortion and infanticide are unspeakable crimes." The proposed amendment of the law, they said, not only "allows the direct and voluntary taking of an innocent life, but opens the door to the broadest interpretations." They repeated the Church's teaching which approved operations to save the mother's life, even if these operations resulted in "the unwanted and unsought death of the foetus." But "direct abortions" they rejected:

> When the mother's life is truly in danger, we understand that there may be a temptation to consider abortion, even direct abortion, as justifiable. Nevertheless, we must point out that this view is contrary to a persistent Judeo-Christian tradition that life is sacred. Likewise, to advocate abortion in order to protect something other than the very life of the mother, even if it be her physical or mental health, is to disregard the sacred right of the fetus to life; also, it is to sacrifice a greater value for a lesser one.

Science, said the Bishops, had "not established a fundamental difference between life in the womb and the child's life after birth." Progress in civilization, they said, "consists in the increasingly clear recognition of the dignity, sacredness and absolute inviolability of the human person, on both the theoretical and practical levels."

The *Globe* reported the Pastoral Letter under the heading "Abortion an unspeakable crime, RC's say in opposing changes."[53] The *Western Catholic Reporter*, though favourable, thought that in places the Bishops could have spoken "in more ringing tones that would have carried their message across the land."[54] The *Prairie Messenger* liked it just the way it was. They are not accusing the advocates of change of evil intent or disdain for traditional morality, it said. The Bishops have stated their position "without equivocation but also without arrogance."[55]

53. *Globe and Mail*, February 8, 1968, w3.
54. Editorial, "Thinking Positively on Abortion," Feb. 8, 1968ff
55. Editorial, "A too simple Solution," Feb. 14, 1968.

CHAPTER *VII*

Winter Hearings

The hearings of the Standing Committee resumed on January 25th, 1968. First the Chairman read Bishop Carter's letter cancelling the presentation of the Canadian Catholic Conference, then he read his own reply. In his own letter he expressed surprise at the Bishops' attitude, claiming that while the Minister of Justice had brought in a bill recommending changes in the abortion law, the perspective had not really changed because it was only *proposed* legislation. In view of the importance of the matter he asked the Bishops to reconsider.[1]

Someone then moved that the Committee accept the Chairman's reaction as its own, and that the Committee, too, urge the Conference to appear and submit a brief in any event. Mr. Ralph Cowan supported the suggestion that the Bishops be asked to reconsider, but objected to concurring in the Chairman's expression of surprise at the Bishops' cancellation of their presentation. "I am not at all surprised," he said. "I cannot criticize anyone who, when they get their face slapped by an interim report before they present their own opinion, reacts the way the... Conference did." Nevertheless, after agreement that the Committee's motion should endorse only the Chairman's invitation to the Bishops to reconsider, it was accepted by all.[2] Two weeks later a reply was received informing the Committee that the Catholic Conference would be happy to send a delegation. It would not submit a brief, however, but if the members so wished, the delegates could discuss the Pastoral Letter which was soon to be published.[3]

Hamilton Right to Life

The first meeting of the resumed hearings received the Hamilton Right to Life Committee, a group formed by Mr. and Mrs. Vincent Calzonetti of Burlington for the purpose of opposing broader grounds for abortion. Chief spokesman for the group was Dr. Gerard Quigley, Chief of Obstetrics at Hamilton's St. Joseph's Hospital, who stated the group's opposition to "health" as a reason for abortion.[4] He explained that there were almost no medical reasons for protecting the health of

---

1. *Proceedings — Abortion*, Jan. 25, 1968, p. 479. "Bishop's abortion brief requested by Ottawa," *Globe and Mail*, Jan. 26, 1968, p. 12.
2. *Ibid.*, p. 480.
3. *Op. cit.*, February 8, 1968, p. 633.
4. *Proceedings — Abortion*, January 25, 1968, p. 481. Also present was Dr. Patrick Beirne, St. Michael's Hospital, Toronto, *op. cit.*, p. 491.

the mother by means of abortion. He himself would never perform an abortion, he said, but he did think that the law should clarify that doctors were permitted to perform abortions when they felt it necessary to protect the life or life expectancy of the mother.[5]

Dr. Quigley's last statement pleased Mr. Knowles and Mrs. MacInnis who were satisfied that he had done their cause an important service. Their view was that as long as an opponent could be persuaded to admit that abortion was acceptable in *principle*, even if only for others and not for himself, the newly proposed legislation stood justified. After such an admission, they felt any discussion about abortion would not be a discussion of conflicting philosophies or ideals but merely a question of deciding the technical conditions. Dr. Brand (PC, Saskatoon) agreed with them. Dr. Quigley explained again, that he was vehemently opposed to abortion on demand, abortion for sexual crimes and abortion for mental retardation or genetic factors.[6] Mrs. MacInnis, too, stated that she did not think the country should have widespread abortion on demand.[7] But, said Mr. Knowles at the end of the hearing, "You have been very helpful, perhaps in a way you did not intend... you seem now to support the position the committee has taken and the position in Mr. Trudeau's bill."[8] The *Globe* printed the proceedings under the title "RC doctor endorses therapeutic abortions."[9]

On the same day as the hearing, the issue of false abortion statistics came to the public's attention again. Mrs. Mary Cooper of the Ottawa Committee for the defense of unborn children, revealed that the figure of 35,000 abortions, which were supposedly performed in metropolitan Toronto alone every year, as well as the figure of 300 supposed annual deaths from these illegal abortions, did not have their original source in the police department but in a newspaper. Further public confusion was caused, she said, by the fact that figures relating to natural miscarriages were listed by hospitals as abortions, which was their proper medical term. As for the estimate of 300,000 abortions in Canada, Mrs. Cooper pointed out that if these commonly used estimates were true, every woman in Canada would average two or three criminal abortions during her 38 years of child-bearing.[10]

Catholic Hospital Association

The Hamilton society was followed by various other organizations such as the London Society for Protection of the Unborn, represented by Doctors L. de Veber, Jack Walters and W. Tillmann, all of St. Joseph's Hospital and the University of Western Ontario in London. Dr. Walters illustrated the various stages of foetal development with

---

5. *Ibid.*, p. 488.
6. *Ibid.*, p. 501.
7. *Ibid.*, p. 505.
8. *Ibid.*, p. 500.
9. John Dafoe, *Globe and Mail*, Jan. 26, 1968, p. 12.
10. "Abortion statistics false, committee chairman charges," CP report, Saskatoon *Star Phoenix*, Jan. 31, 1968; *Globe and Mail*, Jan. 26, 1968, p. 12.

slides including a picture of a foetus sucking its thumb.

On February 8, the Catholic Hospital Association of Canada appeared before the Committee. It was the Committee's most unpleasant hearing. The delegation was led by its executive director Father Maurice Dussault, o.m.i., and the Association's Information Officer, Rev. John Mole, o.m.i.[11] The latter had vigorously protested the December developments. Still angry over the course of events in December and already having made it abundantly clear where they stood, it would, perhaps, have been better for the Association if its officers had boycotted the Committee. Now the hearing was spent in bitter wrangling which was not to the credit of the Association and which did not enlighten anyone.

The aggressive and bellicose attitude on the part of the chief spokesmen of the delegation, the accusatory tone of the presentation, and the suggestion that a Royal Commission would do a much better as well as a non-partisan job, all rubbed the Committee members the wrong way. They retaliated in kind. Mr. MacDonald (PC, Prince), himself a United Church minister, wanted to know why a delegation with three out of five members theologians and clergymen was "more concerned with the physical and mechanical concept of life than with the so-called spiritual, mental and social aspects of life."[12] Mr. Allmand (L, Notre-Dame-de-Grace) attacked the Medical-Moral Code for Catholic Hospitals as "legalistic" and "based on philosophical distinctions."[13] Mrs. MacInnis held forth on pluralism and 'imposing views on society' and managed to read into the record part of a letter received by the Committee from a Dr. James Collyer at the Family Medical Centre at St. Joseph's Hospital in London who expressed his belief "that socio-economic reasons are an adequate and sufficient reason to recommend abortion.[14] Dr. Isabelle (L, Hull) accused the Association of using hospitals to promote a religious movement; he also demanded rectification of the notion that the Bishops had not been consulted, which, he said, was a "monumental falsehood." Although they had been notified of the hearings on July 7, only after a telephone call on September 28th was the Committee told that "they would send a brief but that they would never appear before us." "Moreover," he said "they asked us to present their brief as late as possible during the hearing of witnesses." Did they wish to wait until everything was over before taking a stand?[15]

Mr. Knowles expressed surprise at a hospital association "appearing before us without a single doctor in attendance."[16] He claimed

---

11. Other members of the delegation were Mr. David Dehler, the Association's legal advisor; Father St. Arnaud, consultor on moral medical problems and Mr. Eric Brown, Administrator of the Hotel-Dieu in Kingston. Mr. Brown was also an elder of the Presbyterian Church. (o.m.i.: Oblates of Mary Immaculate, or Oblate Fathers).

12. *Proceedings — Abortion*, Feb. 8, 1968, p. 638.

13. *Ibid.*, p. 642.

14. *Ibid.*, p. 647.

15. *Ibid.*, p. 649.

16. *Ibid.*, p. 650.

that if there had been any consensus at all among the delegations, it had been to the effect that abortion was very much a medical question. Mr. Brand charged that because of their indignation at the Interim Report, the Association had sent a letter to every Catholic hospital in Canada asking them "to write and oppose us in every possible way."[17] Finally, Mr. Stanbury wanted to know whether the delegates were prepared to classify the Presbyterians, the Anglicans and the United Church members as responsible groups even though, in the views of these churches, life exists before birth but does not necessarily have identical value at every stage of its development.[18]

As for the brief which had been submitted, the Committee barely took notice of it.[19] This statement pointed out that abortion would divide hospitals and doctors between "consenting" and "dissenting" groups and that relations between hospitals and doctors would become strained. It forecast that doctors who accepted abortions would resent those who did not, for they would be left doing what most regarded as "distasteful" work. The brief also requested that if the law was amended, an exemption clause be added, as had been done in Britain and Colorado, permitting hospitals to refuse to perform abortions.

The brief was to prove prophetic. Its request that an exemption clause be built into the law was, of course, never passed. Within a few years of the passage of the law in 1969, Ministers of Health in British Columbia and Ontario were both reported talking about cutting off grants to Catholic hospitals.[20] Four years and three months after the brief had been submitted, the Toronto *Globe* suggested that it would be a good thing if all hospitals were taken away from religious denominations.[21]

United Church of Canada

One of the questions which kept recurring was that of the value of life. It had been a major topic of discussion at the hearing with the United Church delegation two days earlier. Rev. W. Clarke MacDonald, Chairman of the Church's Board of Evangelism and Social Service, had explained that in the opinion of the United Church "there is an accruing value" from the time conception takes place, and that in all of this "the primary consideration ought to be for the life of the one who is now living."[22] This notion had captivated several members of the committee though it was not pursued any further. No one inquired about the *nature* of this value, or by what standards it was judged to be "accruing," and whether it continued to accrue throughout life or whether a decreasing value was envisaged for those growing older and feebler.

---

17. *Ibid.*, p. 655.
18. *Ibid.*, p. 660.
19. Ibid., Appendix "QQ," pp. 676-680.
20. See Chapter 10.
21. See Chapter 10.
22. *Op.cit.*, Feb. 6, 1968, p. 603.

Unlike the blundering delegation of the Hospital Association, the envoys of the United Church had a smoothly operating group, well put together, bringing not just two doctors, but two doctors who were women.[23] It also helped that the views of the group fitted those of the majority of the Committee. The brief favoured immediate amendment of the law which it called 'harsh,' 'conflicting' and 'unfair.'

One of the interesting features of this hearing was that it became clear almost immediately that the members of the delegation were prepared to go much further than their brief. The addendum to the brief explained that "the United Church of Canada is not prepared at this time to consider socio-economic grounds for abortion." Dr. White and Rev. MacDonald stated that, personally, they were ready to accept socio-economic grounds such as inadequate housing. Rev. MacDonald suggested therefore that the addendum should now be in the past tense rather than in the present tense, and read "was not," rather than "is not prepared to." Rev. Hord who had drawn it up, agreed, admitting that he himself had "become more liberal as the months have gone by."[24]

The delegation readily accepted the broadest definition of "health," namely that of the World Health Organization which defined it as:

> a state of complete physical, mental, emotional and social well-being and not merely the absence of disease and physical well-being

"I guess on that definition we are all sick,"[25] observed Mr. Chatterton (PC, Esquimalt-Saanich). The delegation denied, however, that it favoured abortion on demand. Both Dr. White and Dr. Moore forecast that doctors would do extensive counselling. On questioning by Mr. MacDonald (PC, Prince) whether this was an "entirely realistic" view of the doctor-patient relationship and whether overworked doctors would not "take the path of least resistance" and simply recommend abortions, Dr. Moore denied that it could happen that way.[26] "I certainly do not think the number of therapeutic abortions is going to multiply," she said a little later.

> The whole problem is going to be brought out in the open, with more counselling and discussion, and more education to prevent the cases ever coming before it (the abortion committee).[27]

---

23. In addition to Rev. W. Clarke MacDonald the delegation consisted of Dr. Marjorie Moore, obstetrician, Women's College Hospital; Dr. Patricia White, psychiatrist, University Health Services, Univ. of Toronto; Rev. J.R. Hord, secretary, Board of Evangelism and Social Service; Mr. Alfred Best, lawyer; all from Toronto.

24. *Ibid.*, p. 612.

25. *Ibid.*, p. 607.

26. *Ibid.*, p. 609.

27. *Ibid.*, p. 613. After legalization in September 1969, less than 300 abortions were performed during the remainder of the year. In 1970 the number was 11,152; in 1971 it had grown to 30,949. (Statistics Canada, *Globe and Mail*, May 6, 1972).

Like the Anglican group, the United Church delegation, too, rested its denial of significant future increases in the number of therapeutic abortions on its faith in the ever spreading use of contraceptives.[28]

The Standing Committee continued its meetings throughout February and early March, hearing the views of a variety of groups and individuals. Six Ottawa women, led by Mrs. Helen Levine and representing no specific organization or group, asked that abortions be allowed on request because women have the right to do as they please with their bodies.[29] Representatives of the Canadian Welfare Council indicated that its interest in abortion was directly related to its concern with family planning. "Both," their brief said, "flow from its objective of promoting social policies which will help to protect and strengthen family life." It noted with approval that the proposed legislation was "permissive, not mandatory" and "that no woman..., no hospital..., no doctor or nurse will be required to participate in an abortion."[30]

Dr. Serge Mongeau, director of the Montreal Family Planning Centre, said that new social policies should be developed to help mothers face unwanted pregnancies and make society more hospitable to children.[31] The Canadian Labour Congress, speaking through Miss Huguette Plamondon, regional vice-president, made a representation in favour of abortion on demand.[32]

Canadian Catholic Conference

On March 5, 1968 the Standing Committee held its last hearing. Before the start of the meeting the Chairman announced that 49,174 persons had petitioned the Prime Minister in opposition to amending the law. No record was available of the total number of signatures of those who favoured a new law, he said, "other than the fact that 252 private submissions, telegrams and letters were signed by one or more persons.[33]

The meeting with the representatives of the Roman Catholic Bishops was not only the last hearing, but in scope and import it was the counterpart to the very first hearing when Mrs. MacInnis had been the star witness. More Committee members were present at this meeting than at any other. It was also the one in which there was the most participation by Committee members and in which substantial parts were conducted in French. While the meeting with the delegation of the Catholic Hospital Association had been strained and burdensome, the hearing with the representatives of the Canadian Catholic Conference was conducted with dignity and proved effortless. Led by Bishop Remi De Roo of Victoria, B.C., the delegation included three professors of theology — Lafontaine, Naud and Sheridan — as

---

28. Contraceptives were legalized in late 1969.
29. *Globe and Mail*, Feb. 14, 1968, p. 12. Saskatoon *Star Phoenix*, Feb. 14, 1968.
30. *Proceedings — Abortion*, Feb. 13, 1968, Appendix "SS," p. 707.
31. *Globe and Mail*, Feb. 16, 1968, p. 11. Saskatoon *Star Phoenix*, Feb. 17, 1968.
32. C.L.C. brief, *Proceedings — Abortion*, pp. 777ff. *Globe and Mail*, Feb. 21, 1968, p. 10.
33. *Op. cit.*, March 5, 1968, p. 820.

well as the Director of the C.C.C.'s Family Life Bureau, Mr. Bernard Daly.[34]

The Bishop delivered the opening statement. He began by recognizing the difficulty of writing a law that in a few words must solve a wide range of problems.[35] Then he went briefly into the history of the Pastoral letter, explaining that the Bishops had originally prepared a statement for the Commons Committee after "consultation with theologians, doctors, sociologists, lawyers and married couples." This draft had been sent to all 100 Canadian Bishops, who in turn consulted other people. But when the Omnibus bill moved the subject "from the stage of being under study in your committee to the stage of actual proposed legislation before Parliament," this document which made no reference to the bill, could not be revised in time. Moreover, the Bishops had been placed under a new pastoral obligation to speak out. This obligation they had fulfilled with their recent Pastoral Letter of February 7th.

Copies of the Pastoral letter had been sent to all the members, the Bishop said, but this delegation "is not here today to present this letter to you or even primarily to discuss it:"

> We are here on your invitation to try to help with a complex and difficult question. We come therefore in a spirit of dialogue. That is, we do not feel that we have the whole answer. We do not want to impose a particular point of view.

But he noted, we bring "not just the private moral opinion nor an isolated specialized point of view." The Church also speaks the views of "men and women who are deeply rooted in the stuff of Canadian life."

In concluding, Bishop De Roo stressed three points: "We are much concerned that a too-open health clause may result in widespread disrespect for, and assault on the life of the unborn child." We wish "to stress the need for research" and the obligation of lawmakers to constantly restudy the consequences of their decision. Finally, we emphasize "the need for the reform... of the socio-economic causes of unwanted children..." In thanking the Committee for the invitation, the Bishop repeated that "we are here simply to bring our little contribution in the spirit of dialogue to help as best we can with the grave responsibility that rests upon your shoulders."

There then followed an exchange of viewpoints and information such as had taken place at no other meeting. Indeed in the history of the abortion controversy, with its difficulties of communication, the hearing of March 5 stood out as a highlight. It illustrated how an almost impossible exchange of opinions between parties of radically different views on matters of prime importance could be carried out in a gracious and dignified manner.

---

34. The theologians were: Rev. E.J. Sheridan, s.j., professor of Moral Theology, Toronto; Rev. Jean-Marie Lafontaine, p.s.s. professor of Social Theology, Faculty of Social Sciences, Univ. of Montreal; Rev. André Naud, professor of Theology, Univ. of Montreal. A Dr. Maloney was unable to attend. (s.j. = Society of Jesus or Jesuit Fathers; p.s.s. = Pères de Saint Sulpice or Sulpician Fathers).

35. For statement see *Proceedings — Abortion*, March 5, 1968, pp. 820-821.

The discussion opened with some factual points about the practice and beliefs of the Catholic Church regarding the foetus. First, Mr. Allmand (L, Notre-Dame-de-Grace) wondered whether religious practice had been consistent with the Church's view of the foetus as human life. Rev. Sheridan explained that the Catholic Church requires baptism of the foetus unless it is evidently dead; and that the foetus is buried in consecrated ground whenever possible. Full funeral rites are not generally held, he said, but funeral services had never been looked upon as essential to the dead person.

Later on, Mr. Enns (PC, Portage-Neepawa) returned to this question.[36] He wondered whether it was not true that some natural terminations of pregnancies happen at such an early stage that mothers might not even advise the Church of it, and that by accepting this situation the Church was admitting that it is "difficult really to spell out the fact that there is human life at that stage?" Father Sheridan did not deny this difficulty, but pointed out that baptism was considered of such importance that the Church would confer the sacrament no matter how slight the chance of human life being present, always on the condition that the foetus was alive. Then, Mr. Allmand asked a second question, this time concerning earlier theories in the Church about the time of animation of the foetus.[37] Rev. Sheridan, speaking once more, explained that the view that life started 40 or 60 days after conception was the common wisdom of early times, inherited from Aristotelian biology, and had been proven by modern science to be without foundation. As long as these theories were held, abortion after 40 or 60 days was considered homicide, and abortion before that time as a lesser offense, but one still gravely criminal since it was the extinction of a process towards life. Mr. MacDonald (PC, Prince) closed this discussion by drawing attention to the Committee's problem of facing contradictory voices among the Churches. Bishop De Roo's observation that despite the different conclusions of the Churches there was a considerable area of agreement on principles, could not resolve this problem, of course.

The remainder of the hearing revolved around the two issues which were on the minds of the members of the Committee: If proposed legislation is unacceptable, then what law is acceptable? And, secondly: Did the Church's attitude towards the divorce-birth control legislation not prove that there is no such thing as a moral absolute?

The question of legislation was first broached by Dr. Isabelle (L, Hull). Assuming the legitimacy of abortions to save the mother's life, and being a doctor himself, he wanted to know why there were objections to adding the term "health." How would the Church, he asked, resolve the dilemma of the doctor in determining when no longer the health, but the very life, of the mother was gravely endangered? When would the mother be "near enough to the point of death?"[38]

Bishop De Roo first pointed out the difference between the moral problem of the physician and the totally different problem of what

---

36. *Ibid.*, p. 837.
37. *Ibid.*, p. 822.
38. *Ibid.*, p. 825.

makes a good piece of legislation. In answer to the first problem, Rev. Naud expressed doubt whether legislation could ever eliminate a doctor's perplexity in borderline cases. And in response to the problem of what makes a good law, Father Lafontaine observed that elements other than the doctor's perplexity were to be taken into account in framing laws — elements such as the mentality which will develop in regard to respect for life.

Following Dr. Isabelle, Mr. Knowles (NDP, Winnipeg North Centre) first expressed appreciation for the way the dialogue was developing. In regard to the delegates' insistence that respect for life must be a major concern in any decision, he wondered whether they would not also agree that concern and respect must be shown for the pregnant woman, the position of doctors, the suffering caused by illegal abortions and the position of unwanted children. "You have criticized our interim report, you have criticized Mr. Trudeau's bill... I do not think you have expressed approval that the law remain as it is. Where are we?" he asked.[39]

Mrs. MacInnis (NDP, Vancouver-Kingsway) agreed with Mr. Knowles. She felt that while one may have much respect for the life "of this tiny beginning," one cannot be blind to respect for the adult life of the pregnant woman. It is not "a simple matter of respecting life or not respecting life," she said, but a matter of weighing one against the other. Let us face the situation squarely and have reasonably broad legislation which will give it legality, she added, and then hope our education and responsibility will increase in this regard.[40]

Bishop De Roo acknowledged the problem of the suffering mother and the sad phenomenon of the unwanted child. But he wondered whether the task was not "to do something about the causes, rather than simply stopping at the consequences."[41] Father Sheridan added that one cannot be totally and exclusively preoccupied with the magnitude and the agonies of the problem to be solved; an eye must be kept on the act, on the proposed solution itself. What are *its* effects? What has pre-occupied the Bishops, he said, is their conviction that the extinction of what is highly probably human life will not resolve this concrete problem.[42] Mr. Daly added that the Government tended to use the narrowest frame of reference as in the case of the new divorce law. In fact, he claimed, it was not just a matter of making a change in the Criminal Code but it involved "the whole question of family policy, educational programs, and so on."[43]

The discussion then moved from the problem of 'what is the best law' to the question whether there is such a thing and whether one can ever arrive at a moral absolute. "If it is serious to write a law which seems to permit what may be the extinction of what might highly probably be life," Mr. Knowles observed, "is it not also a serious

---

39. *Ibid.*, p. 827.
40. *Ibid.*, p. 830.
41. *Ibid.*, p. 827.
42. *Ibid.*
43. *Ibid.*, p. 828.

matter to have a law which forces a woman to go through with a pregnancy under conditions that are... against her health?" He found it difficult to believe that there were absolutes: "the church has changed its mind on things too often through the centuries..."

Mr. O'Keefe (L, St. John's East) rejected the observation that there can be no absolutes. There is certainly an absolute for the child whose life is ended, he observed. Death is an absolute, and he wanted to know whether the beginning of human life was one also.[44] But Rev. Sheridan did not think that revelation, or philosophy, or any empirical science could answer that question. That human life begins at the time of conception, he said, is a high probability, a practical certitude, a moral certitude, but not an absolute mathematical certitude.[45] When Mr. O'Keefe remarked that it had to be either alive or dead, he answered, the important point here was not precisely whether there was life — which was beyond doubt — but whether there was *human* life, an immortal soul. This, he said, revelation neither confirmed nor denied. It said simply nothing.

While Mr. O'Keefe agreed with the Catholic Conference that Parliament should not venture into new legislation without more research, Mrs. MacInnis stuck to the view that everything was constantly evolving and that it was much better to change the law and bring some improvements now. First the Church was opposed to legalizing birth control, she noted. But then it came to accept legalization on the double grounds that the old law could not be enforced and that a great many Canadians looked upon birth control and contraceptive measures with altogether different eyes than the Church. "Wherein is this situation basically different from that?" she asked. "Can you not see that this is a similar situation?" Why, in the one case, are you content to allow people of a different way of thinking to make their own decisions, while in this case you "wish to make the decision for the entire Canadian community?"

Bishop De Roo, having pointed out earlier that the difference in attitudes towards birth control and towards abortion centred around the problem of human life, did not think that the Bishops wished to make the decisions for the entire community. The Pastoral Letter, he said, had "made a clear distinction between two fundamental issues," the moral and the legal. The Bishops had taken their position on the moral issue, but he did not see anything exclusively Catholic about that. The question of what makes a good law he saw as an entirely different issue.

With this remark the hearing moved to the next stage. After having discussed the question of the best legislation and the problem of whether or not there were standards which were morally absolute, the dialogue now raised the issue of the relationship between law and morality. First Mr. Daly noted, apropos the Bishop's remark that the moral issue was not specifically Roman Catholic in character, that the statement that abortion terminated life had also been made quite bluntly by the Presbyterians. Then the Rev. Sheridan added that, while "the business of lawmaking is essentially pragmatic, in moral matters there *are* absolutes." The whole point is, he argued, that it was quite consistent, for instance, for a group to be opposed to divorce as not good morals, yet recognize a law permitting divorce in this society as a good thing. The key question for law is: what makes for the common good. It is "in view of the common good and not because of a religious principle" that we think there can be no concession on something which is so intimately connected with basic human rights, respect for life, and so on:

> It is not a question of allowing people to adopt a position or imposing our position on others or on Catholics. The Bishops are convinced... that a loose law in the matter of abortion is simply not for the common good. It is a bad law because it introduces an element of disorder, a fundamental disrespect for life, which we have great apprehensions is likely to grow.[47]

Returning to the issue of legislation, Mr. Matte (R. Cr., Champlain) wanted to know what practical amendments "would you bring in...so that religious opinions would be respected and doctors enlightened in this matter?" Bishop De Roo, however, declined to answer that on the grounds that he was not a legislator. "We will always be ready to discuss any concrete text," he said, "but we could not ourselves say what it should be."[48] Whereupon Mr. Matte, indicating that he was talking about legislators, asked whether, should abortion come to a vote, Roman Catholics were "morally bound, as some people have stated?"[49] He received only an indirect answer. "In the final analysis," the Bishop said, the legislator "must follow the dictates of his conscience." First, he should see to it that it was a well-informed conscience. Secondly, he should legislate for the common good and not just simply go along with the majority.

This question forced the delegation to refine and clarify its position vis-à-vis the existing as well as the proposed legislation. Obviously, whether or not a legislator acted according to "a right conscience" would relate to whether or not a particular law was for the common good. Thus the delegation had to return to that point again. The Bishop pointed out that one aspect to be considered by the legislator in guiding his people on this question of abortion was the custom of people to regard as moral whatever was legal. Fr. Naud pointed out that such a law should not merely promote respect for life, but effectively assure it. Until now the law considered abortion a criminal act. What will happen to that conviction, he asked, if the clause "health" is added. Rev. Lafontaine observed that even the newly proposed legislation began with the general affirmation that abortion is a crime punishable by life imprisonment. But the legislator, he said, should consider whether a law which could considerably increase the

47. *Ibid.*, pp. 831-832.
48. *Ibid.*, p. 832.
49. *Ibid.*

number of abortions would be compatible with this statement.[50] There are already indications he later remarked on a similar point, that a new collective attitude is being bred, especially through the constant use of "such words as liberalization, broadening, modernization," words which "for many people signified improvement and progress."[51]

Another consideration the legislator had to take into account, the delegation argued, was the mentality which would only consider the value of a human life "in relation to its usefulness or uselessness to others." In reply to a question by Mr. Rock (L, Lachine), what was of greater value, the right to life of the foetus or the right to life of the mother, Bishop De Roo observed that "we do not esteem one higher than the other." "Human life," he said, "is a value in itself and consequently must never be used or exploited for the advantage of another."[52]

Following these points, Mr. Rock quoted from the Pastoral Letter where it said that it "would be a false approach to think that solution of such borderline cases calls for legislative changes of the kind proposed." Does this mean, he wanted to know "that the hospitals that perform such abortions should be allowed to continue to do so without changing any laws?"[53]

Bishop De Roo, cautious not to trespass upon the terrain of the legislator, wanted it emphasized "that we are not saying that the law should not be clarified."[54] We are commenting on the proposed changes, he continued, and we do not find acceptable the introduction of the words "or health." Desirous to make this point clearer, Rev. Naud added that "we believe that any abortion, the fact of directly ending the life of a foetus, is an immoral act." Because "for us Catholics it does not seem possible to stand behind a law that would permit such an act," he said, "it becomes difficult for us to tell you what kind of broadening we would like to have brought into the law." He then repeated what Fr. Lafontaine had stated earlier, namely that as far as the Church was concerned the best law would always be the one which would permit the least number of abortions.

The question of the Church's attitude towards the *making* of law was finally stated as follows:

> The distinction may be the following one: in view of our basic stand, do we have a text to propose? The answer is no. No Bill will be proposed in view of our fundamental stand. But, on the other hand, would we object to another text which would be bound in with the problem of life? This is a different matter. We may not want to propose, but we may or may not protest.[55]

---

50. *Ibid.*, p. 833.
51. *Ibid.*, p. 841.
52. *Ibid.*, p. 834.
53. *Ibid.*, p. 835.
54. *Ibid.*
55. Rev. Lafontaine, *Ibid.*, p. 836.

As the meeting gradually moved towards its close some of the same ground was gone over once more. As Catholicism had been brought up again, Mr. Simard (L, Lake St. John) inquired by what principle of moral theology the Church considered abortion an immoral act.[56] Rev. Naud answered: on the right of any innocent person to life, and the absolute interdiction against the deliberate taking of innocent human life. When Mr. Simard inquired whether that meant that we "cannot start by differentiating between a woman and a foetus?", Fr. Naud said yes.

At this point it was the turn of Mr. Enns. He felt, he said, "like uttering the anguished cry of Pilate and saying, "What is truth?" We have especially listened to Father Sheridan talk about the proba- bility of there being human life at the point of conception and then denying the absolutism of that statement. He wondered with Mrs. MacInnis if the witnesses could not accept that it was "really an evolving tradition."[57] Related to this point, Mr. Chatterton (PC, Esquimalt-Saanich) inquired what the attitude of the Church would be, if it *could* be proven that legalization would decrease the number of illegal abortions.

In reply Rev. Naud asked whether it was not true that, whatever the past or future evolution of moral thought, one must always act according to what one believes to be the right thing today? What counts is what one believes today, he observed. Moreover, just because thought evolves on one point, it will not necessarily do so on others. And in his thinking, evolution was only progressive if it moved towards respect for all human life, not away from it. As for the question of decreasing illegal abortions, supposing a new law would actually reduce them, he said, it still left the question to be answered whether the destruction of life was a good way of doing it.[58]

Towards the end of the hearing the Chairman himself made an inquiry. It seemed to him from what he had heard that the delegation did not necessarily agree with Article 16 of the Moral Code of the Catholic Hospital Association which said, that "direct abortion is never permitted, even when the ultimate purpose is to save the life of the mother."[59] But Fr. Sheridan denied that this was so, stating that this article represented the consensus of Catholic theologians. Does that mean, said the Chairman, "that you wish the Criminal Code amended so that abortion is illegal under any circumstance?" Rev. E.J. Sheridan:

> No. As I understand your question, that abortion is illegal under any circumstances, no. The bishops have never been in favour of tightening the present law so as to exclude abortion. Abortion is permitted under our present Criminal Code, and certainly the bishops have never moved, do not wish to move, in the direction of tightening that. In other

---

56. *Ibid.*, p. 836.
57. *Ibid.*, pp. 837-8.
58. *Ibid.*, p. 839.
59. *Ibid.*, p. 842.

words, we do not believe that our moral principle must be
enshrined in criminal law.[60]

The meeting concluded on an ecumenical note. Mr. Cowan,
speaking as a Presbyterian, wanted to leave with the delegation the
three-word sentence found in the early part of the Presbyterian brief,
"Abortion is murder." Mr. MacDonald ventured the thought that in
emphasizing the importance of respect for life, this delegation hopefully
did not intend to downgrade other church groups. Bishop De Roo
confirmed this, expressing the view that "far from wishing to appear
as sitting in judgment on the other groups or downgrading their moral
principles and convictions... we... recognize in them a similar respect
for life."

Final Report

On March 13, 1968, the Standing Committee on Health and Welfare
presented its second and final Report to the House of Commons.[61]
It had held 29 meetings, received 35 briefs, as well as numerous
resolutions and petitions, and had heard 93 witnesses from many
organizations. In comparing its recommendation of December 19th
with the proposed amendment introduced by the Minister of Justice
in Bill C-195, the Committee gave preference to its own report. It
acknowledged that there had been a "great deal of concern" over the
definition of health. It therefore recommended that the amendment
to permit abortions not read that the continuation of the pregnancy
could be discontinued when such pregnancy "would or would be likely
to endanger her life or health...," but that it read: "will endanger the
life or seriously and directly impair the health of the mother..." A
clear and direct serious threat to the mother's health must be present,
said the Committee, adding that it "intended health to mean physical
and mental health and not the wider definition given to it by the
World Health Organization."[62] Thus the Committee rejected abortion
on socio-economic grounds.[63]

Ten days later Cabinet Ministers were released from their duties
by Prime Minister Pearson in order to campaign for the leadership
of the Liberal party. Following the leadership convention it was
expected that elections would be held during the summer. This meant
that all proposed legislation on the order paper in the House of
Commons was suspended and would not come before parliament unless
re-introduced by a new government.

---

60. *Ibid.*, p. 843.
61. *Proceedings — Abortion*, #24 March 13, 1968, pp. 24-3; 24-4.
62. *Ibid.*, p. 24-4.
63. *Globe and Mail*, March 14, p. w3. *Western Catholic Reporter*, March 21, 1968,
     pp. 1 & 9.

CHAPTER VIII

The Opposition Confused

On March 6, 1968 the Standing Committee on Health and Welfare concluded its business with the hearing of the Canadian Catholic Conference delegation. Within a week the *Globe* resumed its pressure politics. It issued its strongest attack upon the Catholic Church yet, in an editorial entitled "Conscience and the Law."[1] The occasion was a proposal by Health Minister Allan MacEachen that the vote on the abortion amendments be free rather than a vote on party lines as proposed by Prime Minister Pearson and Justice Minister Trudeau. Two months earlier a similar proposal had been made by the Catholic *Canadian Register* in the editorial: A Duty to Follow Conscience.[2]

At the same time that some people were disgruntled about the proposed party vote, the Government seemed to hesitate to proceed with the abortion legislation. Announcing his candidacy for the leadership of the Liberal party at a February press conference, Mr. Trudeau, speaking to a journalist of *Le Devoir*, mentioned the possibility that the proposed amendments to the Criminal Code on homosexuality and abortion might be held over to a later session of parliament in order to give people more time to understand the proposed changes.[3] These hesitations undoubtedly disquieted the *Globe*. On March 11, it published an aggressive editorial starting with the sentence:

> In the light of opposition to reform from Quebec's Liberal caucus, one wonders if once again, the conscience of some Roman Catholic Canadians will be allowed to violate that of millions of other Canadians.

Without further explanation on what other occasions the "conscience" of millions of Canadians had been violated, the reader was informed that "Mr. MacEachen's move toward a free vote and the Quebec's caucus's pressure on Mr. Trudeau to delay reform "raises the... thorny issue of Church and State."

"This issue," said the *Globe*, "first concerns the right of any group of citizens to violate through law the conscience of other citizens. For that is precisely what abortion laws do." The paper then pursued the theme which it had followed for five years or more, namely that

---

1. March 11, 1968.
2. January 13, 1968.
3. *Western Catholic Reporter*, Feb. 29, 1968, p. 1. "Abortion Law may be Delayed," *Canadian Register*, Feb. 24, 1968.

abortion was not forbidden by law because it was harmful to society, but that it was harmful to society because it was forbidden by law:

> The Criminal Code... forces all Canadians — including Protestants, Jews, agnostics and others — to accept the birth of unwanted or deformed children regardless of the mother's health or the family's ability to care for children. It obliges the 12-year-old girl who has been raped to endure a nine-month nightmare; and it orders a wife with German measles to wait out the horror of creating a mental or physical defective. The poor of any or no faith it obliges to deepen their poverty through new financial burdens which may warp or shatter the lives of whole families.

The paper went on to repeat the distinction between morality and law found in the 1966 statement on contraception issued by the Bishops, who had also noted that it was the business of parliament to decide whether or not the common good required that a crime be made punishable by law. It then charged that:

> The bishops are now opposing abortion reform not because it threatens public order or the common good. They oppose it on essentially moral and theological grounds. Their imposition of Catholic morality and dogma on the rest of Canada is incompatible with their own distinction between moral and civil law.

Carefully hedging, yet at the same time claiming certainty that this morality was now being 'imposed' — "the contradiction displays itself most concretely and inadmissibly in the pressure that has apparently been brought on Catholic politicians..." — the *Globe* remarked:

> It would be regrettable if a coherent and vociferous opposition to reform from Quebec MP's were to unleash old demons of anti-French-Canadian prejudice in English Canada. Exasperated English Canadians who strongly wish for a civilized abortion law might be tempted to blame a failure on the "priest-ridden Quebeckers."

It concluded by rejecting the spectre which it had conjured up, finishing with one more parting shot at the Catholics:

> Such a view would not only be unfortunate; it would be wrong. For the man who champions reform is a French-Canadian and a Quebecker... At stake here is neither Mr. Trudeau nor English-French relations. It is a certain high conception of liberal democracy. That means a tolerant respect for the conscience of all — not just the consciences of the most dogmatic.

The General Secretary of the Canadian Catholic Conference, Rev. Gordon George, expressed his "surprise and dismay" at the editorial in a letter to the editor four days later.[4] Underlying the text of this editorial, said Father George, is "the suggestion that the Roman Catholic Bishops of Canada do not have the right to issue a pastoral

---

4. *Globe and Mail*, March 15, 1968, p. 7.

statement opposing a change in a law that deals with the safe-guarding of human rights...." At best, he said, this article "should be dubbed ill-tempered; at worst it is consciously or unconsciously mischievous." The *Canadian Register* phrased its comments somewhat differently. The editorial, it said, "provides classical examples of the use of the half-truth, the smear, the vicious innuendo and the technique of the Big Lie, not to speak of the quite reprehensible effort... to fan the dying flames of racial and religious bigotry."[5] The *Globe* reported these comments to its own readers.[6]

Imposing of Views

The conviction that the Church had no right to impose its views played an important, perhaps even decisive role in the passage of new abortion legislation. According to the Oxford dictionary, to impose means: ...take advantage of (person); practise deception (upon). 'To impose views' clearly conveyed the meaning of forcing beliefs upon people by undue means. For six or more years the *Globe* had been accusing the Catholic Church of 'imposing' its views, and although it had been the most vociferous and the most persistent in doing so, it had not been alone. For instance, an August 1962 editorial in the *Toronto Daily Star*, reprinted in the *Prince Albert Herald* and the *Ontario Medical Review*, stated that while the Roman Catholic view on contraceptives should be respected, it should "not be imposed by law on many other Canadians who disagree."[7] A few years later the Catholic bishops had, in fact, ceased to oppose civil law changes in birth control and divorce legislation.

The changed attitude of the Canadian bishops on birth control and divorce found two different explanations, an official, and an unofficial one. The bishops themselves explained that once they were convinced that existing civil law no longer served the common good, they could resort to distinguishing between moral and civil law, relinquishing opposition to a change in civil law, while maintaining objections to contraceptives and divorce on moral grounds. From then on the Church's views on these subjects was to be reflected only in the behaviour of its faithful and no longer in the laws of the country. On the other hand, the unofficial and more popular explanation disregarded the discussion on the nature and requirements of the common good; it tended, rather, to take the change in attitude simply as factual proof that the Church was withdrawing from the public forum, and that it had finally recognized that it had no right to be there in the first place.

From the early sixties on, the word 'impose' increasingly implied a denial of the right to influence legislation, a denial which was directed especially against the Churches and against religious leaders. In August 1967, the monthly editorial in *Chatelaine* claimed that if the govern-

---

5. "Two standards of Liberty?" *Canadian Register*, March 16, 1968.
6. "Used half-truth-Catholic paper attacks editorial on abortion," *Globe and Mail*, March 18, 1968, p. 5.
7. Reprinted in *Prince Albert Herald*, Aug. 20, 1962. *O.M.R.*, October 1962.

ment "bowed" to the request of the Roman Catholic Church to delay legislation on abortion while the Church prepared a report, "one segment of society will have imposed its views on the whole society again."[8] At the hearing of March 5, 1968, Mrs. MacInnis wanted to know from the Bishops' delegation why the Church insisted on imposing its views upon the rest of society. And the Anglican monthly, the *Canadian Churchman* wrote in April 1968:

> In the area of abortion, contraception and homosexuality the choice is government by the individual's conscience. If his church is opposed then he has a moral obligation to obey his church's rules but he has no right to impose these rules on people of other faiths or no faith at all. There is a clear distinction between moral and civil law.[9]

Thus, there appeared to be agreement among a considerable number of Canadians that somehow or other the behaviour of the Roman Catholic Church was improper. Yet while this accusation was heard more and more frequently, the reasons *why* this behaviour was supposed to be improper remained vague, unmentioned and unexplained, just as if every right-thinking person could do no other than agree. Whatever these reasons were, they seemed related to the notion that the Criminal Code should not reflect 'religious' morality and that law should have nothing to do with the morality of sex and marriage, which, presumably, belonged to "the individual's conscience." That appeared to be the meaning of the *Churchman's* "clear distinction between moral and civil law" and of the *Globe's* "certain high conception of liberal democracy...."[10]

In view of their stand on abortion, the Catholic bishops obviously did not agree that abortion was a matter of private concern only. Yet, in a country with nearly half the population professing membership in the Roman Catholic Church, the new legislation on abortion passed easily and with a large majority. Taking into account the fact that, despite the claims of the *Globe and Mail* and others, abortion was opposed not only by Catholics but by others, there ought to have been a comfortable majority against amendment of the law. Nevertheless the opposite was true.

The explanation for the easy passage of the abortion legislation in Canada must be found principally in the confusion of its opponents. This confusion was directly related to the turmoil within the Catholic Church. As the *New York Times* observed when the state of New York passed new divorce legislation: Every politician agreed that the new law would never have passed if the Catholic clergy and laity had not been in a "state of ferment, in which old dogmas were undergoing an agonizing re-examination."[11] What was true for New York state in the matter of divorce was true for Canada in the question of abortion. Radical changes are not brought about merely because

---

8. "The snail-like battle for progress," *Chatelaine*, August 1967, p. 1.

9. Editorial, "A clear Distinction," April 1968.

10. For further analysis of these statements, see last chapter.

11. Quoted in *Western Catholic Reporter*, May 5, 1966, p. 2.

of increased strength and mounting pressure; they succeed almost as much because of crumbling opposition and confused resistance. In order to understand the crumbling resistance to abortion among the Canadian Catholic population, it is necessary to examine in some detail the causes and nature of the unsettled frame of mind in which the Church found itself during this period.

Vatican Council and Religious Liberty

The state of ferment among Catholics was brought about by the second Vatican council, the first such Council to meet in nearly a hundred years. During the four years of 1962 to 1965, it brought over 2000 bishops from across the world to Rome every fall. Unlike many other Councils of the past which had been called for the formulation of doctrine or the discussion of theological and intellectual problems, this Council was pre-eminently concerned with pastoral affairs and the relationship of the Church to the world. Its liturgical-religious theme was summed up officially by its pontiff, Pope Paul, as simplification and participation, while its political effects were summarized unofficially by one of the participating bishops as the end of "the trilogy of clericalism, triumphalism and legalism."[12]

In the *Pastoral Constitution on the Church in the World*, one of the sixteen documents it solemnly promulgated, the Vatican Council condemned abortion and infanticide as "unspeakable crimes." It did so on the general grounds that it was impossible that there should exist a contradiction "between the divine laws pertaining to the transmission of life and those pertaining to the fostering of authentic conjugal love."[13] But abortion was not explicitly discussed in the assembly, since it was not an issue at the time. Moreover, from the point of view of abortion as a political issue, the Council's most important contribution was not this condemnation which was hardly noticed at the time but two other documents: the section on "The Life of the Political Community" in the same *Pastoral Constitution*,[14] and the *Declaration on Religious Liberty*. These two documents were part of an attempt to redefine the Church's relationship with political society and with other religious communities, to 'declericalize' the bonds with the one and strengthen the ties with the other. Their general tenor rested on greater trust in the effects of practical goodwill and charity, and less on the effectiveness of legalism and dogmatic self-consciousness. Both documents were meant to induce greater respect for the autonomy of these other jurisdictions and, therefore, stressed the dignity of man, personal responsibility, personal rights, and the distinctive roles of state and church.

The *Pastoral Constitution's* section on Political Life touched upon both the autonomy of the political order and the roles of the clergy

---

12. Bishop E. de Smedt of Brugge (Bruges), Belgium. Henri Fesquet, *The Drama of Vatican II*, New York, Random House, 1967, p. 88.
13. See W. Abbot, *The Documents of Vatican II*, New York, America Press, 1966, p. 255.
14. Paras. 73-76, Abbot, *op. cit.*, p. 202ff.

and the laity. It emphasized that the desire for a political-juridical order which protects the rights "of free assembly, of common action, of expressing personal opinions, and of professing a religion both privately and publicly..." was justified.[15] It went on to say that "the role and competence of the Church should in no way be confused with the political community, nor bound to any political system..." Priests, it said, should use means and helps proper to the gospel which "differ from the supports of the earthly city..."[16] Aside from the remark that the Church retained the right to pass moral judgments even on matters touching the political order — "whenever basic personal rights or the salvation of souls make such judgments necessary" — the main thrust of the documents was to bring out more clearly the autonomy of the political order which was basically the affair of the laity, not the clergy.[17] Thus it re-affirmed that "secular duties and activities belong properly although not exclusively to laymen..." The function of laymen, it said, is "to see that the divine law is inscribed in the life of the earthly city..." While they might look for spiritual light from their priests, they ought not to expect them to have a concrete solution "to every problem which arises." Instead, the layman should "take on his own distinctive role."[18]

This emphasis on a just measure of autonomy for the political order as well as for the layman who maintained this order, was parallelled by the *Declaration on Religious Liberty* with its emphasis on the right to freedom of other religious communities. Religious freedom, the Council said, had "its foundation in the very dignity of the human person as this dignity is known through the revealed Word of God and by reason itself."[19]

Religious liberty was the most controversial issue of the four-year-long Council. The preceding, century-long, tradition had been one of opposition to 'absolute' freedom for 'any and all' cults. The *Syllabus* of Pius IX declared "that the civil liberty of all cults and the right of all to manifest openly and publicly all their thoughts and opinions precipitate peoples into the corruption of morals and spirits, and propagate the plague of indifferentism."[20] In a similar vein Pope Leo XIII stated in the encyclical, *On Human Liberty* of 1888, that "...Justice therefore forbids, and reason itself forbids, the State to be godless; or to adopt a line of action which would end in godlessness — namely, to treat the various religions (as they call them) alike, and to bestow upon them promiscuously equal rights and privileges."[21] Both views were consistent with the Church's teaching on the nature

15. *Ibid.*, para. 73, p. 283.

16. *Ibid.*, para. 76, pp. 287-8.

17. *Ibid.*, p. 289.

18. *Ibid.*, para. 43, pp. 243-5.

19. *Declaration on Religious Liberty*, the John La Farge Institute, New York, 1966, p. 10.

20. Proposition 79. The *Syllabus* used the double negative, here omitted. (The following proposition is *condemned*: It is *false* that the civil liberty...)

21. "Libertas Praestantissimum," 1888. See E. Gilson, ed. *The Church speaks to the Modern World*, Doubleday Image Books, p. 70.

of moral liberty which it does not interpret as the freedom to do whatever one likes, right or wrong. Wrongful acts or sinful acts, it teaches, are not acts of liberty, but acts of ignorance, a falling into slavery. Moral liberty, consists "in choosing that good only which is in conformity with the judgment of reason," which in turn conforms the will to the authority of God commanding good and forbidding evil.[22] Still, while the views of the popes were theologically consistent, their frequent repetition by lesser authorities was often the result of an exaggerated pessimistic evaluation of existing political and cultural conditions. In what countries, after all, did *any* and *all* cults demand *absolute* freedom to manifest *all* their thoughts at *any* time *everywhere*?

In the *Declaration on Religious Liberty* the Church took a more optimistic view of existing conditions without denying the earlier statements of the popes. Leaving aside the question what will happen if everyone contradicts everyone else all at once, it stressed the fact that, ultimately, every person is responsible for his own life and that nobody should be forced to believe against his free will. Even so, in his presentation of the first draft of the religious liberty document in the fall of 1963, Bishop de Smedt was careful to reject not only a kind of Machiavellianism (demanding the free exercise of religion for Catholic minorities but denying it to others when Catholics are in a majority), but also the errors of "religious indifferentism," and "doctrinal relativism," so much feared by the nineteenth century popes.

The Declaration bypassed the endless and complicated theoretical arguments of the past most effectively with its biblical inspiration. Revelation, it said, shows that "God calls men to serve him in spirit and in truth; hence they are bound in conscience, but they stand under no compulsion." It went on to say that man is to be guided by his own judgment and that he is to enjoy freedom: "In attracting and inviting his disciples, Christ acted patiently... His intention was to rouse faith in his hearers..., not to exert coercion upon them..." Christ, it pointed out, "refused to be a political Messiah, ruling by force." and refused "to impose the truth by force on those who spoke against it..." The apostles, it continued, followed the same way, making it plain "that each one of us is to render to God an account of himself (Rom. 14:12), and for this reason is bound to obey his conscience... They followed the example of the gentleness and respectfulness of Christ..."[23] The Declaration concluded:

> ...in order that relationships of peace and harmony may be established... it is necessary that religious freedom be every-where provided with an effective constitutional guarantee...[24]

In view of the contrast with previous attitudes, it was inevitable that the positions affirmed by the Council would acquire overtones in the popular mind which were not in harmony with its original

---

22. *Ibid.*, see introduction, p. 55.
23. *Declaration, op. cit.*, paras. 11-12.
24. *Ibid.*, para. 15.

intentions. One feature which almost entirely escaped attention was that the Council did not identify freedom of religion with freedom of conscience. When the document was first presented in the fall of 1963, religious liberty was defined as "the right of the human person to the free exercise of religion according to the dictates of his conscience."[25] When, after two years of postponements and controversy the Schema was finally accepted, however, religious liberty was based on 'the dignity of man' and referred to freedom from coercion, not to freedom of conscience.[26] As one of the architects of the *Declaration*, John Courtney Murray, emphasized, the Declaration did not ground the free exercise of religion on "freedom of conscience":

> Nowhere does this phrase occur. And the Declaration nowhere lends its authority to the theory for which the phrase frequently stands, namely, that I have the right to do what my conscience tells me to do, simply because my conscience tells me to do it. This is a perilous theory. Its particular peril is subjectivism — the notion that, in the end, it is my conscience, and not the objective truth that determines what is right or wrong, true or false.[27]

It was this "perilous theory" which seemed to increase in popularity to the same degree as the Council removed or simplified rules, regulations and legal obligations.

In North America, the two documents had an additional consequence, namely that a number of Catholics, too, began to adopt the idea that it was improper to influence legislation according to one's religious principles because that would be equivalent to 'imposing' views on those who differed in religion or ideals. In February, 1965, an editorial in the United States Catholic weekly, *America*, first drew attention to this. It observed that while "no group in society may demand that its religious beliefs or even its moral principles be accepted by the whole community as the norm of public policy," still, no one should be required to "check his conscience at the door" when he entered the public forum to take a position on one of society's common concerns. "If a person is convinced that abortion is an attack on human life," it noted, he has as much right and duty to say so as he has to denounce racial discrimination."[28] Fully two years later, in 1967, the same periodical was forced to return to the subject. This time it devoted an entire page to the issue with an editorial: "On Imposing Catholic Views on Others." It opened with a quote from a New York Catholic politician who said that "...We're only asking them not to dictate to the rest of the population what they can and cannot do."[29] Describing it as "typical of an argument being heard more and more

---

25. Quoted by Henri Fesquet, *The Drama of Vatican II*, Random House, 1966, p. 24.
26. See Bishop de Smedt's interim report, November, 1964. *Ibid.*, pp. 540-542.
27. See marginal notes by John Courtney Murray, S.J. in *Declaration... op. cit.*, p. 11.
28. Editorial, "Morality and Policy I," *America*, Feb. 27, 1965, p. 280.
29. *America*, Feb. 25, 1967, pp. 273-4.

frequently," the magazine rejected as unsatisfactory such answers as: "When the rest of the population stops telling Catholics what to do, Catholics will stop trying to tell anybody else what to do." The real question, it observed, was to what extent the *Declaration on Religious Liberty* meant "that Catholics should not seek to legalize their morality in a pluralistic society?" After explaining that there was no requirement that everything immoral be made criminal and, indeed, that human freedom and public order pointed "quite the other way," it took its own stand on the grounds that abortion pertains to that type of situation where an immoral act may legitimately be made criminal, namely when it has a harmful effect on someone else, other than the doer.

A second American Catholic weekly, the liberal *Commonweal* edited by laymen, also felt compelled to face the issue at about the same time. *Commonweal* defended its opposition to abortion as perfectly acceptable in a pluralistic state, as long as political pressure was "applied openly, democratically and in a sensible, non-hysterical way."[30] But it observed that Mr. William F. Buckley, a Catholic and a conservative, had argued "that surely the principal meaning of the religious liberty pronouncements of Vatican II is that other men must be left free to practice the dictates of their own conscience... it would appear to contradict the burden of the Vatican's position to put pressure on the law to maintain the supremacy of one's own position." *Commonweal* noted that "many Catholic liberals have argued in a similar way." The weekly itself refused to do so on the grounds that the issue of human life made all the difference. As a consequence it was attacked in its own letter-to-the-editor column as well as in the Protestant weekly *Christianity and Crisis*.[31]

Another result of the Council discussions was the disppearance of the 'argument from authority.' As late as 1964 the American professional quarterly, *The Catholic Lawyer*, had observed that as long as the Church's Canon Law provided a penalty for cooperation in abortions, to vote for the liberalization of present abortion laws would be 'material cooperation.'[32] It concluded that even if there were a grave reason for so doing, it appeared that "a Catholic legislator would be prohibited from voting for a more liberal abortion law."[33] This article was about the last time the point seems to have been mentioned. With the new emphasis on the personal responsibility of the laity and, therefore, of the legislators, no one thought it desirable to return to a relationship of religious and political authority which was characteristic of pre-Vatican Council days.

The editorials gave evidence of a popular interpretation of the Council documents which conservative bishops at the Council had foreseen and feared. The *Declaration of Religious Liberty* was not

---

30. Editorial, "Abortion and Pluralism," *Commonweal*, Feb. 24, 1967, pp. 582-3.
31. See Editorial, "Abortion and Dialogue, *Commonweal*, March 17, 1967, pp. 667-8.
32. "Material cooperation means that one, without giving approval, aids another by an action which is not in itself sinful," *Catholic Lawyer*, Spring, 1964, p. 173, footnote 119.
33. *Ibid.*, p. 173.

interpreted as a declaration in favour of freedom from coercion, but as a confirmation of everybody's freedom of conscience; the latter, in turn, was interpreted by some to mean that each person could believe 'whatever he liked'; by others, that nobody had the right to 'tell' anyone what to do. Catholics, so it appeared, should not try to impose their views upon the nation. Moreover, the de-emphasis of the role of the clergy in affairs of the world and the clarification of the layman's autonomy in this area was now interpreted by some to mean that Church leaders should not only keep out of politics but that they had no right to express an opinion at all. This interpretation was further strengthened and broadened by the sudden growth of the idea among some people within the Church that as celibates, pope, bishops and clergy were not qualified to express opinions on marital questions. Finally, as if to confuse everyone completely, there sprang up a contradictory demand that the clergy and hierarchy intervene in politics and condemn specific political and social conditions.

A similar confusion about the meaning and interpretation of the Council declarations was noticeable throughout the Church in Europe and America, including Canada. The confusion was simply "in the air" and an integral part of a new climate of opinion. It cropped up in letters to the editor of the Catholic weeklies. It was found for instance, in the contribution of Mr. Mark MacGuigan, Member of Parliament and Dean of the Faculty of Law, University of Windsor, to the book, *One Church, Two Nations?*[34] Describing Pope Paul's expression of displeasure at the proposed recommendation for civil divorce in Italy in January 1967 as an "unwarranted intrusion into Italian politics," he hailed the Canadian Catholic Bishops' brief on contraception of October 1966 with its distinction between moral and civil law, as displaying "a much more profound understanding of the legitimate separation of Church and State." Yet, noting that in the same document the bishops expressed their opinions on the projected reforms, he referred to that as "ironic." In support of his objections to this "derogation from principle," he quoted an editorial in the *Canadian Register* which claimed that there was "a degree of contradiction between the responsible freedom of legislators and citizens as described in the first part of the statement and the actual intervention of the bishops."[35]

Authority Crisis

The confusion of Catholics could not have grown so rapidly except for the fact that the state of ferment within the Catholic Church went far deeper and extended far wider than the question of religious liberty or the political autonomy of the laity. These two problems were on the fringe of a re-orientation which dealt essentially with religious and spiritual values. Indeed, it was precisely because of the intense pre-occupation with the re-creation of the Church's authority

---

34. Philip Le Blanc and Arnold Edinborough, ed., Longmans, 1968. M. MacGuigan, "Unity in the Secular City," pp. 146-162.

35. *Ibid.*, Canadian Register, Oct. 22, 1966, p. 153.

and traditions in a more spiritual setting, that 'political' matters such as new legislation on abortion were ignored. It was not an accident that the Canadian Church did not react to the abortion agitation until the middle of 1967; rather, this was a direct consequence of the Vatican Council. It must be understood that like the bishops of other countries, the Canadian bishops spent the fall of four consecutive years between 1962-1965 away from home. The intense preparation preceding each session and the even more strenuous follow-up on their return from Rome undoubtedly absorbed all intellectual, and even physical energy and ability. This became true of the entire Catholic community as the reforms reached downwards and affected ever wider circles.

At the centre of the renewal stood a renovated liturgy, a theme which had been assigned priority over all other issues at the beginning of the Council. Since this decree, promulgated in 1963, concerned the forms and manner of worship and, thereby, touched the heart and nerve-centre of the institutional church, its initial execution required not just the adaptation of rites, the physical alteration of church interiors and a shift in theological emphasis, but a deep and often painful psychological and mental adjustment of both clergy and laity. Simplifications in the central act of worship, the Sacrifice of the Mass, involved abrogations of age-old customs. Some of these had been fixed for centuries, such as many of the detailed ceremonial rubrics, while others dated back a thousand years or more, such as the use of Latin, now replaced by native languages. Mass rites were altered, choirs dissolved, and solemnities simplified. The organ was almost silenced, the Latin hymn was replaced by native folk song and the entire Gregorian musical tradition with its antiphons, propers, prayers and litanies was set aside. While the faithful watched, altars were turned around, super-structures dismantled, communion rails removed, pulpits replaced, and the sanctuary liberated from statues now deemed superfluous.

At no time in its history had the Church experienced such quick change within so few years. It was a time of sudden excitement and expectation, yet also of confusion and irritation. Practices and customs were re-arranged, abolished, replaced or modified. Variations, alterations and novelties succeeded one another in rapid succession to the delight of some and the despair of others.

The sudden spirit of freedom in a hitherto strictly regulated society proved for many of the most committed a turning point in their lives. As the search for new forms and modes of life intensified and penetrated dioceses and religious houses of one kind or another, little was left untouched. Questions created uncertainties; uncertainty caused insecurity. Old forgotten issues, like priestly celibacy believed settled centuries ago, were resurrected, some thought artificially, others thought of necessity. As the turmoil spread from liturgy to theology, then to prayer, and then to faith, the Church discovered that what had started as renewal had developed into a crisis.

From 1965 on, the Canadian bishops, like Catholic bishops elsewhere, faced increasing difficulties in exercising authority. Authority of any kind, of course, had been under assault throughout the Western world from the beginning of the decade or earlier and the Church had not escaped this general trend. At the beginning of the sixties, for instance, questions had been raised about the Church's role during the war. With the help of the furor created by the play, *The Deputy*, the recently deceased, and until his death in 1958 generally admired, Pope Pius XII stood condemned nearly unanimously a half dozen years later.[36] Right or wrong, this condemnation of Pope Pius affected adversely the credibility of the Church's leaders. Now, the critical spirit of Vatican II led to a further questioning of Church authority, this time by its own priests and religious.

Contraception

While the hierarchy was occupied with restraining the bold and the progressive from proceeding too quickly or encouraging the fearful and the reluctant to move at all, a third crisis broke out which deeply affected the faithful at large: the controversy about contraceptives. This controversy was also of direct and immediate consequence to the problem of abortion.

Contraceptives had been condemned as "intrinsically immoral" by Pius XI in the encyclical, *Casti Connubii*, of December 31, 1930, for deliberately depriving the act of procreation of its natural power and efficacy. With the appearance in the late fifties of the pill that could regulate ovulation, the question took on renewed urgency. As a result Pope Pius XII taught that the use of this pill was 'licit' when employed as medicine, that is, when a temporary sterilization was caused indirectly as a result of regulating some uterine or organic disorder. He declared its use illicit when employed to bring on temporary sterilization directly in order to prevent conception.[37]

From the beginning of the sixties and the opening of the Council, there was mounting pressure to review the 'Morality of the Pill.' In February, 1964, the deliberations of a small group of advisors to the Pope on questions of population and birth control failed to reach a conclusion. In June, 1964, Pope Paul officially appointed a Commission for a study "as wide and profound as possible." He hoped, he said, "soon to say our word, supported by the light of human science," but, in the meantime, the norms given by Pius XII "must be considered valid, at least until we feel bound in conscience to modify them."

---

36. Rolf Hochhuth's play, *Der Stellvertreter, (The Deputy)*, was first produced in Berlin in the late fall of 1962. It appeared in book form immediately after and was rapidly translated into various languages. Seven months later, by June 30, 1963, it was estimated that 3000 reviews, commentaries and articles had appeared in the European press. (Fritz Raddatz, *Summa iniuria oder Durfte der Papst Schweigen*, Hamburg 1963, p. 8). Another year later and Eric Bentley could write in his collection of English commentaries that the storm raised by *The Deputy* was "almost certainly the largest storm ever raised by a play in the whole history of the drama." (*The Storm over the Deputy*, New York, Grove Press, 1964, p. 8). The question of 'the right to be silent' and 'the duty to speak' has remained an extremely controversial topic.

37. September 12, 1958. A short but competent survey of the controversy until the beginning of 1967 may be found in Milton Meier, "Why the Vatican is delaying its Statement on Birth Control," in *Report. Perspective on the News*, Jan. and Feb., 1967, reprint.

The Commission had nearly sixty members, including married couples, theologians, and scientists, many of whom questioned the doctrinal status quo. They met in several plenary meetings in March, 1965.

In the meantime, birth control was also debated with considerable passion at the Vatican Council. This led to the formulation of a chapter on marriage in the document on *The Church in the Modern World*, where procreation and mutual love were recognized as two equal ends of marriage. The same chapter carried a controversial footnote warning against undertaking "methods of regulating procreation which are found blameworthy by the teaching authority of the Church..." In February, 1966, the Pope again reorganized the Commission by adding fifteen Cardinals and Bishops to act as an advisory committee. By this time most members had made a choice for or against birth control. News of this division within the Commission leaked out, leading more and more people to believe that the law of the Church was now a *lex dubia*, a law which was officially in doubt, permitting the individual to follow his own judgment. Steps taken by some individual dioceses in providing practical guidelines for their priests, such as Toronto, Munich, Cuernavaca (Mexico), Trier (Germany) and several dioceses in Holland, gave further credence to this position.

During the summer of 1966 the press published the secret reports of the two groups within the Commission. The majority report recommended changes that would permit the use of birth control pills, leaving it to individual couples to plan their families; the minority report held that the traditional teaching should be retained. While the executive Committee held more meetings, leading scientists, Nobel laureates, prominent Catholic laymen, theologians, moralists, the press — both Catholic and non-Catholic — and many of the faithful favoured change. Newspapers were flooded with letters to the editor and Catholic authors favouring contraceptives were published in Protestant magazines.[38] Everyone expected an encyclical soon; some in the summer, others in the fall. While predictions of change were common, the Pope continued to issue warnings against abandoning the old rules, denying that the existing law was in doubt.

Confusion grew steadily while the people went their way. In Britain the *Sunday Telegraph* opinion poll among Catholics of March, 1967, had shown that at that time 66% believed that the Pope should approve the pill for health reasons, while 33% thought he should approve "anyone taking it who wishes." Surprisingly enough, 33% also thought the Pope was right in taking his time coming to a decision.[39]

In the fall of 1967, editors of some Catholic magazines called on the Church to change its teaching;[40] others called for an end to "the

---

38. BIRTH CONTROL! By Robert G. Hoyt. The Catholic Church's most explosive issue reviewed by one of its most outspoken laymen. United Church *Observer*, November 1, 1967. Mr. Hoyt was editor of the U.S. weekly, *The National Catholic Reporter*.

39. Sunday Telegraph as quoted in *The Tablet*, April 1, 1967, p. 361.

40. See, for instance, the Editorial "Contraception and the Synod of Bishops" in the Jesuit weekly, *America*, September 30, 1967, reprinted in *Prairie Messenger*, October 4, 1967, p. 7.

scandalous confusion" on contraception.[41] The Congress of Catholic
Laity, meeting in Rome, advocated individual freedom in the use of
birth control methods.[42] One year later, in May 1968, the British
Cardinal Heenan, one of the two pro-presidents of the Papal Commission, criticized the pressure being put on the Pope "to make a pro-
nouncement before he is ready."[43] Yet, five months earlier, he himself
had publicly expressed the thought that until the Pope announced
the promised decision the Church would continue "to be restless and
troubled."[44]

In Canada the Church was no less 'restless and troubled' than
elsewhere in the Americas and Europe. This was illustrated in three
different areas of the country during the last half of June, 1968. In
Ontario, the *Canadian Register* published an editorial on June 15th,
in which it pointed out that the Pope had resisted the interpretation
that the law was in doubt, yet that large numbers of Catholics had
settled the problem of contraceptives for themselves. It concluded:
"Some Catholics no longer care; but some do. They have a right to
guidance now."[45] About the same time a theologian in Sherbrooke,
Quebec, stated in the official weekly of the Archdiocese of Sherbrooke
that there existed "a positive and reasonable doubt regarding the
morality of some kinds of contraception." According to the principle
of the *lex dubia*, he said, this implied that people were free to follow
the most liberal opinion held by any group of reputable theologians.[46]
On the other hand, in the Archdiocese of Grouard-McLennan in
Northern Alberta, Archbishop Henri Routhier re-affirmed the traditional teaching, and explained again the legitimacy of family planning
and the illegitimacy of contraceptives and the pill except for restoring
regular ovulation.[47] Three weeks later half a dozen letters to the editor
commented angrily on the Archbishop's remarks, especially on his
advice that "wives should make themselves less attractive to their
husbands during their fruitful times."[48]

The suspense within the Church was finally broken on July 29,
1968. Never had a matter of morality been more debated, more
discussed, more studied and more seriously considered; never did a
Papal teaching cause more controversy, more anguish, more disappointment and also perhaps, more relief. After six years of hesitation
the Pope, whom some had described earlier as a man of indecision
and a Hamlet, went against the majority advice of his own Commission.
In his encyclical, *Humanae Vitae*, he spoke an unequivocal 'no' against
pills and other means intended to directly prevent conception. "Con-

41. *Tablet*, as summarized in *Prairie Messenger*, October, 1967, p. 15.
42. *Globe and Mail*, October 18, 1967, p. 4.
43. *Western Catholic Reporter*, May 23, 1968, p. 1.
44. *Ibid.*, January 11, 1968, p. 10, *Canadian Register*, January 27, 1968, p. 4.
45. "The Pope's Silence," June 15, 1968.
46. Father André Bergeron of the University of Sherbrooke, in *Messager*, quoted
    in editorial "Pill Compromise?", *Canadian Register*, June 29, 1968.
47. Published in *La Voix*, official publication of the Archdiocese of Grouard-McLen-
    nan, quoted in *Western Catholic Reporter*, July 11, 1968, p. 1.
48. *Ibid.*, August 1, 1968, p. 4.

forming to fundamental principes of the human and Christian vision of marriage, the Pope said, "we must once again state that there must be excluded absolutely, as a licit way to regulate birth, the direct interruption of the generative process."[49]

The reaction of the press throughout the Western world was mostly one of dismay and disappointment. For many middle-class Catholics the encyclical represented a disaster and caused a spiritual crisis. Others saw it as a set-back to the ecumenical movement and to the *aggiornamento*, the renewal within the Church. Some left that the Church was turning its back on humanity, believing that Pope Paul had completely misread the moral and human issues at stake;[50] however, others believed the opposite, asserting that the Pope had read the issues very well, re-affirming the basic human and Christian values of sacrifice, continence and chastity in a materialistic, hedonistic and sex-saturated society. Whatever their opinions, almost everyone agreed that the Church was in a crisis and that the heart of this crisis concerned the authority and significance of the Papal Office.

During the next three of four months the bishops of every country in the Western world, and of some countries in Africa and Asia, were forced to face the pastoral implications of the encyclical as well as questions of harmony and discipline among their clergy. Some were more successful than others. In Canada, reported the *Globe*, reactions ranged "from stoic acceptance to angry, forthright defiance"; however, "while prominent lay Catholics expressed dismay and disappointment..., most church leaders said the Pope's decision was a hard one but one they would accept."[51] The *Globe* itself acknowledged that the Pope was "not lacking in courage," but it called his decision "insensitive." It saw the encyclical as provoking a crisis of opinion, reaching "into three spheres of ecclesiastical unity: social concern, ethics, and papal authority." The result, it said, might not be "a reaffirmation of authority but a grievous discredit to it."[52]

Among English Catholic weeklies, the *Prairie Messenger* observed on August 7 that reaction to the encyclical had, perhaps, been "too swift and too negative." The weekly emphasized the Pope's "concern for creating an atmosphere favourable to education in chastity," and his misgivings "about putting into the hands of public authorities solutions to community problems which they might in future force upon... people." On the other hand, it denied that "it would be altogether unrealistic to disregard the anguish which the Pope's decision places upon conscientious couples":

> While the Pope has spoken authoritatively, he recognizes that many will not be able to reach the ideal he proposes and urges priests to be compassionate and understanding in counselling them.... Such counselling... might help bring about an evolution of official teaching that will appear more in harmony

49. *Humanae Vitae* (Of Human Life), printed in *Globe*, July 30th: Full text in *Register*, August 3, and other Catholic weeklies.
50. For instance, John Cogley in *Western Catholic Reporter*, August 22, 1968.
51. *Globe and Mail*, July 30, 1968, p. 1.
52. Editorial, "A stern papal ruling," *Globe and Mail*, July 30, 1968.

with contemporary, theological, sociological and biological speculation.

One week later, after observing that... "Surely no encyclical letter from Rome has ever raised such a flurry of opinion, pro and con," it remarked that "guided by the encyclical, Christian couples must prayerfully and prudently form their own consciences..."[53] On August 21 it directed its editorial against extremism and pessimism: "This is no time for extremist statements — on either side of the question," it said, "the encyclical must be given its due, the same due that is paid to the individual conscience..."[54]

The *Western Catholic Reporter* called the encyclical "a hard teaching" and even feared schism.[55] "If only the social teachings of the Popes had provoked similar reactions," it complained. Appealing for calm, it urged that the encyclical be treated "with the greatest respect and loyalty." But this did not mean that "another Pope might not see things differently, that the teaching might not be gradually modified." While every man could not be his own pope, the paper said, there was a legitimate right to dissent: "...there is no use in saying that birth control is a closed issue, now that the Pope has spoken."

In Ontario, the *Canadian Register* actually did think the matter was closed. Noting that the Pope had been under great pressure to give direction in this matter, the editor wrote: "Now he has spoken. It remains only for us as loyal Catholics to accept this ruling, coming as it does from the supreme teaching authority."[56] This statement, as well as sermons in the churches on the following Sunday which took a similar line, were immediately challenged by what the *Globe* described as "a group of Catholic intellectuals, lawyers, teachers and laymen, mainly around St. Michael's College in Toronto."[57] The group presented a statement with 82 names to Archbishop Pocock of Toronto, pointing out that the encyclical was "not an infallible teaching," and that there should be no question about a legitimate right to dissent. The *Globe*, which a day after the appearance of the encyclical had printed an article by Rev. Gregory Baum entitled "Catholics may follow their conscience,"[58] now also reprinted the editorial of the *Canadian Register*.[59] Subsequently, the *Register* denied that the editorial implied "that those who do not give full assent for valid reasons were disloyal." It did mean, however, that one takes the encyclical as "the general rule, the normal course of action...," the editor said, and not just like the 82 signers, as "only one of the many

53. Editorial, August 14, 1968.
54. Editorial, August 21, 1968.
55. Editorial, August 1, 1968.
56. Editorial, "Agonizing but Firm Leadership," August 3, 1968.
57. "RC's attack sermons against birth curbs," *Globe and Mail*, August 6, 1968.
58. "The Pope and the Pill," *Globe and Mail*, August 1, 1968, p. 7. Also appeared in *Commonweal*, August 23, 1968. Reprinted in *The Catholic Case for Contraception*, D. Callahan, ed., London, 1969, pp. 71-76.
59. *Globe*, August 7, 1968, p. 7.

factors which loyal Catholics must consider informing their conscientious attitudes to contraception."[60]

The Pill retained public attention for several more months with opposing opinions appearing not only in the religious, but also in the daily press, with headings such as, "Why the Pope rejected a majority view on the Pill," in the *Globe*, to "A Catholic Mother Answers the Pope, " in *Chatelaine*.[61] Almost every day, during August and September, the *Globe* printed progress reports on the controversy in Europe and the Americas, while the Catholic weeklies continued to cover the same issue in more detail until the end of the year.

In Canada some degree of calm returned only after a hectic, five day, study session in Winnipeg from September 23 to 27, when the Canadian Bishops formulated their own, 'preliminary,' pastoral guidelines. Prior to that date the number of dissenting voices had grown considerably. The Catholic Physicians' Guild in Manitoba declared that not only was the Encyclical unconvincing but "that the doctors had come to the conclusion that conception control was 'not intrinsically evil'."[62] The Western Canadian Conference of Priests submitted a statement bearing the signatures of 351 priests which asked the Canadian bishops to issue "an unequivocal explanation of the conditions for prudent dissent, both internal and practical." Fifteen directors of the departments within the Canadian Catholic Conference signed a statement urging the bishops to give "balanced, positive, pastoral leadership." Opposition was further expressed by the Canadian Association of Theologians. Groups from Toronto, Ottawa and Vancouver reported the results of advertisements placed in local papers asking Catholics whether they thought that the encyclical settled the question once and for all. With about 475 respondents in Vancouver, 350 in Ottawa and 1200 in Toronto, 90 per cent in all three cities said no.[63] During the week of the meeting itself telegrams from individuals kept pouring in, often in favour of the Pope's stand. One telegram, signed by 58 faculty members of St. Francis Xavier University, however, stated that if Canadian bishops could not uphold the right of conscience it would be better for them to say nothing.[64]

At the end of the week the Canadian bishops made a statement which the *Register* summed up as follows:

> They declared their solidarity with 'the Pope and with our people'; urged Catholics to form their consciences with the teaching of the encyclical very prominent in their thinking; and, in the end, recognized the right of everyone to follow

---

60. "A Letter of Protest," P.A.G. McKay, Editor, *Canadian Register*, August 17, 1968.

61. The *Globe* article was by David J. Dooley, Professor of English, St. Michael's College, August 24, 1968; the *Chatelaine* article by Joan O'Donnell, a pseudonym, November, 1968.

62. See survey in Douglas Roche, "Collegiality in Canada," *The Tablet*, October 12, 1968, p. 1022. The 351 priests were out of a total of 1900 priests in Western Canada.

63. "Canadian Bishops toil behind closed doors...," *Globe and Mail*, Sept. 24, 1968, p. 8.

64. Roche, *op. cit.*

the dictates of a mature and open conscience, striving to know
what is best in his practical circumstances.[65]

The editor of the *Western Catholic Reporter* described it as "the most
harrowing week in the history of the Canadian Church." When Friday
afternoon came, everyone was a bit dazed, he said, but "there was
a general feeling that the Church in Canada had crossed the threshold
into a new age."[66]

Summary

Pope and Bishops had always claimed the right to teach on faith
and morals. During the last century this had not infrequently included
matters touching on politics. Wisely or unwisely, the Church had
spoken out on many matters, some of which even its own members
may have regarded as more properly belonging to the responsibility
of the individual rather than to the jurisdiction of religious authority.
Still, the involvement of the Church could not grow less when an
increasing social awareness among people refined moral sensitivity and
thus necessarily expanded the role of society in moral issues. It was
at this moment that through the four-year long second Vatican
Council the Catholic Church became involved in a profound reorienta-
tion of its attitudes and relations with the 'world.' This re-orientation
absorbed all available energy and attention of the members. It assured
the laity new responsibility and autonomy; and it laid the foundations
for a more spiritual Church authority in the future. But it also
weakened the exercise of that authority for the present and, through
ecumenism and pluralism, created a reluctance to stress or defend
traditional positions which differed too sharply from those of Protestant
and other religious bodies.

On the eve of the abortion debate in the House of Commons,
therefore, the largest group of opponents to abortion were in the midst
of considerable turmoil and re-examination. The same group also found
themselves a divided house on the issue of contraceptives which many
regarded as related to abortion. Their religious leaders, moreover, had
experienced many hesitations before making clear that the objection
to legal abortions rested on the same grounds as the objection to
illegal abortions, namely on the inalienable rights of human life that
is innocent of any misdeeds. When the debate finally came, these
leaders discovered that as in the issue on contraceptives, its supporters
either did not accept the authority of their Church leaders or lacked
the courage to defy what an overwhelming majority appeared to regard
as advanced and enlightened legislation.

---

65. "Birth pangs on Birth Control," Michael O'Meara, *Canadian Register*, October
    5, 1968, p. 8. Text of Pastoral Statement, pp. 12-13. See also *Western Catholic
    Reporter*, October 3, *Globe and Mail*, September 28, 1968.
66. Roche, *op. cit.*, p. 1023. See also Roche, "Canadian Catholics and contraceptives,"
    Canadian Churchman, Nov., 1968. Some people strongly disapproved of the
    statement by the Canadian Bishops as unwise, and as an unacceptable concession
    to the spirit of the times.

CHAPTER IX

The Debate in Parliament

New Government

While Roman Catholics were in the midst of a growing crisis, Canada re-elected its Liberal government with an overwhelming majority in June 1968. Mr. Trudeau, now Prime Minister, was succeeded as Minister of Justice by John Turner. On July 6th Mr. Turner announced that the proposed amendments to the Criminal Code would be back in the Commons before the end of the year. "The Prime Minister is committed to it," he said, "and so am I." He did announce, however, that the Cabinet would decide whether to break the Omnibus bill into several parts, permitting free votes on some of its provisions.[1]

The appearance of the encyclical, *Humanae Vitae*, briefly threatened to introduce a new element into the controversy. The encyclical not only asked the Catholic faithful to accept the papal teaching, but also requested leaders of civil governments to adopt it and to outlaw contraception, sterilization and abortion. A *New York Times* and *Associated Press* report called it "an unprecedented appeal."[2] Italian newspapers, ranging from conservative to communist, criticized it.[3] The Toronto *Globe* called the papal appeal "dangerous," and claimed that it would "revive largely irrelevant quarrels between Church and State..."[4]

The *Globe and Mail* immediately inquired what effect the appeal would have in Ottawa. The next day its bureau in Ottawa reported that the "Pope's appeal... will not affect... plans to eliminate legal structures on birth control and to broaden the grounds for abortion." The Prime Minister had no comments, the reporter quoted a spokesman as saying, because he had not read the encyclical; however, plans to proceed with birth control and abortion legislation had not been changed. This "separation of private religion and public business," said the reporter who noted that both the Prime Minister and Justice Minister Turner were practicing Catholics, "is consistent with the position Mr. Trudeau took earlier..."[5]

---

1. "Cabinet may allow MP's freedom on Code votes," *Globe and Mail*, July 8, 1968, p. 1.
2. "Pope asks world leaders to follow RC stand," *Globe and Mail*, July 30, 1967, p. 10.
3. "Editorial, July 30, 1967.
4. "...Church-State in Italy...," *Globe and Mail*, July 31, 1968, p. 9.
5. "Pope's birth-curb stand to be ignored by Ottawa," *Globe and Mail*, July 31, 1968, front page.

Spokesmen for the Church, official and unofficial, affirmed that the encyclical should not make any difference for Canadian legislators. Members of parliament were free to vote on birth control as they saw fit, a professor of theology said a week later, because the principles elaborated by the Canadian bishops in their brief on contraception were still valid. The Pope's "main concern," he stated, was "that some governments, in facing their population and poverty problems, might make laws that would pressure or even compel people to use contraceptives." This, he said, was not the intention of the Canadian legislation which merely allowed the sale of contraceptives and permitted free information about them.[6] Four weeks later, the President of the Canadian Catholic Conference of Bishops, Bishop Alexander Carter, announced the publication of a booklet containing the statements of the Canadian Bishops on contraceptives, divorce and abortion. "The fact that this booklet is being published subsequent to the promulgation of *Humanae Vitae* adds to its interest." wrote Bishop Carter in the preface. "Nothing in the encyclical, to my mind, is in conflict with the position of the Canadian Bishops."[7]

Summary of Positions

The politics of abortion had advanced to what some believed to be its final stage: the debate in parliament and its enactment into law. Positions had been stated and solidified; yet, a certain uneasiness remained, perhaps because few people really understood exactly what had been set in motion. After 1969, of course, an increased radicalization and polarization would occur as each side began to understand its position better.

As late as 1968 there was no answer to the basic question *why* abortions were wanted. Indeed, that question had hardly been asked. Just as there was no reliable data available about the number of abortions, so there had been no scientific investigations about the reasons for abortions. Those who preferred to find their causes on the social-economic level looked for their explanation to such possibilities as inadequate housing. Those who diagnosed cause and effect primarily on the level of ideals found their explanation in the belief that decaying civilizations are always characterized by the evidence of increased selfishness. But neither the one nor the other had contributed any findings of researched investigations or presented a plausible and convincing explanation. Still, it was not necessary to understand why abortions were wanted in order to take a stand on how the law should read, even though the individual answer would probably bear some relationship to that understanding, however vague it might be.

The legal profession, speaking through the *Canadian Bar Association*, was convinced that revision of the law would prove the only

---

6. Rev. Walter Principe, St. Michael's College, Toronto, *Globe and Mail*, August 6, 1968, front page.
7. *Contraception, Divorce, Abortion*, Ottawa, C.C.C., 1968. Quoted in *Prairie Messenger*, September 11, 1968, p. 3. "Bishops still support more liberalized law," *Globe and Mail*, Sept. 9, 1968.

way to avoid the dangers of continued illegal abortions as well as clarify the law for therapeutic abortions. It eventually presented three reasons for widening the grounds for abortions: life or health, rape, and deformity. The last reason was accepted despite strong objections. Health, the Association felt, should include both physical and mental health. The *Canadian Medical Association* had taken the stand from the beginning that it did not want to encourage 'wide' liberalization of abortions, but 'rather to make them legal,' and to provide better protection of both the public and the profession. Consequently, it had accepted life and health as grounds for terminating a pregnancy, but had rejected deformity and criminal assault. Having turned down these two grounds as late as 1966, it approved them at the general council meeting of June 1967. Throughout, however, doctors insisted that what they were proposing could be described simply as making permissible what was already being done in hospitals.

Among the general public, the views of a substantial number of people were represented, no doubt, by the executive of the *National Council of Women* and the Member of Parliament, Mrs. Grace MacInnis. Mrs. MacInnis favoured the British law with its socio-economic clause, but restricted herself to a narrower concept for fear of losing the entire project. She believed that abortion should be removed from the Criminal Code and that, in the desire to improve life, the individual should have the right to prevent unwanted children from being born. The purpose of new abortion laws, said the resolution of the *National Council of Women*, was to "bring these laws into conformity with the realities of Canadian life." Furthermore, the views of some members of the general public were also represented by the Toronto *Globe and Mail* which had made itself the spokesman of the concepts that abortion was a question of private morality and that in a pluralistic society law ought not to be concerned with such questions.

Among the Churches, the *Presbyterian Church* accepted legalization of therapeutic abortion only for serious threats to life or health. It rejected such reasons as 'the expediency of reducing illegal abortions', or abortions as a measure of population control. *The Anglican Church* appeared to be of two minds at once. In one report the Church in Great Britain rejected abortion on demand, and even rape and deformity, as legitimate reasons. The same report, however, wanted the law to be worded in such a way that "the patient's total environment, actual or foreseeable" could be taken into account. A similar duality was present in the brief by the Canadian Church to the House of Commons Committee. It suggested that abortion should not be done for social reasons; yet, it gave the broadest possible interpretation to health.

The *United Church* had cautiously approved legal abortions for physical or mental reasons in 1960. At that time it rejected abortion as a means of family planning or as relief to the unmarried mother. In 1966 it re-confirmed the legality of abortions for reasons of life and health, but the spirit of the resolution was now much different from that in 1960. Little doubt was left that health was to be interpreted widely. In the spring of 1968 the official position still appeared to be that socio-economic reasons were unacceptable, but the delegates to the hearings of the Commons Committee were already prepared to go beyond that restriction. To explain why a choice could be made between the welfare of the mother on the one hand, and the life of the unborn on the other, the delegation presented the theory of "the accruing value of life." Delegates did not expect that legalization would greatly increase the number of abortions.

Members of other Protestant Churches such as Lutherans, Mennonites, Pentecostals and Evangelicals appeared mainly opposed to abortion, as were other religious groups like the Mormons and the Witnesses of Jehovah.[7a] Also opposed were the Greek Orthodox and the Jewish Orthodox. Yet, none of these bodies had taken the effort to issue a detailed refutation. Only the Latin and Greek-Byzantine rite Catholics had done so. After hesitating how to re-assert the traditional condemnation of abortion, the Catholic Bishops had finally taken a stand on a threefold principle: in spite of appearances, human life before birth is not intrinsically different from human life after birth; theology does not provide grounds by which one life may be esteemed of higher value than another; in the absence of scientific proof to the contrary, the date of conception must be taken as indicating the beginning of a new and distinct human life. The best law, their delegation said at the House of Commons Committee hearings, is the one that permits the least number of abortions.

The position of the Canadian Government on abortion was first made clear with the introduction of the Omnibus bill in December 1967. It was further clarified by Justice Minister Turner during the parliamentary debates in the early half of 1969. These debates started with the second reading of the Omnibus bill on January 23, 1969, and concluded with the third and final reading of the bill in mid-April. Third reading did not finish until a month later due to a three week long filibuster by the Ralliement Créditiste directed against the bill's clause on abortion. As for the motivation of the Government's attitude, it could be traced directly to the 1957 British report on homosexuality, better known as the Wolfenden Report.

The Wolfenden Report

The 1957 Report of the Committee on Homosexual Offenses and Prostitution, drawn up under the chairmanship of Sir John Wolfenden, re-introduced the age-old question of the relationship between law and morality into the politics of contemporary legislation. The Committee was forced to consider this problem because of the subject of its investigation, homosexuality. The way the report approached this topic was by asking: What is the connection between crime and sin? Another way of raising the same question was: Should the government be concerned with the enforcement of morals? Should the law forbid immorality and sin?

7a. For instance, the Pentecostal Assemblies of Canada opposed abortion, lotteries and homosexuality at their 26th biennial general Conference in Windsor, August 1968. See *Western Catholic Reporter*, Sept. 5, 1968, p. 8.

The authors of the report replied that the government should not forbid homosexual acts in private between consenting adults. In explaining the reasons for this reply, the Committee presented its views of the function of law in such a way that this interpretation could be applied to subjects other than homosexuality. According to the members of the Committee the purpose of law was "to preserve public order... to protect the citizen from what is offensive and injurious... (and) to provide safeguards against exploitation and corruption of others... particularly the young (and) the weak in body or mind..."[8] To this they added that the law should regard "individual freedom of choice and action in matters of private morality" of the greatest importance:

> There must remain a realm of private morality and immorality which is... not the law's business. To say this is not to condone or encourage private immorality.[9]

Similar ideas were repeated in the Report's section on prostitution: "It was not the duty of the law, to concern itself with immorality as such...," the Committee said; law "should confine itself to those activities which offend against public order and decency or expose the ordinary citizen to what is offensive or injurious."[10] Consequently, the Committee recommended that homosexual behavior between consenting adults in private be no longer a criminal offense because no evidence had been found that its removal from the criminal code would have serious harmful effects on society. In accordance with the Committee's philosophy only proselytizing and the solicitation of minors was to remain forbidden.

The suggestions of the Wolfenden Committee were made law in Britain in 1967, ten years after they were first presented. By then the Committee's philosophy, with its principle of separating law from religious principles and private morality, was almost taken for granted and was rapidly becoming the new basis for modern law. Hitherto it had obviously not been so. After all, prostitution, homosexuality, attempted suicide, duelling, abortion, euthanasia and other similar matters were still on the books.

The Wolfenden ideas provided the philosophy for Justice Minister Trudeau's Omnibus bill of December 1967. At the time of the bill's announcement Sir John Wolfenden's report was explicitly mentioned in explanation of the proposed legislation on homosexuality which was to follow the British model.[11] It was the basis of the Minister's remark that 'the state has no business in the bedrooms of the nation,' a remark which referred to homosexuality but which was soon used in reference to abortion as well. Since Mr. Trudeau treated abortion exactly the same as the other proposed revisions of the Criminal Code, it was clear that like homosexuality he considered it as belonging to private morality.

---

8. Para. 13, *The Wolfenden Report*, New York, Stein and Day, 1963.

9. *Ibid.*, para. 61, p. 48.

10. *Ibid.*, para. 257, p. 143.

11. "Bill Overhauls Criminal Code," *Globe and Mail*, December 22, 1971, p. 1.

In his press conference of February 1968 he confirmed this attitude when he spoke of homosexuality and abortion in the same breath as matters of private morality.[12] The matter was further simplified when during the 1968 summer election campaign he frequently explained the proposed legislation on abortion, gross indecency and related topics, as one of distinguishing between 'crime' and 'sin,' with the implication that sin was a matter of private morality.[13] Three years later, during the agitation for abortion request, Mr. Trudeau had narrowed the question of abortion even further to a matter of concern only to women: "I don't feel I can speak with great authority on this," he said during an address in Halifax, "because I am not a woman."[14]

During the parliamentary debates for second and third reading at the beginning of 1969, the Wolfenden Report was quoted on several occasions by Justice Minister Turner.[15] It clearly inspired his declaration that "we believe that morality is a matter of private conscience. Criminal law should reflect the public order only."[15] In Mr. Turner's opinion this general principle was also the consequence of a practical difficulty which he explained as follows:

> The problem of trying to render synonymous law and morality is that we then come down to the question: Whose morality? Whose standards of behavior? Whose sense of morality? Who is to determine the standard? Who is to attribute blame? Who is to say what is moral and immoral? Who is to decide when moral responsibility exists in terms of freedom of will, and when it has to be diluted in human terms because of environmental or physical causes?... In a pluralistic society there may be different standards, differing attitudes and the law cannot reflect them all. Public order, in this situation of a pluralistic society, cannot substitute for private conduct. We believe that morality is a matter for private conscience. Criminal law should reflect the public order only.[16]

Since Mr. Turner's explanations found favour with the parliamentary majority the abortion clause was approved under a separate vote on May 9, 1969. Of the four parties only the Social Credit party was unanimous in rejecting both the idea that abortion was a question of private morality, and the concept that law should no longer reflect specific Christian principles.

Second reading of the proposed revisions of the Criminal Code started on January 23rd. Justice Minister Turner claimed that "this legislation is the most important and all-embracing reform of the Criminal and penal law ever attempted at one time in this country."[17] He forecast that the bill would be remembered as "a high point" in Canadian penal reform and that it would "be identified in the future

---

12. *Canadian Register*, Feb. 24, 1968.

13. "Sin and Crime," *Ibid.*, July 6, 1968, p. 5.

14. "Women should settle abortion question: PM," *Globe and Mail*, Oct. 30, 1971.

15. *Hansard*, January 23, 1969, p. 4723; April 17, 1969, p. 7634.

16. *Ibid.*, April 17, 1969, p. 7635.

17. *Hansard*, Jan. 23, 1969, p. 4723.

with the indelible imprint of our Prime Minister..."[18] In explaining the section on abortion he stated that "the present state of the law is not clear and one of the overriding purposes of the legislation is to clarify it." This bill does not include "abortion based solely on considerations of eugenics or the commission of sexual offences...," he continued. It "does not authorize the taking of foetal life; it does not promote abortion." After repeating the statement that the proposed legislation did not promote abortion, he added that "it permits it under the restricted circumstance where the mother's life or health might be in danger."[19]

The Liberals

While the new Omnibus bill now included 120 different clauses, abortion proved to be the only truly controversial issue, drawing most of the attention and taking up much of the debate. With the exception of lotteries and homosexuality which were difficult to accept for some members, the remainder of the proposed revisions of the Criminal Code found almost unanimous approval. Among Liberals, aside from official spokesman for the Government such as Mr. Turner, no more than a dozen of the numerous backbenchers in parliament spoke on the bill during second reading, which covered the period January 23rd — February 26th, 1969.

Three of these Liberals spoke against abortion and against Clause 18 which contained the proposed revisions on abortion. All three took their stand on the defense of unborn human life. Gordon Sullivan (Hamilton-Mountain) claimed that Clause 18 contradicted every existing Bill of Rights.[20] On May 14th he was to be the solitary Liberal voting against the entire Bill C-150. Ralph Stewart (Cochrane) argued that abortion was not a question of religion and private morality but a matter of public morality, which, in this case, was directed against public order and natural law. He and John Reid (Lib-Lab, Kenora-Rainy River), who was convinced that abortion was merely a different form of murder, were the only Liberals who voted against Clause 18 when it was presented for a separate vote on May 9th.

The remainder of the Liberal party speakers were content to support their Government. Mr. MacGuigan (Windsor-Walkerville) saw the Omnibus bill as "an entirely new governmental approach to the criminal law..." which "shall no longer be thought of as a mirror of morals." From now on "crime and sin, law and morals, must be distinguished," he said, quoting from John Stuart Mill's essay, *On Liberty,* and from paragraph 13 of the Wolfenden Report to indicate the source of the new philosophy. Although he himself was opposed to abortion, believing "that the foetus is an actual human being from the beginning," he nevertheless accepted the proposed legislation because, in his opinion, the present law did not permit "abortions

---

18. *Hansard,* p. 4717.
19. *Ibid.,* January 23, 1969, p. 4722.
20. *Hansard,* January 24, 1969, p. 4784.
21. *Ibid.,* February 25, 1969, p. 5946.

now taking place in the hospitals... according to the best canons of medical practice..."[22] Dr. Isabelle (Hull), who had been vice-chairman of the House of Commons Committee on abortion, gave an extensive survey of past and present legislation on abortion throughout the world, concluding that Clause 18 embodied legislation with "a fair sense of proportion."[23] At the time of voting, however, he was absent. Mr. Colin Gibson (Hamilton-Wentworth) favoured abortion on request but supported this bill as "an important step forward."[24] Mr. Chappell (Peel South) did not believe a foetus "to be a life, certainly not at the stage when therapeutic abortion is possible." The new British act referred to abortion as "the induced termination of pregnancy," lending support to the view that pregnancy is only a condition of a female."[25]

Mr. Hogarth (New Westminster) agreed with Mr. MacGuigan "that the amendment is not merely clarifying the existing law," though he disagreed with the reasons for a new law put forward by Mr. Lederman in the *Law Quarterly Review*, with which Mr. MacGuigan seemed to be agreeing (that existing law did not permit any abortions). Although he rejected "the suggestion that the unborn child should be destroyed merely at the whim or fancy of the mother" and acknowledged "that unborn life has always been entitled to some protection," he favoured the legislation because a woman ought "to be able to rid herself of a pregnancy she does not want as a result of a crime against her body."[26] Mr. Robert Kaplan (Don Valley) argued that legislative authority could not be used "to express the morality of one group and suppress the freedom of others...;" yet, we must prevent the situation, he said, "where one group's... expression will threaten or undermine the values of the rest to the extent that we cannot co-exist in harmony." Believing in the improvement of the quality of life, he favoured legal abortions, but not "absolutely unlimited abortion."[27]

The mayor of Trois-Rivières, Mr. Mongrain, claimed that there was "no question of legalizing abortion," but only of permitting it when the "mother could be in danger of death or become permanently mentally deficient." He wanted to know what right people had to say " 'My conscience will not allow me to vote for this bill.' Now, I ask that person by virtue of what principle he wishes to impose upon all Canadians the dictates of his conscience?" He announced that, while personally opposed to abortion, he would support the bill, because "I cannot impose the dictates of my conscience upon

22. *Hansard*, January 24, 1969, pp. 4791-4794.
23. *Ibid.*, p. 4804.
24. *Ibid.*, p. 4810.
25. *Ibid.*, January 27, 1969, pp. 4839-4840. On April 28 Mr. Woolliams quoted a letter of Mr. Chappell to a Mr. O'Brien which said: "Although the expression 'unborn child' is used by those who oppose the bill, this is not a life and no religion that I know of anywhere in the world recognizes or claims that the foetus has a soul. Rather than turning the clock back 100 years, the change will bring us forward from the laws of the middle ages." *Hansard*, April 29, 1969, p. 8108.
26. *Hansard*, January 27, 1969, pp. 4867-8.
27. *Ibid.*, February 11, 1969, pp. 5390-1.

others..."[28] Mr. Foster (Algoma) believed that the proposal "simply legalizes what is effectively the status quo in most parts of Canada today," while merely adding the health of the mother as a further ground for therapeutic abortions. The proposed legislation did not resolve the problem of rape, he noted.[29] Finally, Mr. Gilles Marceau (Lapointe), the last Liberal to speak during second reading, replied to speakers of the Social Credit party who had accused members of the government as being either "stupid" or "inhuman," by declaring that he regarded "as an imbecile" the man who failed to make the people in his riding understand "that this legislation was extremely advantageous... because it opened new horizons... and allowed them to make a distinction between religion, morals and law." (*Some hon. Members:* Hear, hear). While acknowledging that he was a Catholic, he joined Mr. Mongrain in thinking that "in our pluralist society everybody has the right to follow the principles that he regards as just and I do not think I have the right to prevent him from doing what he wishes."[30]

Taking the nine speakers as representative of the party as a whole, it is clear that the motivations for accepting new abortion legislation were extremely varied and often contradictory. It was almost a case of nine different people with nine different reasons. One member supported the proposed legislation because he did not think that existing law permitted any abortions at all. Another member favoured it because, like the Minister of Justice, he thought that a law which already permitted abortions needed further clarification. A third did not believe a foetus was human and thought that it was merely a question of preserving a woman's health. A fourth speaker, however, was convinced that the unborn were alive and human, but that society needed compromise. A fifth accepted the proposals only as a step forward on the road to abortion on demand, contradicting others who favoured the new law but who vigorously denied that abortion on demand was either desirable in itself or would result from the proposed legislation. A sixth gave criminal assault on a woman as his sole reason — without noticing that the Government specifically meant to exclude abortions for rape. Finally, several speakers who presumably had voted numerous bills into law against the wishes of the opposition, asserted that in the matter of abortion they did not have the right to impose their views upon society. Moreover, they vigorously denied that party discipline had any bearing on their view.

The question of whether or not party discipline was being imposed upon the Government side, as well as the propriety of having one vote for a 120 clause Omnibus bill, were two major issues in the debates. Prime Minister Trudeau had never approved the request of party members and others to permit a free vote. Now, there were frequent denials by supporters of the Government that any Liberal was being forced to act or vote against his conscience. Yet, it remained difficult to believe that both the expected party vote, as well as the fact that

---

28. *Hansard,* February 13, 1969, pp. 5476-7.

29. *Ibid.,* February 25, 1969, p. 5920.

30. *Ibid.,* February 25, 1969, p. 5928.

abortion was wrapped up together with other proposed reforms of
which everyone approved, did not have a profound influence on the
attitude of many, not only during the vote, but ever since the original
introduction of the legislation in December, 1967. The Government,
however, did permit a motion for the elimination of Clause 18, thus
allowing the House to have a separate recorded vote on abortion
towards the end of the third reading, on May 9, five days before the
vote on the entire reform bill.

Vote on May 9
(on the elimination of Clause 18)

	For	Against	Absent	General Standing June 25, 1968
Liberal	2	85	68	155
Progressive Conservative	25	7	40	72
New Democratic Party	1	15	6	22
Ralliement Créditiste	8	–	6	14
Independent	–	–	1	1
	36	107	121	264 [30a]

The Progressive Conservatives

Like the smaller parties, the Progressive Conservatives who formed
the official opposition in the Commons, left members free to vote as
they saw fit. Their opposition to the proposed legislation was motivated
partly by a sense of duty to oppose legislation coming from Government
benches and partly by a true rejection of some of the proposed reforms.
Just as Liberals were tempted to vote with the Government regardless
of their true feelings about abortion, so Conservatives were already
inclined to vote against the Government regardless of the legislation
proposed. Nevertheless, the vote on May 9, as well as the debates,
made it abundantly clear that the Conservatives viewed abortion much
more critically than the Liberals.

The debate was opened with a general evaluation of the entire
Omnibus bill by Eldon Woolliams (Calgary North) speaking for the
party. Mr. Woolliams demanded that the Standing Committee on
Justice and Legal Affairs which, under new ground rules just introduced was to receive the bill after second reading, be instructed to
bring out four distinct and separate reports: on abortion, on homosexuality, on lotteries and gambling, and on all the remaining clauses
of the bill, in order that separate votes could be taken.[31] He attacked
as "utter nonsense" the suggestion that "Canadians, who were one
of the first peoples to be guaranteed their religious freedom by the
common law, by the Bill of Rights and by other statutes, can separate
their spiritual and temporal responsibilities..."[32] Without taking a
position on abortion at this time, he declared that there simply was
no question that abortions to save the mother's life were permitted.

30a. For details, see appendix 7.
31. *Hansard*, January 23, 1969, p. 4725.
32. *Ibid.*, January 23, 1969, p. 4727.

He forecast that "the great quarrel" about the proposed legislation would centre around the addition of the word "health," which had been left undefined by the Government. In the future, he said, "health could have a very wide definition. Words grow with sociological changes."[33]

Following Mr. Woolliams' address in the name of the party, Erik Nielsen (Yukon) was the first of sixteen Conservatives who spoke on the bill. Mr. Nielsen argued that together with the new birth control and divorce legislation, these proposed reforms on homosexuality and abortion made Mr. Trudeau's "just society" look more like a "permissive society."[34] He objected to the abortion provisions as simply killing "human beings unborn" and as entirely inconsistent with the recent abolition of capital punishment which had been brought forward on the ground that "we must not kill."[35] Noting that he was not a Roman Catholic, he announced he would vote against the bill if present when the vote was called. While Mr. Nielsen made it very clear how he regarded abortion, Mr. MacEwan (Central Nova), though demanding a free vote and intimating opposition, did not speak on abortion.[36] Former Prime Minister John Diefenbaker of Prince Albert demanded that the bill be split; he objected to both the legalization of homosexuality and of abortion, and rejected the argument that they "are taking place and, therefore, we ought to legalize them."[37] On the other hand, New Brunswicker Gordon Fairweather (Fundy-Royal) complained that they had "been flooded with extreme statements on this issue...." Abortion, he said, was a topic "which concerns something that womanhood should decide...." Claiming that there was no law on abortion in Britain "until 1801" and that "there was no dogmatic rule concerning abortion in the Roman Catholic Church until 1865," he repeated that a decision on abortion should be left to the pregnant woman. If he had doubts about any issue in this bill, he explained, it was about lotteries, which he feared would "diminish... the national prestige of the country."[38]

The wide spectrum of opinion, as well as the feeling of many of being at a loss what to do, was illustrated further by the remainder of the speakers. Robert McCleave (Halifax-East Hants) first indicated he had serious doubts about the wisdom of all three controversial sections: lotteries, homosexuality and abortion. On the question of abortion, however, his objections proved only of a technical nature. He was satisfied that "if a Roman Catholic woman feels strongly enough about her religion, presumably she would not consent to an abortion in any case."[39] James McGrath (St. John's East), expressing approval of much of the Omnibus bill, objected strongly to the "dealing

33. *Hansard*, January 23, 1969, pp. 4733-4.

34. *Ibid.*, p. 4789.

35. *Ibid.*, p. 4788.

36. Mr. MacEwan voted against the entire bill on May 14.

37. *Hansard*, January 27, 1969, p. 4838. Mr. Diefenbaker voted against the bill on May 14.

38. *Hansard*, January 27, 1969, pp. 4841-2.

39. *Ibid.*, pp. 4861-2.

at once with the very sacred laws of life itself and the rather mundane laws of lotteries and gun control." As he agreed with the reasons given by the Liberal member for Hamilton, Mr. Gordon Sullivan, he, too, intended to vote against the bill.[40] A representative of Prince Edward Island, Melvin McQuaid (Cardigan), denied that any "religious group in this country is trying to force its ideas down the throats of the Canadian people." Those who oppose abortion, he said, oppose it "because they are convinced that foetal life is human life and that to destroy human life at any stage is deliberate, premeditated, cold-blooded murder."[41] He declared himself opposed, as did Ambrose Peddle (Grand-Falls-Labrador). Mr. Peddle, who acknowledged that he was a Catholic although he claimed not to speak as one, attacked the bill as an example of Mr. Trudeau seeking "to impose his particular belief upon members of this House." This legislation, he said, "is not concerned with fostering unity but more with spreading discord and disunity."[42] Mr. Walter Carter (St. John's West), like all his colleagues, attacked the package character of this bill. Aside from the moral arguments, he wondered about the social consequences of the bill's philosophy and of such notions "that because a lot of people do something, that makes it natural and acceptable." A government, he said, "which relaxes... curbs on drugs, makes divorce easier, permits abortion and homosexuality, is in the process of remaking our society. The question which we must ask is, in whose image and likeness?" The proposed legislation on homosexuality, he said, indicates that "what we are legislating is a kind of well-mannered, sedate, controlled Canadian type of vice." What kind of society are we building which permits the destruction of unborn life "because of social convenience or possible embarrassment?" he asked.[43]

David MacDonald (Egmont) thought that as "a person who passes from time to time as a theologian", he should become involved.[44] He forecast that the provision on abortion would "satisfy almost no one." In some way "we are going to legalize abortions in this country," he said; yet, from the minister's own speech and those of other members we have come to realize that "the definition that will be given to these clauses is exceedingly narrow..." Therefore, he said, "we cannot call the proposed bill a reform measure."[45] Still, he favoured the bill, as did Mr. Gordon Ritchie (Dauphin) of Manitoba who saw the differences on abortion as irreconcilable. In his opinion, the bill would "not make abortion any easier in this country, although it may make it more available in certain parts of the country..." He forecast that it might even "further restrict the carrying out of a therapeutic abortion because these were now to be reserved to 'accredited' hospitals only.[46]

40. *Ibid.*, pp. 4870-1.
41. *Hansard*, February 11, 1969, p. 5383.
42. *Ibid.*, p. 5407.
43. *Ibid.*, pp. 5410-11.
44. Mr. MacDonald is a Minister of the United Church of Canada in P.E.I.
45. *Hansard*, February 13, 1969, pp. 5472-3.
46. *Ibid.*, pp. 5499-5500.

Mr. Noble (Grey-Simcoe) saw the bill as "the thin edge of a wedge which (will) open the door to removing all provisions in respect of abortion..." "Wanton abortion is murder," he said and "my conscience will not let me support murder."[47] On the other hand, the leader of the opposition, Mr. Robert Stanfield (Halifax), considering the bill on the whole as "constructive," was not certain whether the section on abortion "will not make it more difficult in fact to obtain abortions in some of the more remote parts of the country." While accepting that for homosexuality criminal law may not necessarily be "the proper instrument for society to use," he rejected the view "that society has no right to be concerned about the moral climate in private society."[48] Mr. Stanfield's general approval was supported by Mr. Baldwin of Alberta's Peace River district, who discussed the nature of crime and sin, indicating that he did not count himself among those "who feel that the family has outlived its usefulness"; the criminal law, he said, must "give effect to certain moral principles." He forecast that long after this bill had become law people would remember how "issues, involving certain moral and conscientious questions which should lie far outside the range of political partisanship laws, were in fact placed on the statute books by most questionable means."[49] While Mr. Baldwin left his views on abortion unspoken, Steven Paproski (Edmonton Centre) made it very clear that he was not about to vote for a bill which refused to protect life from being "destroyed for the most frivolous reason." Finally, the Hon. Hugh Flemming (Carleton-Charlotte) objected especially against "the homosexuality feature." He indicated he had not studied the abortion question, but after hearing Mr. Fortin (R. Cr.) earlier, he felt worried that the proposed legislation might lead to "a lessening of the restraint and respect for embryonic human life."[50]

The New Democratic Party

While a majority of Progressive Conservative speakers expressed opposition to the abortion clause or reflected a hesitant groping for answers mixed with fear for unknown consequences, the majority of NDP members demonstrated confidence and approval with only one member opposing the proposed revisions. Spokesman for the party was David Lewis of Toronto (York South), who first denied Mr. Turner's claim that the revisions represented a radical reform: "Important social matters," he said, "are treated with timidity." In his view, the general proposition which "ought to govern public law" was that "in our criminal law we ought to amend everything that is a relic of the past and not consistent with modern morality." He noted that when he studied the history of law as a student, he learned that:

47. *Ibid.*, p. 5502.
48. *Hansard*, February 25, 1969, p. 5920. Mr. Stanfield voted in favour of the bill on May 14th.
49. *Ibid.*, pp. 5921-5923.
50. *Ibid.*, pp. 5950-1.

Much of our law developed during a period when society was governed by the church as well as the state. A good many of our laws can be traced to that historic fact. As society develops, and as the separation of church and state developed, the influence of the church in the formation of laws has become less and less. I urge that we do not term public crimes those actions which are matters for an individual's conscience.

Mr. Lewis rejected the idea that abortion or homosexuality were being legalized: "all these sections do is remove the taint of crime to certain actions which are merely personal matters to the person concerned, actions which do not impinge on the public good..." He stressed the educational value of law, and pleaded for a law "which is modern, humane, compassionate, responsive to the technological age in which we live..." Speaking on Clause 18, he regretted that the proposed legislation would "not have have the slightest effect" on the number of illegal abortions in this country "because it did not add anything new to the old law." He said that adding the word "health" merely clarified things a little and suggested that "the only intelligent and modern way to deal with this question" was "to remove from the Criminal Code any reference to abortion" altogether. "I have," he said, "complete confidence that all but the unethical members of that profession... would be as careful about doing an abortion, or advising a woman to have an abortion, as any law on the statute books could require..."[51]

The next day, other New Democrats like David Orlikow (Winnipeg North) also expected "that the present proposal on abortion will do very little."[52] Mrs. Grace MacInnis (Vancouver-Kingsway) gave the longest speech of the NDP members on the subject. She noted profound disagreement even with those members of her own caucus who "want no part of legislation designed to deal with abortion." Those who believe in the concept of abortion, she said, should be allowed "the right to follow the dictates of their consciences and remain within the law." Do opponents insist, she asked, "on imposing their views on those who consider it their right to follow their consciences in this matter?" They ought to realize "that public crime and private sin are entirely different matters," she continued, commending "the Prime Minister because he was quite right in saying the law has no business in the bedrooms of the nation." Mrs. MacInnis claimed that the existing law "makes criminals of pregnant women who are caught in the trap of pregnancy and need to have an abortion..." In answer to an earlier reference by a French speaking member of the House that those who favoured the amendments "love darkness," she countered that, in her opinion, "the people who love darkness are those who are closing their eyes to the terrible predicament of women from one coast to the other who are caught in the pregnancy trap and have no recourse because the lawmakers of this country... have given them no recourse." Surely, she said, this "is not a situation that can be met by quotations from religious or philosophical authorities who

51. *Hansard*, January 23, 1969, pp. 4755-4759.
52. *Ibid.*, January 24, 1969, p. 4808.

lived centuries ago." She regretted that the proposed legislation excluded social reasons and even rape and possible deformity. To her
mind it was "the height of irresponsibility for people to bring into
today's world children who are deformed." A new law would "give
the foetus the right, in many cases, not to be born. To my mind the
right not to be born is very important in a great many cases."[53]

Mr. Stanley Knowles (Winnipeg North Centre) spoke on abortion
on February 11. When voting on this bill, he stated, "we will not
be voting for or against abortion... (but) whether abortion is a crime
or a human problem." Let us "get into the 20th century on this issue,"
he said, and "admit that this is a human and social problem to be
dealt with in a humanitarian manner." He noted that there was a
"tendency for some people to assume that the churches will be
narrow-minded and traditional." He thought it significant, however,
"that in the main the churches and the church people who have been
thinking about this are saying to us, 'Apply reason, apply psychology,
apply compassion, apply human understanding to these problems.' "
"Serious-minded and thoughtful people in this country," he said, "will
be going along." Mr. Knowles approved of the remainder of the bill
with the exception of lotteries. "Whatever else we may agree to," he
said, "let us not make the social and economic mistake of establishing
or even permitting state lotteries..."[54]

Arnold Peters (Timiskaming) spoke on the same day as Mr.
Knowles after members from Newfoundland had expressed opposition
to both the homosexuality and abortion clauses. He invited them to
"the twentieth century" and suggested that "even those who have
spoken for the dinosaur class" might be "broadminded enough to allow
the rest of the country to develop in a reasonable manner." Referring
to abortion, he wondered how many people "have been to a church
service for a foetus. So far as I know, no church will bury a foetus
that is under seven months of development." Moving from churches
to statistics, he claimed that "according to the legal profession half
a million abortions a year are performed in Canada which has a
population of 20 million."[55] Continuing his address the next day, Mr.
Peters suggested that "a woman seeking an abortion ought to be viewed
by a doctor as he would view a woman seeking to have her tonsils
out." Repeating his statistics of "half a million abortions a year,"
he concluded with the observation that "religious convictions are
forcing (people) into a position which is out of touch with the realities
of our society and which, in the final analysis, contravenes the concepts

53. *Hansard*, January 27, 1969, pp. 4842-4847.
54. *Hansard*, February 11, 1969, pp. 5375-5378. Mr. Knowles is a former minister
    of the United Church. Dr. Robert McClure former moderator of the United
    Church expressed similar views as follows: *On Lotteries*: "As a civilization decays
    it goes in for lotteries. Chance takes the place of frugality and planning." *On
    Abortion*: "It's sweeping the world. I hope it comes to Canada on an even keel.
    I am against repeated abortions..." Quoted in United Church *Observer*, December
    1971, p. 22.
55. *Ibid.*, pp. 5413-5. On the burial of a foetus, see Chapter 7, Canadian Catholic
    Conference. Peters MP obviously did not attend this meeting of March 5, 1968.

of their religion."[56] Andrew Brewin (Toronto Greenwood) recognized that abortion was a "delicate subject which involves people's deepest religious feelings" ... and that they were "discussing the sanctity of life." Nevertheless, he thought it "more humane to take abortion out of the field of criminal law," thus agreeing with Mrs. MacInnis that "we should remove it from the sphere of criminal law altogether."[57]

Harold Winch (Vancouver East) opened his speech with the remark that he wished that "those who have said there should be the opportunity to vote according to their religion and conscience had added the words, and knowledge and understanding." Recalling his years as member of the British Columbia legislature and his annual visits to provincial institutions for children, he described his feelings as follows:

> In going through an institution in New Westminster I have looked down into a baby's crib and have seen what I considered to be a six or seven year old child who was nothing but skin and bone, and later discovered this child was breathing but certainly not living. I have no hesitation in saying that not only must we consider the right to be born but we must also consider the right not to be born a vegetable that medical science can keep alive until you and I are probably long dead.[58]

"As I say," he repeated, "we should think of the right not to be born as a vegetable." John Gilbert, (Toronto Broadview), disagreed with those who had said that there really was no change brought with the new law except for a few clarifications and the addition of the word "health." It creates "a different atmosphere and different attitudes" he noted; "we are beginning to regard the problem of abortion as a human or social problem rather than as a criminal act... Therefore this amendment is a step in the right direction."

The last New Democratic speaker was John Burton (Regina East), the only one of his party opposed to Clause 18. "The state has an obligation and duty to protect human life where it exists," he said; "it is clear that human life does exist prior to birth." He rejected justification of the new legislation with the argument "that the state through other actions, such as in police action, war, execution of criminals, etc., has been deemed to have the right to take lives or take action that may or will result in loss of life." "Surely," he said, "no comparison can be made between an innocent unborn child and an adult who has no regard for life or who may be defending other lives." Mr. Burton wondered whether health was not "a very vague term"; whether hospitals that did not want to perform abortions were protected; and whether "there should not be provision for a review after five years, such as is the case with capital punishment?"[59]

56. *Hansard*, February 12, 1969, p. 5451.
57. *Ibid.*, February 13, 1969, p. 5479.
58. *Ibid.*, p. 5496.
59. *Hansard*, February 25, 1969, pp. 5947-9.

Ralliement Créditiste

While almost every member of the NDP, with the exception of Mr. Burton, was in wholehearted agreement with the proposed legislation or, if dissatisfied, dissatisfied only because the legislation did not go far enough, the 14-member Créditistes, representing rural Quebec ridings, were even more wholeheartedly opposed to it. All were Catholics and none hesitated to quote Pope or Bishops in support of their cause, while the large group of Catholics in the Liberal party who had studiously ignored these authorities, watched in silence or absented themselves from the debates.

The first to speak was Bernard Dumont (Frontenac). After expressing the party's objection to the clause on homosexuality and the fact that the bill had not been split, he expressed his sentiments on abortion as follows:

> Mr. Speaker, my 4-year-old child accompanied us when we went to visit relatives during the Christmas holidays of 1968-69 and getting close to his aunt asked her: "Auntie, may I hear your baby move?" How happy he was when he told us: "Mother, the baby moved!" When a 4-year-old child is able to detect the presence of life in the womb of a woman who is 5 months pregnant, one wonders why they try to make us believe in this house that the presence of life in a child only appears in the 9th month of pregnancy or at birth. No, Mr. Speaker, we cannot as Christians accept that theory.

To show that he did not stand alone in believing that the unborn have rights, he quoted from the bible, the Canadian Bill of Rights, papal documents, and the Canadian Bishops' Pastoral Letter.[60] Mr. Romuald Rodrigue (Beauce), too, put the weight of his arguments on the right to life "as a basic human right on which depend all the others that every human being is entitled to claim." He thought it "truly ironic" that "shortly after abolishing the death penalty... we want to pass legislation which will destroy life instead of protecting it."[61] Mr. Adrien Lambert (Bellechasse) argued that the abortion amendment was of "the utmost importance since it is likely to change the meaning of the term 'homicide.' " Rejecting the assumption that "for a human being life only begins the moment a child is born," he said that, "human capital, the inhabitants themselves are the greatest wealth of our country." He noted that when a few decades ago material conditions were far less advanced, "there was no question of seeking abortion as is the case today." Having witnessed the birth of everyone of his twelve children, he was convinced "that life is... of exceptional value." Quoting extensively from medical sources to show that there were almost no medical reasons for abortions, he concluded with an expression of faith in the wisdom of God who "has indeed provided our earth with sufficient resources of all kinds to satisfy the need of each one of us."[62]

---

60. *Hansard*, January 24, 1969, pp. 4778-80.
61. *Hansard*, January 27, 1969, pp. 4863-4.
62. *Ibid.*, February 11, 1969, p. 5388.

Léonel Beaudoin (Richmond) read a long quotation from the association of medical officers of Quebec hospitals showing the extreme rarity of medical grounds for abortions. He noted that Justice Minister Turner on a television program the previous December 27th had "asserted that the word 'health' would not be interpreted by courts of justice, but by the various therapeutic abortion committees," confirming "our apprehension that abortion committees would make the law themselves." He forecast that "to legalize therapeutic abortion on grounds of physical or mental health would alter the moral standards of an entire nation and could "lead a country to its downfall and its death."[63] A similar view was expressed by Henri Latulippe (Compton), who believed that because all our freedoms are based on respect for man, "the survival or disappearance of society in general (was) at stake."[64] The next day he continued the explanation of his pessimistic philosophy of man and society and declared that "the modern state is the enemy of man," who, as far as the state is concerned, "is a material, a thing, a number, a file and nothing more." There is "no solution in the world of law," he said, "there are only irreconcilable inconsistencies, we must get out of this tragic dilemma... Society must recognize the importance of every individual." He declared that "apart from being pernicious, the provisions in this bill dealing with homosexuality and abortion will lead the nation to its own destruction." Mr. Latulippe refused to accept the separation of law and morality, and claimed it was up to the state to promote morality so as to maintain, as far as possible, a well-balanced human personality." He attacked "our diabolical system which prevents people from having decent housing..." and could "see nothing but increases in capital gains... and an increase in taxes and contributions that reduce the income of small wage earners who cannot afford to rent decent houses for their children yet to be born..."   Roland Godin (Portneuf) was equally pessimistic. He, too, attacked the proposed legislation on homosexuality and abortion. Quoting a French journalist who claimed that there were two million homosexuals in Great Britain, he believed that "like monkeys we are imitating England."[66] While speaking on abortion, he quoted the encyclical, *Humanae Vitae*, which pointed out to the legislators that they "must not allow 'a degradation of the moral tenets of nations through legal processes... through practices which are contrary to natural and divine law.' " Then he recalled the history of mass murders from "the slaughter of the Holy Innocents" at the time of Christ to the "30 million" who died in Russia under Stalin, and wondered, considering the background of the member of Mont-Royal (Mr. Trudeau), whether "the present government with its loathsome laws on divorce, on abortion, on homosexuality, is not simply the tool of a dreadful plot against our civilization."[67]

---

63. *Hansard*, February 11, 1969, pp. 5402-6.
64. *Ibid.*, February 12, 1969, pp. 5453-4.
65. *Ibid.*, February 13, 1969, pp. 5467-70.
66. *Hansard*, February 13, 1969, p. 5482.
67. *Ibid.*, pp. 5493-4.

Mr. Gilbert Rondeau (Shefford) claimed that Mr. Winch's references to people suffering from some kind of physical illness as 'vegetables', made "the blood of the members of the Ralliement Créditiste boil," and were a sample of the philosophy of materialism which dominated the mass media. After he had defended the Social Credit philosophy against communists, socialists, and other enemies he returned to abortion by quoting Father Paguin's book, *Morale et Médecin*, that "the murder of an innocent person is always a murder and it is the more hateful that the victim is defenceless." After presenting selections from various Bills and Declarations of Rights in favour of protecting life, and noting that "at one time, the execution of pregnant women condemned to death was deferred until the birth of their child," he showed that the precepts of the Church and its penal legislation had condemned abortion from the Council of Elvira in 300, the Council of Ancyra in 314, the Council of Lerida in 546, and the Council of Constantinople in 692 onwards to Pope Pius XI, Pius XII, and the second Vatican Council.[68] "Whom shall we obey?" he asked, "Shall we obey now Caesar or... God?"[69]

André Fortin (Lotbinière) was happy to welcome 'the updating' of the Criminal Code. We must bring forward "legislation which is humane, and promotes freedom and security for individuals," he said. Examining the proposed legislation on abortion he found that it could "only warp the scales of values." The term therapeutic abortion "constitutes a formal contradiction," he said. In the sentence 'would or would be likely to endanger her life or health,' he objected to the term 'would be likely.' In fact, he objected to the entire clause with words like 'endanger,' 'would be likely,' and 'health' being left vague and undefined. "Those provisions," he said, "are much too broad, when one realizes that a pregnancy is not too dangerous."[70]

The views of the party leader, Réal Caouette (Témiscamingue), were summed up when he described the entire bill as "a general abortion." Lotteries, he said, "will be the abortion of the financial system;" the law on guns "might be considered as the abortion of understanding between individuals"; homosexuality "is in some way the abortion of marriage between a man and a woman..."; the "breathalizer test... is the abortion of sobriety or of breweries"; parole "is the abortion of justice. Mr. Speaker, this is a bill of abortion."[71] Mr. Gauthier (Roberval) declared "the medicine" of Clause 18 "by far too bitter, especially for Roman Catholics." He attacked the Liberals who now claimed that the bill "was imposed upon them" and that "abortion

---

68. In his Address to Italian midwives on Sept. 12, 1958, Pius XII had repeated that: Every human being, even the child in his mother's womb, owes immediately to God, and not to his parents, to society or to human authority his right to live. Therefore, no man, no medical, eugenic, social, economic or moral counsel can produce or confer a judicially valid right to dispose directly and deliberately of an innocent human life, that is, to dispose of it with a view to its intended destruction considered either as an end or as a mean to achieve an end which perhaps in itself is not at all unlawful. (*Hansard*, February 13, 1969, p. 5505.

69. *Hansard*, February 13, 1969, pp. 5502-8.

70. *Ibid.*, February 25, 1969, pp. 5912-4.

71. *Hansard*, February 25, 1969, pp. 5952-7.

is not so serious since the bill tends only to save the mother's life..."
He attacked the members of the New Democratic Party as "well known
for their avant-garde ideas, that they call sophisticated." In reference
to Mr. Lewis' remarks about society evolving from "a time when the
clergy... (influenced)... popular beliefs and morals," he himself did not
think it "progress to follow the downward path of a materialistic and
atheistic minority." "Whether they admit it or not," he said "when
passing this legislation on abortion, the Government legalizes murder."

The Final Round

Following the close of second reading, the bill was referred to the
Standing Committee of Justice and Legal Affairs which, beginning
on March 4th, considered technical details of drafting and amendments, permitting a few legal and medical experts to present their
views. It concluded its work on March 28, 1969, by accepting the
provision that abortions could be performed also at hospitals approved
by provincial Ministers of Health.[72] Third and final reading started
on April 16. The Créditistes refused to enter into an agreement to
establish a time-table for limited debate. Gérard Laprise, House leader
of the 14-member group, said the agreement "amounted to nothing
more than a Government effort to impose closure."[73] Instead, the
Créditistes were determined to introduce a long series of amendments
and discuss each amendment fully "to m. .e sure that the act will
correspond to the wishes of the Canadian people."[74] It ensured much
procedural wrangling while the Government attempted to have the
Speaker declare as many amendments out of order as possible. This
was evident already on April 16 when the discussion started with the
clauses on buggery, bestiality and homosexuality.

A number of Conservatives and Créditistes declared themselves
against the revisions on homosexuality. Robert McCleave (PC, Halifax-East Hants) summed up the position of the opposition. What is
the whole criminal law about, he asked, if "it is not to enact something
that imposes sanctions against what we regard as behaviour that is
anti-social or against the interests of our society?" He answered his
own question with a quote from *Western Catholic Reporter* that 'the
Government has an obligation to promote the acknowledged norms
of decency.'[75] It was in response to the opposition's denial of the desired
separation of law and morality that Justice Minister Turner raised
the question, "Whose morality?" and answered it with the assertion
"morality is a matter of private conscience. Criminal law should reflect
the public order only."[76] This roused Mr. Dinsdale (PC, Brandon-
Souris) to reply. The Wolfenden report, he said, "is not the law of

---

72. "Committee approves abortion law changes," *Globe and Mail*, March 28, p. 1.
73. "Créditistes scrap...plan for...debate limit," *Globe and Mail*, April 17, p. 10.
74. André Fortin, *Hansard*, April 16, 1969, p. 7599.
75. February 9, 1969. Mr. McCleave noted that as a Presbyterian he did not read
    this periodical but it had been given to him by Mr. Woolliams of Calgary.
    Hansard, April 17, pp. 7632-3.
76. *Hansard*, April 17, 1969, p. 7635. Also, see above.

the Medes and Persians." As advice for those who believed that the moral impact of a bygone era had no significance today, he quoted three conclusions of the historian Charles Beard:

> First 'the mills of the Gods grind slowly, but they grind exceedingly fine'; second, 'when it is dark you can see the stars.' Morally, it is very dark right now in many parts of the world. Possibly there will be light at the end of the tunnel before very long. The third and most significant is, 'He whom the Gods would destroy, they first make mad.'

What we are embracing, said Mr. Dinsdale, "is the *Playboy* philosophy." He concluded with quoting Dante, who "at another time of darkness" said: "the hottest places in Hell are reserved for those who in a period of moral crisis maintained their neutrality.' "[77]

When the debates on homosexuality and lotteries were concluded after more than a week of verbal duelling, the debate on abortion finally started on Friday, April 25th, although it did not get properly underway until the following Monday, April 28th. Both Créditistes and Conservatives submitted amendments to the proposed wording of the new legislation in Clause 18 which together numbered almost fifty. Some amendments were frivolous; others were serious. The final amendment proposed the elimination of Clause 18 itself, thereby giving everyone an opportunity to take a stand for or against the entire legislation on this subject.

The first amendment was defeated within minutes of its introduction.[78] The second amendment was moved by Eldon Woolliams of the Conservatives in the name of Mr. McCleave who was absent. It read:

> Nothing in this section shall be construed as obliging any hospital to establish a therapeutic abortion committee or any qualified medical practitioner to procure the miscarriage of a female person.[79]

The purpose of the amendment was to ensure that no hospital should be required to set up an abortion committee and no doctor should be required to perform abortions. Such guarantees were built into the laws of Great Britain and of those states in America which were contemplating similar legislation. The Minister of Justice, however, took the view that there was "no evidence that questions of conscience posed a practical problem"; there was "nothing in Clause 18... which would in any way impose a criminal obligation... on a hospital"; Section 237 as amended "imposes no duty on the board of a hospital to set up a therapeutic abortion committee," and "it imposes no duty... to perform an abortion."[80]

Mr. Baldwin spoke in favour of the amendment. Créditiste Gérard Laprise (Abitibi) pointed out that doctors had expressed fears of coercion and that the Canadian Bishops' Conference only "a few days

---

77. *Ibid.*, pp. 7637-9.
78. Hansard, April 28, 1969, p. 8056.
79. *Ibid.*
80. *Hansard*, April 28, 1969, p. 8058.

ago" had renewed their request that the Criminal Code "would at least respect the freedom of all physicians and hospitals."[81] His colleague, René Matte (Champlain), complained of being "at a loss to find a way to have our arguments taken into consideration." Everything has been decided in advance, he said. He pointed out that the Association of the Hospital Medical Boards had made a similar request for a guarantee the previous January. But "this chamber... is on the way to becoming a modern Sodom and Gomorrha," he exclaimed.[82] NDPer John Burton proposed his own version of the guarantee. Créditistes Roland Godin, Romuald Rodrigue, and André Fortin illustrated the desire for such a clause with more documentary evidence. In the middle of it all Dr. Rynard (PC, Simcoe North) wanted to know whether abortions were to be paid "out of medicare hospitalization," which Mr. Turner answered with "Oh, no."[83] Dr. Rynard forecast that the pressure which would be brought to bear on hospitals "will be great indeed."[84] Marcel Lambert (PC, Edmonton West) forecast that Clause 18 would attack the doctors' freedom of practice and that hospitals already had "no freedom with regard to their financing" and were now directly controlled by the provincial authorities. Mr. Asselin (PC, Charlevoix) quoted an article in *Le Devoir* warning against this bill and its consequences. It was all in vain. Mr. Turner saw no need for the amendment and the motion went down to defeat 94 to 36.[85]

Eldon Woolliams introduced a second motion for the Conservatives. It was intended to prevent abortions being performed just before the act of birth under the guise of a miscarriage, in case "doctors become so ruthless that they interpret the law to mean that any action they take may be considered necessary." At the same time Mr. Woolliams attacked the general attitude of the Government:

> Clearly this government is talking out of both sides of its mouth. To those who want abortions it is saying, "Look at what a great reform party we are," and to those who do not want abortions it is saying, "We are really not that kind of party after all, we just want to be very careful in this area."[86]

The amendment was defeated the next day, April 29.[87]

The next amendment was introduced by a Liberal, Mr. Gaston Clermont (Gatineau), who proposed to delete the words "or would be likely to" in the phrase: ...or would be likely to endanger... He claimed that as the expression stood now it was much too vague and would leave the interpretation wide open. Quoting from the proceedings of the Standing Committee on Justice and Legal Affairs at its March 27, 1969 sitting, he pointed out that while it was the Govern-

---

81. *Ibid.*, p. 8060.
82. *Ibid.*, pp. 8061-2.
83. *Ibid.*, p. 8078. Since 1969, of course, abortions have been paid for by medicare.
84. *Ibid.*, p. 8079.
85. *Hansard*, April 28, 1969, p. 8087.
86. *Ibid.*, p. 8090.
87. *Ibid.*, p. 8122.

ment's intention that the term health should not be given the wide
interpretation of the World Health Organization, the word did not
have a clear definition. Hence the Committee recommended:

> that a simple amendment to the proposed legislation should
> establish that a clear and direct serious threat to the mother's
> health must be present.[88]

But Justice Minister Turner once again turned down the amendment,
claiming that the elimination of these words would require that a
doctor needed absolute certainty there was a serious threat. Such
certainty could never be the case. "Health," he admitted, "is incapable
of definition and this will be left to the good professional judgment
of medical practitioners to decide."[89]

From then on the debate began to carry bitter overtones. Outside
the House the Créditistes were being blamed for 'filibustering.' Indeed,
the *Globe and Mail* had attacked them as early as April 18 when
the debate had barely started, simply for having refused "the unanimous consent the House requires for establishing a timetable for
debate..."[90] News reports were blaming the Créditistes for holding up
progress. On May 1 a *CP* news report printed under headings like
"Criminal Code bill inches forward despite Créditistes" appeared in
the *Edmonton Journal,* Saskatoon *Star Phoenix, Regina Leader Post,
Winnipeg Free Press* and the *Montreal Gazette* despite the fact that
of the four amendments discussed by April 30, two had been introduced
by the Conservatives and one by a Liberal.

Exchanges between Quebec Liberals and Créditistes in the House
became more acrimonious. The Créditistes made the most of the fact
that a Liberal had introduced an amendment which revealed once
more the uneasiness about the legislation which existed behind official
party unanimity. They were constantly taunting Liberals to speak,
who as Mr. Fortin said, "seem to be seated on six inches of Lepage's
glue, and we do not hear a peep out of them."[91] Mr. Gaston Isabelle
(L, Hull), answering a few digs directed at him earlier, stated that
if future generations read the speeches delivered by the Créditistes
"one of their descendants might say to his mother: Good were it for
that man if he had never been born."[92] Mr. René Matte replied to
the "dull member for Hull" that "I want at least posterity, that is
to say my own children and others, to know that we stood our ground...
Sooner or later we shall overcome." Mr. Matte also wanted to know
why, if the Government intended to separate sin and crime and "really
believes that abortion may be only a sin, why does it not delete any
mention of it in the Criminal Code?" He forecast that the words as
now phrased would "give complete freedom to those who wish to evade
the law."[93]

---

88. *Hansard,* April 29, 1969, p. 8123.
89. *Ibid.,* p. 8124.
90. Editorial, "Blocking a Reasonable Limit," *Globe and Mail,* April 18, p. 6.
91. *Hansard,* May 2, 1969, p. 8282.
92. *Ibid.,* April 29, 1969, p. 8130.
93. *Ibid.,* p. 8133.

From the beginning of May the Créditistes began in earnest. They covered old grounds and new protests and read 'into the record' lengthy quotations from medical, legal, religious, and philosophical sources, if not for the benefit of their contemporaries, then for the sake of history. They persisted in bringing up various aspects of one and the same theme: the difference between what the government intended the legislation to mean and what the proposed wording might permit people to believe the legislation meant.

As Liberals felt embarrassed and Créditistes experienced despair because all their arguments were rejected, accusations grew more heated. Mr. Gauthier accused the government of being a "military dictatorship."[94] Mr. Mongrain sarcastically described Créditistes as "guardians of virtue..." who moved silly amendments "which enable all the members..., one after another, and with a kind of masochism and parliamentary 'auto-eroticism' to wallow in these dirty things which are hidden in good families."[95] This, in turn, led Mr. Gauthier to utter the statement "that abortionists are about to exterminate the Canadian race" and that "we are heading for a society of absolute licence where socialism and communism will prevail." Mr. Henri Latulippe stated that "there are no more morals, there is no more conscience on the other side at the present time."[96] By May 7 Pierre de Bané (L, Matane) referred to the Créditistes as "fossils and demagogues," while Bernard Dumont defended his group as "champions of truth and Christianity."[97]

The vehement exchanges only exasperated an increasingly impatient press. In an editorial called "The Créditiste Filibuster: Futile and Obstructive," the *Ottawa Journal* still gave the Créditistes credit for "sincerity" and for "having made their case admirably." But there comes a time, it said, when no new arguments are left to be advanced...[98] An editorial in the *Vancouver Sun* claimed that "it was scandalous that a minority party should be able to thwart the processes of Parliament and democracy..."[99] Further disapproval came from the *Calgary Herald* which also objected to the "filibuster."[100] Columnist Charles Lynch thought it interesting to present the views of the 14-member Créditistes to his readers "at tulip time" by means of an anthology of quotes from the speeches of Henri Latulippe.[101] Columnist George Bain wrote a similar article for the *Globe*, using a somewhat wider selection.[102] By lifting the more extreme statements out of their context and stringing them together, Bain and Lynch made the Créditistes look foolish and boorish.

---

94. *Hansard*, April 29, p. 8141.
95. *Ibid.*, April 30, 1969, p. 8189.
96. *Ibid.*, May 2, p. 8272; May 5, 1969, p. 8328 and p. 8336.
97. *Ibid.*, May 7, 1969, p. 8447 and p. 8455.
98. *Ottawa Journal,* May 7, 1969.
99. *The Vancouver Sun,* "A Case for Closure," May 7.
100. The *Calgary Herald,* May 8, 1969.
101. The column appeared in the *Ottawa Citizen,* May 7, and on May 8 in the *Calgary Herald* and *Edmonton Journal.*
102. George Bain, "The Abortion Debate," *Globe and Mail,* May 7, 1969.

During the next few days the Créditistes introduced three amendments. The first one proposed that a female person under age must obtain her father's consent for an abortion.[103] The second one proposed that approved hospitals be restricted to those of not less than 400 beds.[104] The third amendment moved that the abortion committee include a gynecologist approved by the Board of the hospital involved and by the College of Physicians and Surgeons.[105] The Minister of Justice rejected all three motions, the first one for belonging to the jurisdiction of the provinces and the other two as too restrictive.

On May 5 the Progressive Conservatives introduced an amendment that a psychiatrist as well as a clergyman be part of abortion committees. The mover, Walter Dinsdale, expressed alarm at the "direct antagonism" expressed in some of the proposed legislation to what "has become known down through the centuries... as the Judaeo-Christian ethic." He rejected the notion that "law does not concern itself with questions of morality" as well as the "fundamental shift" from "concepts that derive... from our Judaeo-Christian traditions" to the "direction of humanistic moral relativism." Taking a dim view of the "chief architects" of contemporary ideas, Darwin, Marx, Spencer and Freud, Mr. Dinsdale could not refrain from describing the believer of progress and perfection, who appears to know all "there is to be known" and who exercises "all the functions that we used to attribute to God", with a little doggerel.[106] But in the debate that followed Mr. Turner rejected the need for both psychiatric and spiritual help because the decision to be made, he said, was "a medical decision." Mr. Woolliams (PC) then called the entire bill "window-dressing," and Mr. Fortin (RCr) complained that, while this therapeutic abortion committee was really the "cornerstone which supports all the legislation on abortion," any attempt to clarify the "competence, the specialization and the scientific affiliation" of its members was once again doomed to failure.[107] The amendment was defeated.

Surprisingly, the last attempt to clarify the nature of the proposed legislation was introduced by Liberals. Norman Cafik (L, Ontario), speaking in support of the mover Warren Allmand of Montreal, proposed that the words "or would be likely to endanger her health" be replaced by "endanger her life or seriously or directly impair her health." Mr. Cafik argued that as "evidence certainly leads me to believe that the foetus is in fact a human being," abortions should be permitted only for the most serious reasons. The operative words, he said, were 'seriously and directly impair her health.' While rejecting the idea that he or the government had any responsibility to legislate morality, we are under an obligation, he said, to "protect the lives

---

103. *Hansard*, April 30, 1969, p. 8175.

104. *Ibid.*, p. 8180.

105. *Hansard*, May 2, 1969, p. 8277.

106. Man used to be a tadpole learning how to swim,
    And then he was a frog with his tail tucked in,
    And then he was a monkey hanging from the tree
    And now he is a professor with a Ph.D.
    Hansard, May 5, 1969, pp. 8318-9.

107. *Hansard*, May 5, 1969, pp. 8321-3.

of our citizens, including the unborn child."[108] Léonel Beaudoin (RCr), speaking in support of the motion, repeated that almost everything in the bill was too vague and evasive. Mr. René Matte (RCr), thoroughly discouraged and pessimistic by now, took the view that adding 'seriously and directly' would not change anything because when a woman absolutely wants an abortion there will always be a doctor "who will find a way to say that her health is or can be 'seriously impaired.'[109] Mr. Laflamme (L, Montmorency) also agreed with the motion. Mr. Réal Caouette, leader of the Créditistes, welcomed it, pointing out that his group had been speaking in defense of human life for sometime. "A few people only understand what is going on," he said; "the others are all at sea."[110]

Almost the last one to speak was the mover himself. Mr. Allmand recalled that he had been a member of the Health and Welfare Committee which had sat for six months studying the abortion question. In its Interim Report of December 19, 1967, this Committee recommended that therapeutic abortions be permitted "where a pregnancy will seriously endanger the life or the health of the mother," he said. In its final report of March 13, 1968, the Committee used the terms "seriously and directly impair." Some people, Mr. Allmand noted, say that an abortion is no different from removing "an appendix." But, he added, "I must say that the vast and overwhelming majority of the... witnesses who came before our committee denied that contention." As for the argument that parents should be free to do whatever they want to do, he observed that we certainly don't take that attitude when it comes to non-support by a father, or battering a minor, or education. Science showed, he said, quoting evidence given before the Committee, that a foetus was a clearly identifiable human life with a distinct identity as early as nine weeks. I maintain, he concluded, that we must make up our minds whether we want the child before it comes into existence. "Once it has come into existence we have forfeited any right to dispose of it for any reason whatever." Yet, after regretting that the Créditistes whose behaviour he declared "deplorable" might use his amendments to continue their filibuster, he contradicted his own conclusion by suggesting that abortions should be allowed after all when related to "serious" threats to the life or health of the mother.[111]

Aside from being backed by Créditistes and Conservatives, Mr. Allmand's motion was also supported by his fellow Liberals John Reid and Mark MacGuigan. Mr. Turner, however, was not amenable to the motion. He followed up the idea of Gordon Blair (L, Grenville-Carleton) who had answered that the word 'endanger' was "a good, old, Anglo-Saxon word. It is strong, forceful and carries great significance."[112] The words in the bill itself, Mr. Turner said, "more adequately and conclusively convey the meaning" that Mr. Allmand

108. *Ibid.*, May 6, 1969, pp. 8374-5.

109. *Ibid.*, p. 8379.

110. *Hansard*, May 6, 1969, p. 8383.

111. *Hansard*, May 6, 1969, pp. 8384-7.

112. *Ibid.*, p. 8387.

and supporters wish to convey "than do the words that they are offering to the house."[113] We are comparing, he said somewhat impatiently, the significance of 'endanger' with the significance of the words 'seriously and directly impair.' All other issues are irrelevant.

The bill has rejected the eugenic, sociological or criminal offence reasons. The bill limits the possibility of therapeutic abortion to these circumstances: It is to be performed by a medical practitioner who is supported by a therapeutic abortion committee of medical practitioners in a certified or approved hospital, and the abortion is to be performed only where the health or life of the mother is in danger.

The word 'endanger,' he concluded, "imports or connotes the elements of hazard, peril or risk... The meaning of the word 'endanger' is every bit as clear and significant as is the meaning of the words "seriously and directly impair'..."[114]

After the amendment had been defeated, the Créditistes tried twice more. First they introduced a motion requesting the elimination of the word "health" in order that abortions could be done only to save the life of the mother. This motion enabled them to read more scientific evidence into the parliamentary records but could achieve little else; yet, it gathered the most votes of any amendment, winning support from 26 Conservatives, 2 Liberals and one New Democrat: it was defeated 151 against 41.[115] After a further motion requiring unanimous decisions from abortion committees had been defeated, the final vote of the abortion debate was taken on the motion to eliminate the entire Clause 18. On May 9 the motion was defeated 107 against 36,[116] thereby ensuring its acceptance as the new law of Canada.

The next day the *Canadian Press* report "Abortion Clauses Remain" made the front pages of the *Edmonton Journal*, the Halifax *Chronicle Herald*, the *Winnipeg Free Press*, the *Toronto Daily Star*, and the *Regina Leader Post*. Only the two last named papers printed it in headlines. *The Calgary Herald*, the Saskatoon *Star Phoenix*, the *Ottawa Citizen*, the *Ottawa Journal*, and the *Montreal Gazette* printed the report on inside pages. The *Vancouver Sun* which had not reported any of the abortion debates did not report the end either. The *Toronto Telegram* carried its own news report on the front page as did, of course, the *Globe and Mail* which presented it under headlines as the major news item.

The news that the entire Omnibus bill had been approved on May 14 was given prominent display by nearly all papers, yet during the following days there were few editorial comments. The *Ottawa Journal* approved of the news as "a Victory for Reform of our Criminal Laws," noting that not everyone agrees with everything. It did not

113. *Ibid.*, p. 8389.
114. *Hansard*, May 6, 1969, pp. 8397-8.
115. *Ibid.*, May 8, 1969, p. 8474.
116. *Ibid.*, May 9, 1969, p. 8543.

mention abortion.[117] The *Vancouver Sun*'s editorial was entitled "Sanity in Sight." It noted that "the broadened interpretation of what constitutes a legal abortion" was "a marked advance... (which) hopefully will put an end to much personal tragedy and misery."[118]

The expected exception to the generally cool reception was, of course, the Toronto *Globe and Mail*. In an editorial entitled "It was a great day," it presented the May 14 vote as "an important moment in Canadian history":

> This bill is important because it is honest, because it cuts clean through the hypocrisy which the puritan ethic had engendered in Canada and writes law that conforms with the views of the majority of Canadians. When then Justice Minister Pierre Trudeau introduced it in December of 1967, it was an act of courage. He was mounting a public defense of personal liberty; he was saying that there is a difference between public morality and private morality, and that the state has no business dictating the conduct of individuals when that conduct injures nobody else. He was saying that the moral or religious views of one group shall not be imposed on another.

After noting its disagreements on some things in the bill, it continued:

> But it was the spirit of the bill that was important. It stepped boldly into a great many areas where legislators had never dared to step before. This is an essential spirit in our rapidly changing world...
>
> ...The man to whom most of the honor must go is Mr. Trudeau.

---

117. *Ottawa Journal*, Editorial, May 15, 1969.
118. *Vancouver Sun*, Editorial, May 15, 1969.

POSTSCRIPT
AND
A PERSONAL VIEW

CHAPTER **X**

Postscript and a Personal View

In our democratic society people believe that political problems, whatever their nature, can always be "worked out". All that is needed is a little give and take and a sense of compromise. This attitude is reasonable as long as it is understood that compromise in daily life *presupposes* that there is agreement on basic principles such as the nature and ultimate destiny of man. When this presupposed agreement disintegrates, the much lauded ability to compromise disappears. Society becomes divided into mutually opposed groups whose views cannot be reconciled. Needless to say, under such circumstances government becomes increasingly difficult and eventually impossible.

To my mind the abortion movement is significant from the moral-political point of view because it indicates that this necessary agreement on basic principles is breaking down. We may well ask the question: to what degree is it breaking down? And, again: what exactly are the principles which are in dispute?

The answer to the first question can only be tentative, especially if we consider it in its quantative form of how many people are deeply disturbed by the developments surrounding abortion. Perhaps it suffices here to note that the opponents of legal abortions are neither restricted to Roman Catholics nor do they number a mere handful. Moreover, much more important than mere numbers is the character of the opposition, especially the nature, the depth, and the tenacity of their convictions. As these convictions are the consequence of an attitude which leaves little room for manoeuvre, it may be well to summarize them.

Opponents of legal abortions hold that abortion is an act of violence against (unborn) human life which is innocent of any misdeeds. They know that in western civilization, governments have traditionally, i.e. for two thousand years or more, condemned and supressed such acts of violence. Now, within a matter of a few years some governments have suddenly decided to change the nomenclature and make these acts of violence "legal" in order to escape from what is admittedly a difficult situation. But in doing so these governments undermined the traditional use of language, and, above all, introduced into western society principles of behavior contradicting concepts essential to the older heritage generally known as the Judaeo-Christian tradition. As this new view directly contradicts the traditional view it will ultimately force every person into one camp or another, because the new principles implied in the legalization of abortions will have a whole train of consequences, conscious and subconscious, foreseen and unforeseen, political and philosophical, personal and social. Together, these consequences will profoundly affect society and affect it, not for the better, but for the worse. Already, it is argued, abortion has contributed to confusing the virtue of compassion, the rights of women, the rights of unborn life, the rights of hospital personnel, the functions and rights of private and public hospitals, the meaning of the Hippocratic oath, the nature of the Criminal Code, the role of legislators and the purpose of law. To ask, then, in the name of a pluralistic society to accept such a situation is to ask, not for compromise on matters of secondary importance, but for surrender on a matter vital to society. Such is the view of opponents of legalized abortions.

Many people do not understand this opposition to publicly approved abortions. Hoping to appease both opponents and advocates, and mistaking the nature of the problem, they will offer solutions which in the eyes of opponents, are not solutions at all. Take, for instance, the following proposal offered by the famous cultural anthropologist, Dr. Margaret Mead:

> "The simplest way of dealing with this is to repeal all abortion laws. Do not nave laws. The medical profession is perfectly capable of licensing surgeons and keeping them in order. Catholic hospitals can protect Catholics' consciences and Protestant hospitals can protect Protestants' consciences. To ask Roman Catholics, who believe that the taking of any human life is wrong, to respect, pass or endorse a law approving such an act, is to ask them to behave unethically. On the other hand, to pass a law restricting the action of Protestants and humanitarians who believe differently in this matter is also to ask them to behave unethically"[1]

On a first, casual, reading this proposal appears attractive and sensible. But on closer inspection it becomes clear that this proposal will not, and, indeed, cannot, satisfy the opponents of legalized abortions.

First, there is the minor point of an improper division between Catholics and Protestants. As noted before, there are many Protestants and others who are as much opposed to abortion as Catholics, though it is true that Catholics as a group stand our more distinctly. Secondly, there is an erroneous distinction between Catholic hospitals and Protestant hospitals. The correct distinction is between *private* hospitals, often under denominational control, and *public* hospitals. But as the latter are financed by the taxes of all citizens, they are, therefore, even more the concern of all, whether these citizens are for or against abortion.

More important than these distinctions, though they are by no means to be neglected, is the implied suggestion that everyone will

---

1. Quoted in *Cross Currents*, Spring 1971, p. 231 from *Who Shall Live* (Philadelphia, Fortress Press).

agree: 1) that abortion is a question of private concern; 2) that in this matter there are no objective ethical standards applicable to all citizens. But the first suggestion is proven wrong by such facts as described below, while the second one is the very idea which opponents of abortion reject as invalid.

It appears, then, that a compromise solution will satisfy no one. Seen in the light of two diametrically opposed views of life, abortion as a moral-political controversy is a first confrontation of what may become a much wider clash between rival points of view. In the broadest sense, this clash concerns the understanding of the relationship between God and man. In the narrower framework of the abortion issue itself, this conflict turns principally around two issues: on the one hand, the perception of the nature and dignity of human life, and, on the other, the understanding of the relationship between law and morality. Under both headings I propose to make some observations. In the section 'Recent Trends' my remarks concern the question of human life, the general dissatisfaction with the 1969 law, the threat of coercion, the divisions and discriminations in the medical profession, and the question of theology.

In the last part of this chapter I will discuss the question of law and morality. The defenders and promoters of the new law refused to accept abortion as a moral problem involving society. They presented it as a medical problem, or at the most, as a moral problem which concerned nobody but the individual. Thus they were determined to see it removed from the Criminal Code on the grounds that sin is not the same as crime, and that law should not concern itself with morality.

Recent Trends

I have attempted to explain how and why those who opposed a permissive law were so slow in reacting: the middle and late sixties proved to be years of crisis for any and all traditional authority and wisdom, not in the least for the wisdom and traditions of the institution which has inspired our civilization for so long, the Christian Church. The entire atmosphere inhibited a leisurely examination by principles—be they religious or philosophical—while favouring immediate action inspired by a search for pragmatic "solutions". By 1969, the pressure from pro-abortion ranks was so intense and the government already so fully committed that it proved psychologically impossible for members of parliament to change the seemingly inevitable course of events. Thus these members went along out of inertia or otherwise favoured or accepted the proposed change in the Criminal Code for different and, often, contradictory reasons.[2]

It is not surprising, then, that the final legislative product, too, is intrinsically contradictory. Three years before the passage of the

---

2. See the summary of the Liberal party speakers in Chapter 9. It may be recalled that in 1967 the Justice Minister had expressedly included abortion in an Omnibus bill in order to strengthen the forces of inertia and make resistance more difficult

law an observer wrote as follows:

> The fact of the matter is that there is no half-way house between complete prohibition of abortion on the one hand and complete freedom of abortion on the other... For moral codes just cannot be averaged by saying that many people believe that abortion is right and many believe that it is wrong, so let us make it legally half right and half wrong... Simple reason suggests that if abortion is wrong, it should be absolutely proscribed; while if it is not wrong, it should not be proscribed. But to say it is wrong and then permit it, or to say it is not wrong and then proscribe, is clearly unreasonable.[3]

For Canada such a law is now on the books. It declares the destruction of the unborn to be a crime punishable with imprisonment for life in its first paragraph, while explaining in the remainder of the act how this same deed may be done legally, that is, by having it done under professional supervision in sanitary conditions.[4]

Human Life

The preceding historical study indicates that the 1969 change in the Criminal Code of Canada was accomplished partly as a consequence of ignorance about the nature of the 'foetus' and partly as a consequence of changing morals. We may well ask, where do we stand on the question of human life today?

As noted above, at the time not a few people seriously maintained that the foetus was not alive; others that it was merely a blob of tissue; others again that it was not human in the same sense as life already born. On the other hand, science leaves no doubt that the foetus is alive from conception onwards. This life has an identity of its own and is separate from, though not, of course, autonomous of the mother. Indeed, at ten weeks the foetus is a miniature baby with all the proper organs, fingers, toes, etc. It is therefore with some astonishment that one discovers that during the crucial years of the abortion debate, the years 1965-1969, this fact seemed thoroughly obscure to many people.[5] Only towards the end of the public debate did the understanding that abortion does not concern the mother alone but also involves another autonomous life, begin to spread in parliament beyond the ranks of the handful of French-speaking, Catholic, Créditistes.[6]

Science and common sense tell us that the foetus is human in the sense that it is 'of man', not of a horse or elephant. However, science cannot tell us when the foetus becomes human in the same sense as life already born. Christians believe that this happens when

---

3. Dr. Colin Harrison, *Canadian Medical Associal Journal*, Vol. 95, August 20, 1966.
4. See Appendix 2.
5. For examples of this confusion which was undoubtedly widespread, see Chapter 3, the Canadian Bar Association debate; Chapter 5, the CBA spokesman; or Chapter 9, Mr. Chappell (Lib.) speaking on January 24. 1969.
6. One reflection of this growing uneasiness was the last minute amendment proposed by members of the Liberal party. See end of Chapter 9.

the soul is infused. In view of the fact that the vast majority of parliamentarians in Canada profess Christianity, the almost complete absence of any discussion on the human soul, is also perplexing. The soul is the all important life-giving power which provides the spirit for the body, transforming mere tissue into a human being. It survives the death of the body and is the basis for the dignity of each individual man and woman and the equality of all people before God. Christianity is meaningless without a firm belief that each person has a soul, that this soul is infused by God, and that it is immortal. Yet, during the committee hearings, the existence of the soul was only brought up by the delegation representing the Roman Catholic Bishops; during the debates in parliament it was mentioned only by Créditistes.

Today the debate has shifted ground. On the one hand medical persons in England and elsewhere are openly experimenting with life 'foetuses' in their laboratories. On the other hand, it is forecast that it will soon be possible to keep 'foetuses' alive from as early as six weeks on. Consequently, it is no longer denied that we are dealing with something alive and human. Some people, of course, still argue that this 'humanness' is sufficiently different from that of persons born, to permit killing it. But they have provided no scientific evidence to indicate how and in what way a ten week old, or an eight months old foetus *is substantially* different from a one day old baby. Meanwhile, the argument has moved from denying that the *foetus* is alive to denying that that is at all important. What *is* important, so it is said, is to save the quality of life of those already born. When Mrs. MacInnis said something similar in 1967, though apparently more in the heat of argument than by deliberate intention, the remark made headlines in Canadian newspapers.[7] This utilitarian philosophy, whereby some lives are held more important than others according to some undetermined standard of utility, appears increasingly acceptable and is openly defended today.[8]

Dissatisfaction

It is not surprising that the government's solution has proven not to be a solution at all. Indeed, its handling of the abortion clause, its forecasts and expectations, its rejection of amendments as unnecessary, have proven to be mistaken. What has happened in the short time since 1969 may be listed under four headings:

   a) increased dissatisfaction on the part of everyone, both supporters and opponents.

   b) increased demands for more state intervention, not only for abortions, but also in areas of contraceptives, birth

---

7. See Chapter 5.

8. For instance, by some pro-abortion speakers and members of the philosophy department, University of Toronto, at the May 1972 Canadian Abortion Conference held at St. Michael's College, Toronto. Dr Lise Fortier, speaking at a Canadian Bar Association Conference in Montreal declared that a human foetus is a living human being, but its life does not have to be respected above all else: "what is most important is not the life itself... but the quality of that life, and its purpose." Saskatoon, *Star-Phoenix,* Sept. 1, 1972.

control, sterilization and family planning.

c) threats of using coercion and force.

d) more and more reports of experimentation with aborted foetuses, forecasts of selective breeding, and pressure to legalize the "voluntary" death of the incurably ill and the old (euthanasia).

After the passage of the abortion law, dissatisfaction broke out almost at once. Doctors became divided, nurses upset, hospital boards confused, patients irritated, public hospitals found themselves pitted against private hospitals, and all of them were left to wonder just exactly what the law meant. It could not have been otherwise.

Hospitals were requested to set up abortion committees of three doctors to "rule" on so-called "therapeutic" abortions. But as many private hospitals refused to do so, public hospitals had to deal with the flood of applicants. The inequality of available services from city to city and province to province led to charges of inequality before the law and "unwarranted" delays. In some cities, delays of one kind or another have on occasion made it impossible to perform the abortion at an early stage of the pregnancy. Unlike Britain and other countries, however, Canada has no restrictions whatever on the time abortions may be performed. Thus British Columbia Health Minister Ralph Loffmark informed the public in a matter of fact way that "there have been instances known... where removal of a foetus had produced a life in being whose chance of survival was better than some natural premature births..."[9]

Meanwhile, doctors in public hospitals feel that they have been given an impossible task. Some of them are upset because they are asked to make *moral* rather than *medical* decisions in ruling on abortions, thus refuting almost at once the oft repeated assertion that abortion is a question of medicine only.[10] Often they do not even *see* the applicant; they merely make the decision on the basis of the applicant's file.[11] Those who sit on the committees have been accused of "playing God," and they would now like to see the three-doctor rule abolished.[12] Many doctors, no doubt, wondered how all of this was to be reconciled with the Hippocratic oath by which they were sworn to preserve life. But the Canadian Medical Association recently modified this oath which has stood for 2500 years, by eliminating its condemnation of administering abortifacients.

There is no unanimity on the meaning of the term "therapeutic". Some committees approach their set task seriously, but they tend to cause delays which make operations more difficult. Other committees are rubber stamp committees, approving every case which comes before

9. *Globe and Mail*, October 9, 1970, p. 11.

10. See the October 6, 1967, Globe editorial, Chapter 5, and the editorial of December 21, 1967, Chapter 6. Also Justice Minister Turner, May 2, 1969, Chapter 9.

11. Letter in *Globe and Mail*, June 6, 1970, p. 6.

12. *Globe and Mail*, June 19, 1970; October 19, 1970, p. 14. Compare also L. Augenstein's book, *Come Let Us Play God* (Harper, 1969).

them.[13] They interpret the term "therepeutic" so broadly as to practically grant abortions on demand. This is the most prevalent approach in Canada today. Abortions are performed for such reasons as extreme youth, substantial risk of deformity of the foetus, pressure of parents and a variety of socio-economic considerations, all of them *illegal* according to the intentions and declarations of its sponsors, the Liberal government, though not according to the letter of the law as it was finally formulated and passed.[14]

It is still somewhat puzzling why the government refused to adopt more specific conditions. This refusal, in fact, has permitted people to do as they please.[15] The Créditistes of Mr. Caouette, together with some members from each of the other parties including the Liberal party, proposed some 50 amendments intended to make the bill reflect this restrictive attitude which the government claimed as its own. These proposals were dismissed out of hand. Even the government's own appointed Committee recommended that the law read: "will endanger the life or *seriously* and *directly* impair the health of the mother..." It also stated that it rejected the all encompassing definition of health by the World Health Organization.[16] But its recommendations, too, were simply ignored. It is difficult to believe that the two successive Ministers of Justice, Mr. Trudeau and Mr. Turner, were not aware that speeches in parliament do not become law unless they are incorporated into the text itself. Why, then, did the government refuse to make the law more precise?

As already mentioned, it is easier to ask for an explanation than to provide it. The reading of the debates leaves one with the feeling that the attitude of the government was one of extreme self-assurance, mixed with a good measure of aloofness and unwillingness to note objections. This reflected a widespread attitude of the pro-revisionists. But if contempt for the views of its opponents is perhaps stating it too strongly, no doubt a good measure of disdain on the part of the government, especially for the views of the Créditistes, contributed to that position which judged further qualifying conditions in the law unnecessary. A similar self-assurance explains the slogan often used by the pro-revisionists that to change the law was not to "legalize" abortions, as well as the equally frequent denials that the changes in the law as proposed by the government would not "open the gates to abortion on request" at all, nay might even make the getting of abortions more difficult.[18] The facts were to prove

---

13. *Globe and Mail,* June 6, 1970.

14. See Justice Minister Turner's comments on January 23, 1969, Chapter 9.

15. Compare the remarks of Mr. Eldon Woolliams (PC) on April 28, 1969, Chapter 9.

16. See conclusion of Chapter 7.

17. See Mr. Bazos at the CBA law convention of 1966, Chapter 3; or Mr. Turner in parliament at the start of the bill's second reading on January 23, 1969, and Mr. Mongrain (Lib) speaking on January 27, 1969, Chapter 9.

18. See the submission of Mr. Herridge (NDP), Chapter 5; the submissions of Drs. White and Moore, members of the United Church delegation, Chapter 7, of Mr. Turner on January 23, 1969, of Mr. Gordon Ritchie (PC) on February 13, and Mr. Stanfield (PC) on February 25, 1969, Chapter 9.

otherwise without delay. Between August 1969, the date the Bill received Queen's approval, and the end of that year, abortions in Canada numbered 268. In 1970 they rose to 11,152; in 1971 to 30,949. And in 1972 they numbered 38,905. During these years there were other abortions as well, such as the thousand or so abortions done annually by Dr. Morgenthaler in his Montreal clinic.

Coercion

Apart from its refusal to write in qualifying conditions,—and leaving aside the question whether the Criminal Code should have been changed at all—the government irritated opponents of abortion most by its refusal to have a written "conscience clause". Having failed all along to understand the difference between the question of abortion on the one hand and all the other changes in the Criminal Code including homosexuality and divorce on the other, the government failed to provide opponents of legal abortions with even that minimal safeguard which might have guaranteed them some immunity from direct involvement in abortions.

Since 1969 there has been a serious deterioration of tolerance concerning the freedom *not* to perform abortions. This is only too understandable: tolerance, which is based on respect for the other viewpoint in matters which are not vital, cannot survive when agreement on basic principles breaks down. Respect is replaced by misunderstanding, then by contempt, and finally the other point of view comes to be considered a threat to the successful fulfillment of one's own plan. To some this may be surprising, first because of the claim that nobody would be forced to participate in abortions, and secondly because abortions were supposed to be a private and not a public matter. Indeed, from 1965 on, those who attacked the opponents of a permissive law constantly repeated, "that there was no question of forcing abortions on anyone."[19] This, too, was the position of the government which argued that it was self-evident that no one should be forced to participate and that a conscience clause, therefore, was unnecessary.[20]

For a few months it appeared that the government's interpretation might be correct, with people using the phrase conscience clause as if such a thing actually was on the books. But as the memory of the parliamentary debates grew fainter, the resistance of opponents became an increasingly intolerable irritant to the pro-abortion forces. Finding this challenge and defiance more and more difficult to bear, and knowing the weight of the law to be on their side rather than on the side of their opponents as hitherto, they built up pressure to make everyone conform. In December 1970 the Toronto *Globe and Mail*, which by then referred to all religious denominations as "sects" and called private hospitals "sectarian" hospitals, published a survey on abortions in Quebec. It discovered that only 14 out of 250 provincial

---

19. See the presentation of Mrs. MacInnis, Chapter 5, or that of the Canadian Welfare Council, February 13, 1968, Chapter 7.
20. See the debate on April 28, 1969, Chapter 9.

hospitals had abortion committees and that all but one of the 181 abortions during the first 10 months of 1970 had been performed at English-language hospitals in Montreal's West End. The next day it published an editorial in which it implied that the conscience clause was "an abdication of responsibility on Ottawa's part", bewailed the fact that French-speaking Quebec "had absolutely no justice under the law", suggested that the now empty maternity wards be changed into abortion clinics and demanded that authorities—in Quebec and elsewhere—"exert themselves".[21]

In British Columbia, Mr. Loffmark, the provincial Minister of Health, had similar thoughts. The Minister claimed that his province had the highest per capita rate of abortions in the country. Noting that Catholic hospitals did not have abortion committees, he warned on October 5, 1970, that he might "order *all* B.C. hospitals to grant legal abortions." This, he said, was to be done "on the grounds that· hospitals supported by public funds will have to face up to their public responsibilities."[22] Some time later the Minister of Health of Ontario made similar remarks only to withdraw the idea after his office received a number of protests.

Instead of being able to rely on rights anchored in the law, opponents of legalized abortions have been reduced to safeguarding their rights by means of organizing protest actions. Until now, attempts at coercion have been stopped through constant watchfulness and the efforts of individual men such as the outspoken Manitoba MLA, Joseph Borowski, who sacrificed first his position in the NDP and then his political career in his attempts, in both the Manitoba Legislature as well as on national television, to stop publicly financed agencies from aiding and encouraging abortions. Since 1969 the organization of protest actions, the formulation of counter proposals and the presentation of the anti-abortion point of view have gained much in efficiency, principally through the development of the so-called Right-to-Life Committees, united nationally under the umbrella of the Alliance for Life under chairmanship of the Toronto gynecologist Dr. Heather Morris.[22a]

Yet the abortion pressure does not let up. Doctors and hospitals doing abortions periodically launch appeals to their provincial governments that all accredited hospitals should share in performing abortions. One such appeal came from the abortion committee of City Hospital in Saskatoon in March, 1973. This appeal, no doubt, was typical of hospitals and doctors elsewhere. In 1972 the Family Planning Federation of Canada, which receives large subsidies from the Federal Government, officially urged all Canadian provincial and territorial governments "to require all hospitals receiving public funds to provide abortion services." In March 1973, MP Stuart Leggatt (NDP., New Westminster) demanded in the House of Commons that there be an investigation of hospitals refusing to set up abortion

21. *Globe and Mail*, December 18, 1970, p. 6.
22. *Globe and Mail*, October 9, 1970, p. 11.
22a On May 9, 1973 Alliance for Life presented the Prime Minister with a petition carrying 353, 652 signatures.

facilities.[23] On January 17, 1974, the official blueprint for a radically new system of provincial health care in British Columbia, written by Dr. Richard Foulkes, recommended the removal of abortion legislation from the Criminal Code and the laying down of requirements for all public-funded hospitals with surgical facilities to permit abortions and sterilizations. On January 18, 1974, the Toronto *Globe and Mail* in an editorial demanded the same thing. The editorial concluded with the following note:

> It seems obvious that hospital boards should never have been allowed a choice in the matter. The Government should change the discretionary portion of the law and simply require hospitals which receive public grants to establish abortion committees.[23a]

Thus, as the declarations of yesterday are forgotten, some people are prepared to compel everyone to participate in the acceptance of abortions. As mentioned earlier, in view of the nature of the conflict it is not surprising that the issue has reached this stage. Nor is it surprising that those who threaten coercion, count among them the same people who only a few years ago accused others of "violating the conscience of millions." It has come to the point now where some spokesmen of Catholic hospitals have suggested that they would rather surrender control of their hospitals than have abortions done there. Others argue that in view of the rights and principles involved, these threats of coercion should not be countered by surrendering control of hospitals, but that they should be countered by resistance and non-cooperation.

Medicare

Much of the pro-abortion appeal among the general public derived from the claim that abortion should be a private, not a public, matter. In spite of the fact that by 1969 it was clear that a not inconsiderable number of people cared to have nothing to do with abortions, most of the general public seemed undisturbed because "private" abortions were not expected to affect society or demand participation from anyone. When Mr. Turner was asked whether abortions would be paid for by medicare he exclaimed quite spontaneously: "Oh, no!"[24] It was one more example of the atmosphere of unreality that surrounded this issue. Today, in most if not in all provinces abortions are to a very large extent paid for by medicare. In an age of spiralling health costs with hospital beds and the use of medical facilities and personnel at a premium, this cost to the public is not likely to decline. Still,

---

23. Re Saskatoon's City Hospital, see *Star-Phoenix*, March 5, 1973. The F.P.F. resolution was reprinted in the Federation's Newsletter, *Family Planning and Population*, Spring 1973, Vol. 1. For Leggatt, see *Hansard*, March 27, 1973, p. 2643.

23a. For Dr. Foulkes, see *CP* report, Saskatoon *Star — Phoenix*, January 18, 1974, p. 26. The *Globe*'s editorial was entitled "Law that denies equality", January, 18, 1974.

24. Hansard, April 28, 1969, p. 8078. See Chapter 9.

whether or not the 31,000 abortions in 1971 might have cost the Canadian taxpayer millions of dollars is not in itself very significant. Neither is the fact that a proportion of abortions require blood transfusions using up the not too plentiful supplies of bloodbanks, nor the fact that having priority over operations which are not absolutely urgent, abortions take up needed space in the gynecology departments of hospitals. Cost-accounting of this type rarely is, at least on a question which is basically a moral one, but these facts do illustrate that abortion is not a 'private' matter.

Nurses and Indoctrination

Some nurses who work on the gynecology floors of hospitals where abortions are performed, have become very upset. When they entered the profession of nursing, they believed that they would help alleviate pain and preserve life. Now they may be placed in a position where they must destroy life, though efforts are made to present it in a different light. Pro-abortionists hope that eventually nurses, and people in general, will get used to the idea and will become "educated" and "enlightened". The process which is required to bring such a situation about was described in a story about Mount Sinai Hospital in New York.[25]

The Director of Nursing noted that when the New York law came into effect, there was considerable opposition among nurses. Some left the hospital; others requested transfers to different departments. "Most nurses find the destruction of life the very antithesis of what they believe", she observed as if she were talking about some strange phenomenon, and added, "the concept of euthanasia and abortion is very difficult for them to accept." However, the picture is much brighter today. The Director explained that after extensive group therapy and counselling services, the remaining nurses have now been properly conditioned, though in spite of this 'conditioning', she had to admit that:

> periodically we still have problems. Recently a baby emerged from the salting out still alive. There was no hope for ultimate survival but the heart beat. The nurses were upset.

The story continued by pointing out that both the Director of Nursing and the psychiatrist who did the counselling were optimistic about the future. As the latter observed: "with the new nurses it is easier because the situation is established." It must not be supposed that these events are restricted to New York: similar sessions are held in Canadian hospitals and the same hope for the gradual indoctrination of people induced Ontario's Minister of Health, Mr. Lawrence, to predict confidently in February, 1972, that within two or three years abortions would be done by *all* Ontario hospitals.[26]

---

25. *Globe and Mail*, February 4, 1972, p. 13.
26. *Globe and Mail*, February 1, 1972, p. 5.

In spite of these hopes and in spite of some "fully adjusted" nurses, gynecology departments have difficulty finding the required number of personnel. They are constantly borrowing nurses from other departments or floors. Naturally, nurses whose consciences bothers them feel alone. A so-called floating or casual nurse may be told that her contract requires that she serve wherever she is sent. Permanent staff is more difficult to handle, but as abortion is an embarrassing subject barely discussable in non-emotional terms, a few casual sarcasms are often sufficient to make a person feel isolated and helpless. After all, in Canada abortions are now legal and, by implication, acceptable. Moreover, proponents of free and public abortions have succeeded in making the controversy between pro and con appear as a self-evident battle between the broadminded and the narrowminded, the forward and the backward, the enlightened and the obscure. And who wants to be identified with religious obscurantism?

One person who did defy the new legal and social code was nurse Frances Martin of Henderson General Hospital in Hamilton, Ontario. She refused to assist at abortions and was demoted from head nurse in the labor-delivery unit to regular duty nurse with a pay cut of $100 a month. Her subsequent complaint with the Ontario Human Rights Commission was rejected. The Commission claimed the demotion was caused by her inability as an employee to carry out lawful hospital policy. To sweeten this judgment the Commission recommended that she be reinstated as head nurse as soon as a position became available outside the obstetrical department.[27] But the point had been made: according to the Ontario Human Rights Commission it is legal to attempt to coerce or penalize nurses who oppose abortions. Thus we have the situation that the state supports or finances abortions on the grounds that every woman has "the right to control her own body", but at the same time denies nurses in public and state hospitals freedom of conscience in refusing to assist at abortions.

Doctors and Discrimination

Just as the confused and illogical legal position of nurses illustrates what is happening to freedom from coercion, so the position of doctors presents us with further clarifications of what is involved. While the abortion law has divided doctors from the beginning, it now appears that the new law will also provide for future discrimination in the medical profession and for the exclusion of a certain group of doctors from an important medical specialty. An illustration of what is happening may be found in England.

In the *British Medical Journal* of June 26, 1971, C. K. Varton of London, England, in answer to H. P. Dunn of New Zealand, who was concerned about the effect of increased abortions upon the selection of candidates for certain hospital posts in Obstetrics and Gynecology, states the case boldly. He tells us that those who are not prepared to perform abortions should train in some other branch

---

27. *Western Catholic Reporter*, Edmonton, July 25, 1971.

of medicine.[28] In England this advice has already become standard practice.

In January 1972, the Lane Committee, set up to study the workings of the Abortion Act in Great Britain, received a long memorandum from the committee set up by Catholics in March 1971 to prepare their own submission to the Lane Committee. The excerpt on doctors (Section VII) reads as follows:

> "The evidence supplied to us shows that at various places throughout the country, appointments committees of public hospitals regularly enquire in regard to obstetrical and gynaecological positions whether a candidate is a Catholic and/or what his/her attitude is about "fulfilling the responsibilities for doing abortions." It is all too clear that Catholic doctors who might well be appointed are passed over because of their attitude to abortions. As also are non-Catholics who are opposed to abortion in principle...

> "The view that those who will not terminate pregnancy should train for some other branch of medicine has been voiced recently in the *British Medical Journal.* So important is this whole matter that we have set out in an appendix what certain of our doctors have said about it."

In the above mentioned appendix we find the following letter from a doctor to a Member of Parliament:

> "...I am a Catholic, aged 33, and a medical practitioner with five years' postgraduate training in obstetrics and gynaecology and a member of the Royal College of Obstetricians and Gynaecologists. Recently, I have applied for registrar appointments at three university teaching hospitals and have been unsuccessful. At each interview I have been asked my views on the abortion law and have stated my conscientious objection to abortion on demand. At my last appearance before an appointments board I was directly asked if my conscientious objection was due to religious conviction. After the interview was over, I was recalled by a member of the committee, himself a Catholic, and told that, although I was the most senior and well-qualified of the group shortlisted I was not given the job as I was a Catholic. It was considered that to give me the job would be doing me a long-term disservice and I was directly told that "there is now no place for a Catholic obstetrician and gynaecologist in the United Kingdom". As I have recently done part of my training in Canada, I was advised to 'cut my losses and get out of England as soon as I could or, if not, change my specialty'. Recent advice from consultants in a teaching hospital not far from the House of Commons was in the same vein."

> "I have personal knowledge of at least six similar cases in which highly trained and well qualified doctors have been forced to leave the United Kingdom because they are Catholics."[29]

---

28. Compare A. Adams, M.D. in "Abortion": A matter of fundamental concern" in *Our Family*, November 1971, p. 2.

29. *The Tablet*, London, February 5, 1972, pp. 120-122.

Thus in medicine too, the effects of legalizing abortions have been very different from what its promoters had expected. A 'private' matter has turned out to be very public; what was supposed to be a purely medical decision, has proved a most moral controversy; and a new law which meant to clarify has become the source of confusion, division and discrimination. In Canada, moreover, none of this has been without its bitter irony for the doctors. The Canadian Medical Association has been the foremost semi-public body in the nation in favour of legalization, acting with disregard of any aspect other than what it considered its own interest. It had demanded a change in a law under which no doctor had ever been charged or prosecuted on the grounds that "we must end our life as lawbreakers".[30] It remains somewhat puzzling why this action was taken. Perhaps after years of bitter opposition to the introduction of comprehensive public medical insurance and other measures, the executive of the society was anxious to gain for once the goodwill of the nation. Whatever the reason, the moral side of abortion was completely ignored as of no concern to doctors.

Meanwhile, some doctors are still breaking laws in the name of an ethic of their own while receiving public support for it from representatives of their profession. They treat 16 or 17 years-olds without prior parental consent although the medical age of majority is 18.[31] Already some doctors openly advocate infanticide and euthanasia and do not hide that they are prepared to apply it. But the most blatant example of lawbreaking, Dr. Morgenthaler of Montréal, has been hailed as a folk hero. Having done 5000-6000 abortions in his clinic illegally, that is, without permission of a hospital abortion committee and outside the premises of an accredited hospital, he was acquitted on a technicality of law which, if upheld, will make a mockery of all control of abortion. The pro-abortion wing of women's liberation groups hailed it as a great victory. One newspaper accorded this man "a hosannah or two — or three". Four days later the same newspaper lectured the Ontario Minister of Energy for having decided to give the conservation of energy priority over auto pollution by declaring that "it is not for Mr. McKeouch to say what laws are to be upheld and what laws ignored. If he wants to change the law he can debate it in the Legislature or make representations to the federal government..."[32]

The abortion program may also be promoted in other ways. In 1971, it was announced, for instance, that Toronto school trustees intended to introduce abortion teaching into the public schools.

30. See the presentation of the CMA to the H.O.C.'s Committee, Chap. 5.

31. "Laws broken for patients, president says," Saskatoon *Star-Phoenix*, July 18, 1973, p. 1.

31. In March 1974 the medical-legal consultant to the Ontario Ministry of Health, Dr. Frederick Evis, simply announced that a new provincial regulation had lowered the age of parental consent for abortions to 16. There is no evidence of consultation with anyone beyond an inner circle of civil servants and doctors.

32. Editorials in *Globe and Mail*, November 15 and 19, 1973. One recent advocate of infanticide, the nobel prize winner Dr. James Watson, proposed that a child not be declared alive until three days after birth to allow the elimination of malformed infants. *Time*, May 28, 1973.

The *Globe* lauded the decision, stating that "to teach is not to advocate." Yet, it immediately added that Catholic children would be allowed to leave the classroom.[33] Here we have another illustration of the muddle in which the revision of the Criminal Code has put the nation. The introduction of a subject like abortion into the public school system is presumably justified according to the notion that abortion is not a moral but a medical and, therefore, an "objective" and "neutral" subject. The true state of affairs is then revealed by the concession that Catholic children be permitted to get up and leave. From other aspects, of course, that concession itself is a highly dubious form of pedagogy. At the same time the false impression is created once again that only Catholics oppose abortion. What about Lutherans, or Mennonites, Pentecostals, Greek Orthodox, Jewish Orthodox and Evangelicals whose Churches oppose abortion, not to mention numerous Presbyterians, Anglicans, or even United Church members who disagree with the stand of their Board of Evangelism? Will the Alliance for Life or other pro-life groups be permitted to show science movies illustrating how at ten weeks a so-called foetus has all the human features and organs? And what, may one ask, is supposed to be accomplished with all this confrontation in a school system which professes to serve all children?

And so it goes. Few people notice how these forms of coercion creep into our lives. No one commented publicly when Dr. Bette Stephenson, then president of the Ontario Medical Association, proposed that those who have had abortions should be *forced* to consider *voluntary* sterilization.[34] (my italics)

Theology and the United Church

In Canada the group of Christians who have most outspokenly accepted the legalizing of abortions are the members of the United Church. In so doing, this Church has lent its support to the overthrow of a two thousand year old tradition, which has been accepted unanimously by the teaching authorities of all Christian Churches until recently and which is still accepted by most of them. This tradition holds that abortion cannot be reconciled with the law of God and, consequently, that it cannot he reconciled with the law of man, because the latter depends on the former. God alone is the Source of life and death. Man, who has been made in the image of God, has the right to rule and order the world. Society also has the right to defend this order and lock up those who threaten it, or defend itself against those who attack it. But society does not have the right to kill life created by God when such life has committed no crime or act of violence.

In view of the formidable tradition, arguments, and weight of history, one would have expected extreme caution on the part of Christians who were contemplating a change. But what strikes a historian looking at the recent years of debate on the part of the United Church — as well as of some of the other Christian bodies

---

33. *Globe and Mail*, Editorial January 14, 1971, p. 6.
34. *Globe and Mail*, October 19, 1970, p. 14.

who have come to accept abortions as legitimate — is not their deliberate caution, but their precipitate haste; not the length and depth of their theological reflections, but the *absence* of such reflections.

The United Church of Canada has defended abortion since 1960 when it accepted abortions for reasons of life and health, both for medical and mental reasons. Nevertheless, at that time the United Church Council also stated that "the Christian conscience cannot approve abortion". Moreover, it rejected abortion as a means for family planning. Following this very important change from non-acceptance to acceptance, which apparently was brought about almost without debate, other changes came quickly and in pace with the latest popular views. Six years later, in 1966, the Church's General Council made it clear not only that abortions were justified "when the life of the foetus threatens the life or health of the mother", but that the term 'health' should be interpreted broadly, and that the air of guilt surrounding abortions should be rejected. At this time the General Council's official position was still that abortions for socio-economic reasons were unacceptable. But two years later, in 1968, the United Church delegation to the House of Commons Committee on Abortion was prepared to go beyond that restriction. Finally, in 1970, the United Church declared abortion to be purely a private matter between a woman and her doctor. This position was re-affirmed in August 1972 though the Church then indicated that it would like to see abortion on request restricted to the first twelve weeks of pregnancy.

During the various stages of this rapid evolution, there is no evidence of serious theological reflection. The impression is that the issue was introduced in 1960 without understanding what theological and basic general principles were involved and that during the following years the original stand was upheld because it seemed to fit a socially progressive image. In 1966, 400 delegates let pass such statements as "Every child has a right to be well born and in some cases this means the right not to be born at all."[35] Now rights are possessed only by the living, not by what has never come into existence. Therefore, there is no such right as the 'right not to be born at all'. And the statement that 'every child has a right to be well born' is equally incomprehensible. The wisdom characteristic of Christianity is the wisdom of the cross, a sign of suffering and a sign of victory over suffering.[36] In the Christian theological tradition — and I dare say in all of human history — there is no such thing as a 'right to be well born'.

In 1968 the United Church made a more formidable attempt at justifying abortion. As explanation of why a choice may be made between the welfare of the mother on the one hand and the life of the unborn on the other, the United Church delegation to the House of Commons hearings presented the theory of "accruing value". From the time conception takes place, the delegation stated, there is "an

---

35. See footnote 11, Chapter 3, (For similar statements by MP's MacInnes and Winch, see Chapter 9.)

36. cf. 1 Corinthians 1, 17 ff.

accruing value of life" and "the primary consideration ought to be for the life of the one who is now living."[37] This statement sounded attractive and some committee members were duly impressed. Unfortunately, no member of the Committee attempted to examine this theory. As a general theory of society its truth stands unproven. As a Christian theology the theory is untenable. Christians believe that once God has created the soul, what is of man in the purely biological sense becomes human and therefore immortal. This human soul does not 'accrue in value' in the sense that one day it is mortal and the next day immortal. Once created it is equal in the sight of God for all, old or young, rich or poor, born or unborn. If there is no absolute certainty precisely when 'body tissue' receives the soul, and if there is no proof when a human being exists, then no action may be taken, and surely no action which means life or death, as if there were no human life at all. Thus the Roman Catholic delegation to the House of Commons Committee on Abortions explained that revelation does not reveal *when* the soul is infused, transforming life into *human* life. But as no one can tell when this takes place the only course of action at all respectful of human dignity and God's design is to base it on the knowledge provided by human reason. Science confirms that life begins at conception. Consequently, life should he treated with the utmost respect from that point on. The United Church delegation, however, followed the exact opposite approach. Their Brief stated — and it was repeated later on in a 1970 publication — that:

> "We believe it is futile to decide when the foetus receives a soul... We rather regard the foetus, especially during the first seven months, as potentially a human being, though not one yet."[38]

The same theory of the "accruing value of life" should have been questioned by members of the House of Commons Committee from a more general point of view. *What* value is supposed to be accruing? By what *standards* is it judged to be "accruing" (by increased brain power, or heart beat, or muscle power, or size, or ability to move)? Does this value continue to accrue throughout life, or is there a decreasing value for those growing older and feebler, with all the consequences this involves about the rights of these older and feebler people to continued life? Are crippled people less valuable than healthy ones? Are brainy people superior to those of ordinary intellect? And so on.

To my mind, the theory of the "accruing value of life" cannot be reconciled with Christian thinking. It undermines the concept that all human lives are equal and replaces it with the notion that the value of each human life depends on its utility, its usefulness, to society. It endorses the notion that the end justifies the means. Today, it justifies abortion. Tomorrow, it may be used to justify euthanasia and infanticide. The theory provides a new way of thinking for those

---

37. See "United Church", Chapter 7.
38. The United Church of Canada, *Abortion, A Study*, 1970, p. 19.

who will want to determine who or what is useful to society. But it has failed to provide the theological justification for abortion which is a prerequisite within the Christian community. It has presented no adequate answer to the three points elaborated by the delegation of the Canadian Catholic Bishops in March 1968:

1. In spite of appearance, human life before birth is not intrinsically different from human life after birth.
2. Theology does not provide grounds by which one life may be esteemed of higher value than another.
3. In the absence of scientific proof to the contrary, the date of conception must be taken as indicating the beginning of a new and distinct human life. Since all men are given an immortal soul nobody may destroy life which is not guilty of a criminal act.[39]

Morality and Law

The abortion controversy is especially important because it has drawn attention for the first time to certain recent developments and arguments regarding the relationship between law and morality. In the attempt to refute opposition to legal abortions from Churches or religious quarters, the argument was heard with increasing frequency that sin is not the same as crime and that the law should not concern itself with morality. The answer to this question is crucial to the understanding not only of the problem of abortions, but also of all other issues, present or future, which involve 'morality' in any way whatever. The following section treats the question of religion and politics in Canada, analyzes the argument of the Wolfenden Report, and discusses the history of the relation between morality and law in our own civilization.

Politics and Religion in Canada

To say that religion or ideas about religion — whether by their presence or their absence — seriously affect the thinking of every person and every politician is to note the self-evident. But that does not explain the relationship between politics and religion. Mr. Trudeau made a sensible remark when he observed in 1971 that "it would be pretty awful if Canadians came to choose political leaders not for their political ideas and actions but because of their devotedness to one faith or another."[40] Adherence to a particular faith is not a guarantee of statesmanship. If, in the past, politicians were not free from religious ties, it was, in part, because they believed that the connection between a man's religion and his politics was important. In an age of sectarianism that meant sectarian politics. In an age of broadmindness which

---

39. See Chapter 7. For a short survey of abortion in the earlier Christian tradition see Appendix 10.
40. See the interview of Prime Minister Trudeau in the *United Church Observer*, September 1971, pp. 16-20.

borders more and more on indifferentism, it means that people are divided on this issue. Some politicians have adopted the view that religion and traditional morality are private and of no concern to the state and the law. Others cling to the older tradition and consider that matters such as prostitution, homosexuality, divorce, pornography, abortion and a host of other matters should be a concern of the law. An inquiry about how present leaders of Canada's political parties regard their relationship to religion and the Churches indicates a considerable range of views. Each of the present political leaders has come to this position in his own way but the leader of the French-speaking Social Credit party is the only one who forthrightly rejects the view that religion ought to be private only and that the state should be "neutral" instead of Christian. He believes that Canada should have laws which reflect Christian moral principles. This opinion is no doubt part of the reason why some newspapers in English Canada have been almost consistently derisive of his views and those of this party.

There is no mathematically accurate evidence to determine how closely the religious views of the leaders of the Canadian political parties reflect those of individual party members. But it *is* clear that these views reflect an increasingly dominant characteristic of contemporary thought on church-state relations in English-speaking countries: religion, whether regarded as good or indifferent, must be kept private and out of public affairs. This does not necessarily mean that politicians will be opposed to Christianity in principle. It may merely mean that in politics and public life they are unwilling to allot a special status to religion in general or to any Christian Church in particular. It may mean that they do not accord Christian leaders special influence, not even on political issues which involve moral problems. It may mean that they do not feel that the religious dimension of man should require State support or protection. Finally, it may mean that in politics and public life they do not recognize the theological or religious authority of any Church as qualitatively more important than that of any other. Any and all of these things have been present in the past and are part and parcel of the separation of church and state theory which most Western countries have adopted in varying degrees since the French revolution. This theory is useful in the regulation of the everyday intercourse between churchmen and statesmen, principally by recognizing the legitimate autonomy of each in their respective spheres of activity. But it is of no use whatever as a philosophy of life, as a guide by which to regulate one's inner convictions, or as inspiration for the conduct of either the private or the public body. Such philosophy or guidance or inspiration has to come from a source which is both moral and religious. In our western societies this has been Christianity; in other societies it has been Mohammedanism or Buddhism or, as lately in Eastern Europe and in China, Marxist atheism, a religion which worships a god which is within, instead of above and beyond this world. It is these religions or philosophies of life which shape a country's public moral code. They have done so in the past and they will do so in the future. And this brings us to the final question: whether or not law should reflect religious morality.

Morality and Law

The question of the relationship between law and morality is as old as man himself, yet it keeps re-appearing in new forms. When it does re-appear, it indicates that some major change is underway in society or that basic institutions or customs are being challenged in order to clear the way for that change. In spite of an almost natural inclination of modern man to believe that it must be so, not every change is necessarily an improvement. At any rate, the removal of abortion from the Criminal Code reflects the increasing acceptance of a new concept of law, a concept of law which some believe to be necessary and appropriate for the so-called "pluralistic" society, a concept which promotes the *complete* separation of moral and civil law. Its most effective expression to date is to be found in the already mentioned Report of the Committee on Homosexual Offences and Prostitution of 1957 or the Wolfenden Report, described above as "the intellectual turning point in the history of the abortion controversy and, perhaps, in that of modern criminal law in general...".[41] The spirit of the Wolfenden Report was very much the spirit of John Stuart Mill's essay, *On Liberty*. This essay has been a key inspiration for nineteenth and twentieth century liberalism and the liberal philosophy of society. Above all, it expressed the need of the individual to be free from interference from society.

Mill argued that in order for individual man to develop his personality and pursue happiness, freedom is necessary. Only in a free society is there a possibility of progress, of making new discoveries in the realm of morals and elsewhere and of keeping old truths alive. Man ought to be able to act and think for himself. Only in such a society would truth become known and a continuous process of experimentation and debate "refine and develop morality to the common advantage."[42] Therefore, Mill attempted to design a society in which the individuality of the thinking man, the intellectual, would be protected against the pressure of the masses. In other words, he looked for a way which would allow the man of reason as much freedom as possible from the encroachments and demands of society. Regarding "the dealings of society with the individual", he thought he had found a guarantee for such freedom in the "one very simple principle", namely "...that the only purpose for which power can be rightfully exercised over any member of a civilized community, against his will, is to prevent harm to others."[43] Thus society's power over the individual would be restricted to an absolute minimum of socially necessary values. In Mill's mind 'the harmful effects' were clearly restricted to matters which could be proven to be necessary for the maintenance

---

41. See Chapter 1, "Background in Britain"; also Chapter 9.
42. cf. Basil Mitchell, *Law, Morality and Religion in a Secular Society*, Oxford University Press, 1967, p. 89.
43. J.S. Mill, *On Liberty*, Crofts Classics, p. 9.

of society by *human reason* alone; and the social utilitarianism of
Mill did not include as part of that minimum of socially necessary
values morality derived from revealed religion.

The essay, *On Liberty*, has remained a key inspiration for modern
liberalism. But as Professor Basil Mitchell of Oxford has pointed out,
the new liberalism has acquired a basic premise which is quite different
from that of John Mill.[44] This different premise is expressed in the
claim that "the identity and continuity of a society resides not in
the common possession of a single morality, but in the mutual
toleration of different moralities."[45] Mill envisaged that the exchange
and clash of opinions would refine and develop a morality held in
common. He thought that while the truth might not be known now,
it might become known in the future. But modern liberalism assumes
that moral truth is not knowable at all. It holds instead that society
is marked by a *variety* of moralities. The individual will choose one
of these moralities which, consequently, is entirely private and personal
because it holds no more authority than the authority which the
individual who has chosen it, intends to bestow upon it. Under this
scheme the only *moral* idea which needs to be shared is tolerance.
Naturally, this tolerance will not be based on the belief that by debate
and experiment one may discover the right answers to moral questions.
It will be based on an appreciation of having many ethical beliefs,
that is to say, on an appreciation of the pluralistic society.

Like Mill, the new liberalism does not deny that in order to
preserve society people must share *some* principles. But those basic
principles are minimal and are distinguished from 'morality' by being
rational and utilitarian. If these principles also become designated
as 'morality' then it becomes necessary to distinguish between, on
the one hand, "a social morality which is rational, utilitarian, and
necessary to society", and on the other hand, "moral ideals which
are non-rational, non-utilitarian, and peculiarly personal."[46] Under this
scheme, then, any action, which does not prove 'harmful' to society
is classified as private and falls outside the proper jurisdiction of the
law. Religious principles or religious ideals also belong to private
morality because they are classified 'non-rational'. And sexual morality
and mores, too, will fall under private morality and private judgment,
because they are based on 'variable tastes and conventions'. To
complete the picture, according to the same view, religious morality
— being private — ought not to encroach upon, or attempt to determine
the common (social) morality.[47]

Such appears to be the position of modern liberalism. It also
appears to be the position of the Toronto *Globe and Mail* when
it speaks of religion endangering "a certain high conception of liberal

---

44. B. Mitchell, *op. cit.*, Chap. 6, *Varieties of Liberalism*, pp. 87ff.
45. As explained by Professor Wollheim in *Encounter*, November, 1959 quoted in
    Mitchell, *op. cit.*, p. 89. Other theorists of liberalism agree with Prof. Wollheim.
46. B. Mitchell, *op. cit.*, p. 91.
47. cf. P.F. Strawson, "*Social Morality and Individual Ideal*," in *Philosophy*, 1961,
    p. 1. Quoted in Mitchell, *op. cit.*, p. 91.

democracy".[48] That which represents 'religious morality' is declared to be 'private', and any attempt to have this private morality reflected in the laws and customs of the nation becomes an act of usurpation and tyranny. Even if this 'private morality' were supported by a majority, it would still be a case of unduly 'imposing' private and personal views.

As we have seen, this concept of law, with its avowed aim of separating legislation from religious principles and morality, achieved its first series of victories during the nineteen sixties. Contraceptives have been legalized. Attempted suicide and homosexuality have been removed from the Criminal Code. Divorce has become available almost by consent. Laws against obscenity and pornography in films and literature are without real meaning, if they exist at all. Finally, the jurisdiction of the Criminal Code has been withdrawn from abortion, if not in every technical detail, certainly so in common practice. Only with the removal from the Code of the latter did the new theory for the first time run into strong opposition. While other amendments have been accepted as reasonable or considered necessary as the lesser of two evils, the legalization of abortion raised questions about the nature and implications of the ideas behind it. But proponents of the legalization of abortion, having the momentum of the earlier victories of birth control, divorce and homosexuality as a decided advantage, were able to press forward relentlessly with the air of men whose premises were simply unassailable. But rather than taking the Wolfenden Report's interpretation of the relationship between crime and sin for granted, it ought to be seen for what it is: the overturn of a fundamental principle.

Western Society

In western society law has not generally been regarded as co-extensive with morality. This is most clearly seen in their differences of sanction and scope. The law imposes a physical sanction—deprivation of property or liberty or perhaps even life — while the moral sanction is interior. Law is concerned with external conduct; morality is concerned with interior attitudes. Law aims for the good of the community; morality also aims for that but goes beyond that to the individual. Yet, in the past the two jurisdictions frequently overlapped and supported one another, presumably where people believed that a moral offense was not only harmful to the individual but also to society. One of those areas was the subject of the Wolfenden investigation which concluded that in the case of homosexuality it could find no evidence that this 'sin' also had effects which were harmful to society. Whether or not its analysis was correct will not be discussed. What is important here is that in recommending the removal of homosexuality from the jurisdiction of the law, at least as far as it is a private act between adults, the Report did so in language which suggested that *any* connection between law and morality was a mistake. This gave rise to the popular notion that sin and crime have nothing in common,

---

48. See appendix 6, Editorial, March 11, 1968.

reinforcing, in turn, the very heart of the new theory, which rests on the assumption that while society cannot function without a body of socially necessary principles, this minimum set of laws is a body of universal values on which all men will agree simply by following reason, rather than religion.

The first to recognize the revolutionary character of the Wolfenden recommendation was Lord Devlin who from 1959 on took issue with its premises, primarily in an ongoing public debate with Professor H.L. Hart.[49] Lord Devlin argued that crimes such as euthanasia, suicide, duelling, abortion, incest between brother and sister, are all acts "which can be done in private and without offence to others and need not involve the corruption or exploitation or others." Yet all of them are regarded as crimes because the basis of criminal law has always been that:

> There are certain standards of behaviour or moral principles
> which society requires to be observed; and the breach of them
> is an offence not merely against the person who is injured,
> but against society as a whole."[50]

Thus the idea that acts should simply be left outside the scope of the law merely on the grounds that they belong to private morality is to be rejected. Society has *always* claimed the right to pass judgments on moral matters; moreover, it has used the weapon of the law to enforce this public moral code, even though it remains a matter of prudent decision whether or not the law should be enforced in all cases or only in some.

As further evidence that society passes moral judgments all the time, Judge Devlin pointed to the Wolfenden Report. When the Report recommended that solicitation of youngsters and minors by homosexuals be still a punishable crime in order to prevent their 'corruption', it did so, he said, only because it judged homosexuality to be morally wrong. By the same token, when the Committee used terms such as "to preserve public order and decency...", "to protect the citizen from what is offensive or injurious...", "to provide sufficient safeguards against exploitation and corruption...", it constantly made moral judgments. Words such as order, decency, offensive, injurious, exploitation and corruption, are all words implying value judgments. They indicate the difficulty, if not the impossibility, of distinguishing between what is private and what is social in individual action. They illustrate why John Stuart Mill failed to resolve that problem in his practical examples which were meant to elucidate his 'simple' principle of the socially harmful.

It is not enough to admit merely that society needs a shared morality of some kind about what is right and wrong. The fact of the matter is that this shared morality is basically a religious morality

---

49. Most of Lord Devlin's arguments may be found in his book *The Enforcement of Morals* (1965) and Professor Hart's in *The Concept of Law*, 1961, *Law, Liberty and Morality* 1963 and *The Morality of the Criminal Law* (1965) Basil Mitchell, to whom I am indebted for my remarks, surveys the Devlin-Hart debate in Chapter 1 of his *Law, Morality and Religion in a Secular Society*, Oxford, 1967.

50. Lord Devlin, *The Enforcement of Morals*, Oxford, p. 6.

152   MORALITY AND LAW IN CANADIAN POLITICS

simply because morals and religion are inextricably joined. In our Western civilization this shared morality is a *Christian* morality while outside Christendom other standards derive from other religions. While in Mohammedan countries a man is permitted to have four wives at once, Christianity is the reason why western societies have adopted the monogamous marriage. It is only one example how deeply law in our society is immersed in religious principles which, moreover, are all interconnected.

The observation that our law is permeated with the spirit of Christianity is commonplace. It is true for Roman law, which was penetrated, reshaped and transformed by the new light emanating from the Christian message; it is even more true for the common law of England before the nineteenth century as well as American law since the eighteenth century.[51] The historian of English law, Theodore Plucknett, has observed that "the Church brought with it moral ideas which were to revolutionize law." He noted that in Christianity the salvation of each separate soul was dependent upon the actions of the individual. "This contrasted strongly," he says, "with the custom of the English tribes which looked not to the individual but to the family group of which the individual formed a part. Necessarily such a system had little place for an individualistic sense of morals for the group can hardly be credited with moral intention in the sense that an individual can. With the spread of Christianity all this slowly changed. First, responsibility for actions gradually shifted from the whole group to the particular individual who did the act; and then the Church (and later the law) will judge that act, if necessary, from the point of view of the party who committed it."[52] It is not surprising that a Chinese scholar noted that he found in the jurisprudence of Christian nations "a far greater respect for the dignity of man as man" than in the jurisprudence of non-Christian nations.[53]

According to the thinking of great philosophers as well as great legal minds, eternal and human law form a whole, with eternal law as the vine as it were, and human law its branches. But as already noted, this did not and does not mean that it is the purpose of human law to forbid or proscribe every moral evil. Sin and crime do indeed differ and this has been the standard rule throughout the Christian epoch, from Augustine in the fourth century to Aquinas in the thirteenth and the moderns in the twentieth century. Using Aristotle's *Metaphysics* as foundation, Aquinas remarks in answering the question, "Is it the business of human law to restrain all vice?" that:

> The ability... for acting in a certain way springs from our interior disposition or habit; the same course of action is not possible for a man who has a habit of virtue and for a man who lacks it, nor for a grown-up and a child: this is why

---

51. cf. John Wu, *Fountain of Justice* (New York, 1955), Chapter 18. This book provides evidence for the relationship between law and Christianity in western society.

52. Th. Plucknett, *A Concise History of the Common Law*, pp. 8-9.

53. J. Wu, *op. cit.*, p. 222.

the same laws do not apply, for many things are allowed in the young for which older people are punished or at least blamed... Law is laid down for a great number of people, of which the majority have no high standard of morality. Therefore, it does not forbid all the vices, from which upright men can keep away, but only those grave ones which the average man can avoid, and chiefly those which do harm to others and have to be stopped if human society is to be maintained...[54]

However, to assert that civil law does not aim to remove every moral flaw from society is a long way from insisting that law and morality are 'clearly distinct', or that crime and sin 'have nothing in common', or that there should be 'freedom *from* religion', or that the law 'does not look to what is morally desirable'. Aquinas continues with the remark that "the purpose of human law is to bring people to virtue, not suddenly but step by step." In the context of the problem he himself had posed, the emphasis falls on the 'step by step'. In our context, however, it is important to note that Aquinas never loses sight of the wider meaning of the law, namely to bring people *to virtue*. Throughout his treatise he insists that the end of law is the *good*, and that every law is shaped to the common good. In support of this he constantly draws from the great philosophers, but especially from Aristotle who tells us among other things, that "legislators make the citizens good by forming habits in them."[55]

Unlike Aristotle, who lived in pre-Christian times, Aquinas insists that the guidance of human conduct requires the divine law as revealed in the Scriptures. This is so not only because human law cannot forbid or punish all wrong doing, as noted above, or because of the untrustworthiness of human judgment; it is especially true because human law cannot legislate for the interior motions required for the full flowering of the "virtuous" man, nor direct man to the ultimate end for which he is made, the life with God. Human activity cannot and may not be divorced from this ultimate end. Consequently, human law which provides a kind of direction for this human activity, must be guided by divine law. Thus we read in Psalm 118:

Lord, how I love your law
It is ever in my mind.
Your command makes me wiser than my foes
for it is mine for ever.

I have more insight than all who teach me
for I ponder your will.
I have more understanding than the old
for I keep your precepts...

Psalm 118, vs. 97-8.

Naturally, materialists and the supporters of utilitarian positivism will not accept such a view of law at all. But for Christians, the precepts

---

54. Thomas Aquinas, *Summa Theologiae*, I-II, Q90, art. 2, Vol. 28 "Lawand Political Theory", Blackfriars-McGraw-Hill, 1966, pp. 113-5.
55. Ethics, 11, 1, 1103b3. Quoted by Aquinas, *op. cit.* Q 92, p. 43.

and commands of divine law should be constantly before them, with their fullest expression in the teaching and example of Christ. Jesus presents an indispensable hierarchy of values, for example in the judgments that laws are made for man, not man for laws; or, that we should give to Caesar what is Caesar's and to God what is God's; or that we should reject "blind guides who strain out a gnat and swallow a camel." (Mt. 23,24). In the last case Jesus denounced the scribes and Pharisees because, meticulous as they were in tithing mint, anise and cummin, they forgot about the weightier things of the law — love, mercy and justice. That is the position in which we find ourselves today. It is the reason why it is so important that the abortion controversy be settled. With the other 1969 revisions of the Criminal Code we have strained out gnats; with the revision of abortion we have swallowed a camel.

Conclusion

To say that opponents of legalized abortions are primarily encouraged in their stand because of their religious convictions is basically correct. Christians in general have always believed that the divine Revelation in which they believe was not an accident but a necessity. They have always maintained that the great principles of the Judaeo-Christian heritage are essential to a vital, dynamic and just society. They believe that without these principles society remains stagnant or reverts back to inferior forms of human culture and justice, or possibly even to new forms of barbarism. Christians believe that Revelation shores up and illuminates human reason. They believe that in the practical order of daily life the great principles of their faith have proven essential to human needs and to a more profound recognition of what belongs and what does not belong to the common good. That is why in our society the standards of law have been Christian standards.

The fact that those who profess the Christian religion may have failed to live up to their ideals from time to time, does not flaw the nature or invalidate the value of the ideals themselves. But in the practical order, of course, this failure does weaken the power of those ideals. So, above all, does the fact of divided counsels. It has been the contention of this author that this division among Christians regarding abortion is more apparent than real. Ultimately the truth of this or that theory depends on whether or not it is true and valid theology. Unless it can be integrated as part of theology and as a consequence flowing from first principles, such theories cannot be designated 'Christian'. To my mind those religious bodies who have attempted to speak in favour of legal abortions specifically as Christain bodies, have done so erroneously. They have not provided answers to important theological questions. While undoubtedly well-intentioned, their actions in this respect are only to be regretted as one more illustration of the evils of division which have plagued Christianity for centuries.

Meanwhile, when utilitarian philosophers and spokesmen demand the removal of "morality" from the law, they are asking for the removal of *Christian* standards of behavior in favour of their own standards. The latter consist of a minimum shared morality founded on reason. It is the aspect of the minimal which will always make this demand attractive because man's natural inclination gravitates towards the minimum rather than the maximum, towards the least, rather than the most. The legalization of abortion has been a consequence of their theory. This legalization is the first instance in Canadian history, I believe, where an element has been introduced into the legal system which is diametrically opposed to the common good as Christian theology understands and defines it. It has introduced the notion that human life innocent of any crime may be snuffed out for reasons of utility. This principle is so important to our civilization that opponents of legalized abortions who base their opposition on these grounds will never be reconciled to it. If the law is not repealed, one of the consequences of the 1969 revision of the Criminal Code will be the permanent alienation of a large number of people. This sense of alienation will grow as the implications of the new philosophy begin to demonstrate themselves in other areas.

Opponents of the permissive abortion law have not had much to cheer about during the last ten years. They are very much aware that time, pressure, the prevailing moral climate, the process of indoctrination, and man's general inclination to seek the way of least resistance in difficult situations work against the principles they are trying to uphold. Already girls grow up in a milieu in which abortion is one of several alternatives should they become pregnant. Among social workers and psychiatrists there is a wide-spread tendency to think of abortion as a first solution to difficult cases. Family Planning organizations throughout the country do their utmost to make it acceptable. Moreover, the number of those who justify abortion must be ever growing. Once people have voluntarily participated in abortions, whether as patients or staff, they will feel bound to defend it.

Most important of all, the oft-mentioned "educational role" of the law now works in favour of abortions. The Canadian government has adopted the stand of the neutral arbiter in a pluralistic society. But the abortion controversy has shown that there are limits to pluralism and that these limits have now been transgressed. The presumed neutrality means, in fact, permissiveness and approval, because the popular mind believes that whatever is legal is permissible. In matters of life and death neither the citizen nor the state can be "neutral". A vacuum will be filled, if not by one view of life, then by another.

Those who believe that abortions are not permissible in spite of their being legal will have to find ways to keep this belief alive. This they are now doing, principally in two ways: legislative pressure and practical aid. The task of influencing future legislation is being exercised by the so-called Pro-Life groups. Until now their activity has consisted in counteracting the pressure for abortion on demand. But in future they must work to remove the present law, so destructive of the dignity of human life.

The movement to extend practical and immediate help to pregnant girls and women in need of aid has also grown steadily. It has taken on new and modern forms, especially under the sponsorship of the "Birthright" groups. Founded in 1968 by Mrs. Louise Summerhill, a Toronto housewife and mother of seven, the organization had reached 325 legally, incorporated chapters by 1973, extending to practically all principal cities in Canada and the United States. Manned and supported by volunteers, it has already been extraordinarily successful in extending a practical alternative to abortion.

If it proves impossible to change the law in Canada, it will be the task of grass root movements of volunteers to keep the idea alive that the common good of society is threatened by the concept of legalized abortion and the entire philosophy and psychology it represents. As pointed out sometime ago in regard to the organization of society, "the choice that is actually before us is not between an individualistic humanism and some form of collectivism, but between a collectivism that is purely *mechanistic* and one that is spiritual."[56]

That is the choice which confronts us today about life itself. If a sufficient number of people believe that man is a machine, he will be treated as one. Brutes are treated brutally; machines are treated mechanically. Abortion and its future cousins such as infanticide and mercy killing are signals that a mechanistic spirit which has already influenced society in many other ways is now encroaching upon the territory of human life itself. But people who believe that man is above all a spiritual being, must live that belief, it not with the support of human law, then in spite of it.

If it is politically possible to repeal the present law it should be repealed in order to return to a sane tradition. If the government permits or is forced to continue the present situation, the consequences of legal abortions will fester like an open wound, gradually infecting other areas. 'Legalizing' abortions has resolved nothing. On the contrary, it has added new and graver problems which in their philosophical implications will create far more dangerous conflicts than the practical problem of how to stop illegal, backstreet, abortions. For a society to have many illegal abortions is no doubt a very serious situation. It will be very difficult to stop them. But to legalize abortions is to corrupt the law and, thereby, ultimately to corrupt society. It will prove far more difficult to stop that corruption than it will be to stop illegal abortions.

---

56. Christopher Dawson, *The New Age*, p. 100.

Appendices

APPENDIX I

Criminal Code of Canada

Statutes of Canada, 1927.
Section 303, Chapter 2.

Everyone is guilty of an indictable offence and liable to imprisonment for life, who, with intent to procure the miscarriage of any woman, whether she is or is not with child, unlawfully administers to her or causes to be taken by her any drug or other noxious things, or unlawfully uses on her any instrument or other means whatsoever with the like intent.

Statutes of Canada, 1953-54.
Section 237, Chapter 51.

Intent to Procure Miscarriage: (1) Everyone who, with intent to procure the miscarriage of a female person, whether or not she is pregnant, uses any means for the purpose of carrying out this intention is guilty of an indictable offence and is liable to imprisonment for life. (2) Every female person who, being pregnant, with intent to procure her own miscarriage, uses any means or permits any means to be used for the purpose of carrying out her intention is guilty of an indictable offence and is liable to imprisonment for two years. (3) In this section "means" includes: (a) The administration of a drug or other noxious thing. (b) The use of an instrument. (c) Manipulation of any kind.

Statutes of Canada, 1953-54.
Section 238, Chapter 51.

Unlawfully supplying Drug or Noxious Thing: Everyone who unlawfully supplies or procures a drug or other noxious thing or an instrument or thing, knowing that it is intended to be used or employed to procure the miscarriage of a female person, whether or not she is pregnant, is guilty of an indictable offence and is liable to imprisonment for two years.

Statutes of Canada, 1953-54.
Section 209, Chapter 51.

Causing Death of Child Not a Human Being: (1) Every one who causes the death of a child that has not become a human being, in such a manner that, if the child were a human being, he would be guilty of murder, is guilty of an indictable offence and is liable to imprisonment for life. (2) This section does not apply to a person who, by means that, in good faith, he considers necessary to preserve the life of the mother of a child that has not become a human being, causes the death of the child.

Statutes of Canada, 1953-54.
Section 195, Chapter 51.

When Child Becomes a Human Being: (1) A child becomes a human being within the meaning of this Act when it has completely proceeded in a living state, from the body of its mother whether or not: (a) It has breathed. (b) It has independent circulation. (c) The navel string is severed. (2) A person commits homicide when he causes injuries to a child before or during its birth as a result of which the child dies.

Statutes of Canada, 1953-54.
Section 45, Chapter 51.

Surgical Operations: Every one is protected from criminal responsibility for performing a surgical operation upon any person for the benefit of that person if (a) the operation is performed with reasonable care and skill and (b) it is reasonable to perform the operation, having regard to the state of health of the person at the time the operation is performed and to all the circumstances of the case.

APPENDIX II

Criminal Code of Canada

(after 1969 amendments)

ABORTION.

Procuring miscarriage — Woman procuring her own miscarriage — "Means" — Exceptions — Information requirement — Definitions — Requirement of consent not affected.

251.   (1) Every one who, with intent to procure the miscarriage of a female person, whether or not she is pregnant, uses any means for the purpose of carrying out his intention is guilty of an indictable offence and is liable to imprisonment for life.

(2) Every female person who, being pregnant, with intent to procure her own miscarriage, uses any means or permits any means to be used for the purpose of carrying out her intention is guilty of an indictable offence and is liable to imprisonment for two years.

(3) In this section, "means" includes
    (a) the administration of a drug or other noxious thing.

(b) the use of an instrument, and

(c) manipulation of any kind.

(4) Subsections (1) and (2) do not apply to

(a) a qualified medical practitioner, other than a member of a therapeutic abortion committee for any hospital, who in good faith uses in an accredited or approved hospital any means for the purpose of carrying out his intention to procure the miscarriage of a female person, or

(b) a female person who, being pregnant, permits a qualified medical practitioner to use in an accredited or approved hospital any means described in paragraph (a) for the purpose of carrying out her intention to procure her own miscarriage.

if, before the use of those means, the therapeutic abortion committee for that accredited or approved hospital, by a majority of the members of the committee and at a meeting of the committee at which the case of such female person has been reviewed,

(c) has by certificate in writing stated that in its opinion the continuation of the pregnancy of such female person would or would be likely to endanger her life or health, and

(d) has caused a copy of such certificate to be given to the qualified medical practitioner.

(5) The Minister of Health of a province may by order

(a) require a therapeutic abortion committee for any hospital in that province, or any member thereof, to furnish to him a copy of any certificate described in paragraph (4) (c) issued by that committee, together with such other information relating to the circumstances surrounding the issue of that certificate as he may require, or

(b) require a medical practitioner who, in that province, has procured the miscarriage of any female person named in a certificate described in paragraph (4) (c), to furnish to him a copy of that certificate, together with such other information relating to the procuring of the miscarriage as he may require.

(6) For the purposes of subsections (4) and (5) and this subsection

"accredited hospital" means a hospital accredited by the Canadian Council on Hospital Accreditation in which diagnostic services and medical, surgical and obstetrical treatment are provided;

"approved hospital" means a hospital in a province approved for the purposes of this section by the Minister of Health of that province;

"board" means the board of governors, management or directors, or the trustees, commission or other person or group of persons having the control and management of an accredited or approved hospital;

"Minister of Health" means

(a) in the Provinces of Ontario, Quebec, New Brunswick, Manitoba, Alberta, Newfoundland and Prince Edward Island, the Minister of Health,

(b) in the Province of British Columbia, the Minister of Health Services and Hospital Insurance,

(c) in the Provinces of Nova Scotia and Saskatchewan, the Minister of Public Health, and

(d) in the Yukon Territory and the Northwest Territories, the Minister of National Health and Welfare;

"qualified medical practitioner" means a person entitled to engage in the practice of medicine under the laws of the province in which the hospital referred to in subsection (4) is situated;

"therapeutic abortion committee" for any hospital means a committee, comprised of not less than three members each of whom is a qualified medical practitioner, appointed by the board of that hospital for the purpose of considering and determining questions relating to terminations of pregnancy within that hospital.

(7) Nothing in subsection (4) shall be construed as making unnecessary the obtaining of any authorization or consent that is or may be required, otherwise than under this Act, before any means are used for the purpose of carrying out an intention to procure the miscarriage of a female person.

Supplying noxious things.

252.   Every one who unlawfully supplies or procures a drug or other noxious thing or an instrument or thing, knowing that it is intended to be used or employed to procure the miscarriage of a female person, whether or not she is pregnant, is guilty of an indictable offence and is liable to imprisonment for two years.

APPENDIX III

Resolution-Canadian Medical Association
Passed at Annual Meeting, Edmonton, June, 1966

Therapeutic Abortions

It is recommended that legislation be enacted to ensure that an operation for the termination of pregnancy is lawful in the following circumstances:

(A)   where it is performed by a duly qualified licensed medical practitioner after consultation with and approval of a hospital-appointed therapeutic abortion committee.

(B)   and if performed in an active treatment hospital approved by a qualified accrediting board.

(C)   and performed with the written consent of the patient and with the consent of the spouse or guardian where the Committee deems necessary.

(D)   and where the continuance of the pregnancy may endanger the life or the physical health or mental health of the mother.

It is proposed that this recommendation be referred to the Minister of Justice, with the suggestion that the Criminal Code be amended to incorporate the recommendations as written above.

APPENDIX IV

The Position of the United Church of Canada Re Abortion

The 19th General Council, 1960, approved the following statement:

Christian conscience cannot approve abortion, either as a means of limiting or spacing one's family, or a relief to the unmarried mother, because it involves the destruction of human life. However, if in the judgment of reputable medical authorities the continuation of pregnancy seriously endangers the physical or mental health of the mother, therapeutic abortion may be necessary.

The 22nd General Council, 1966, passed the following resolution on Therapeutic Abortion and related Issues:

Whereas the Christian Gospel requires us to use our knowledge and skills to combat disease, save life and promote the well-being and dignity of every person;

Whereas we believe that therapeutic abortion would be justified when the life of the foetus threatens the life or health of the mother;

Whereas the sections of the Criminal Code of Canada pertaining to abortion are conflicting, leaving the impression that abortion is wrong and even murderous, in all circumstances;

Whereas the air of secrecy and guilt surrounding abortion dissuades a harrassed mother from discussing her problems openly and honestly with her doctor and discourages doctors from dealing straight-forwardly with this situation, thus driving many women to attempt to abort themselves or to seek an illegal abortion, which is often carried out by unskilled persons, under very primitive conditions and which threatens the future health and even the life of the mother: BE IT RESOLVED THAT THIS GENERAL COUNCIL:

(1) Petition the Government of Canada to revise the Criminal Code to permit therapeutic abortion when continuance of pregnancy is likely to endanger the mother's life or seriously impair her physical or mental health, when the following safeguards are observed:

(a) permission is secured from a Therapeutic Abortion Committee of at least from three to five persons, the majority of whom would be doctors, except that in cases of emergency, the judgment of a patient's doctor, who has consulted, if at all possible with one or two other doctors, would be regarded as sufficient;

(b) written consent is obtained from the patient, or parent or guardian of a minor, except in cases of emergency when the life of the mother is in danger;

(c) that the operation should be performed by a qualified doctor, in hospital or other suitable treatment centre, elsewhere only in cases of extreme emergency.

(2) Recommend that Government and voluntary agencies co-operate in providing adequate Counselling Services whereby mothers could receive financial and legal aid and moral support which would encourage them to have their babies.

(3) Appeal to all responsible citizens and groups to co-operate with the Government in seeking to do away with the illegal abortion traffic.

(4) Petition against the Government of Canada to amend 150 (2) (c) of the Criminal Code which forbids the advertising and sale of Birth Control knowledge and devices in order that all parents may have the advantage of planning the size and spacing of their families.".

Proceedings of Health & Welfare
February 6, 1968

APPENDIX V

ROMAN CATHOLIC BISHOPS

Canadian Catholic Conference Statement on proposed change of Canadian Law on Abortion

About a month ago, draft amendments to the Criminal Code were introduced in the Canadian House of Commons. One amendment would so change the law on abortion that a medical doctor, with the approval of a hospital committee, would be permitted to perform an abortion when continuation of a pregnancy "would endanger, or would be likely to endanger, the life or the health of the mother".

With Parliament about to discuss a law of such serious consequence, careful study of the question is a duty of conscience for everyone, especially for doctors, lawyers, politicians and all who influence public opinion. Therefore we, too, must try to set before you as clearly as possible what we believe to be in harmony with Christian faith, moral norms worthy of man, and the requirements of civilized life. Our concern for the common good compels us to do this. While speaking primarily to Catholics, we hope to receive sympathetic hearing from all who want to serve the best interests of the Canadian people in the study of this grave and complex problem.

I
ABORTION AND RESPECT FOR LIFE

The Mind of the Church

Although it did not deal at length with abortion, the recent Vatican Council repeated in general yet forceful terms the traditional teaching of the Church. "God, the Lord of life," it said, "has conferred on men the surpassing ministry of safeguarding life — a ministry which must be fulfilled in a manner which is worthy of man. Therefore, from the moment of its conception, life must be guarded with the greatest care, while abortion and infanticide are unspeakable crimes" (Constitution on the Church in the Modern World, Art. 51). The Council's teaching, it is clear, condemns the direct taking of foetal life, but not treatments needed to save a mother's life even if they sometimes result in the unwanted and unsought death of the foetus.

No one should be surprised that the Church takes so firm a position on this question. Her words in this case are but a faithful echo of God's solemn and grave commandment, "Thou shalt not kill." They also give witness to the great law of Christian love (Rom. 13, 8-10). These words touch on something that is fundamental for any true civilization or real progress — respect for life and for the human person.

It is clear that this commandment of God obliges in conscience, no matter what legislation may be in force in a country.

Must Respect for Man Apply to the Foetus?

"The Church's principles," it is sometimes said, "are noble in themselves but do not take into account the basic difference between life in the womb and life after birth." This prompts us to make the following points which will clarify the Church's position on abortion.

First, we note that science has not established a fundamental difference between life in the womb and the child's life after birth. Instead, scientific findings lead us to look upon the whole development that begins with conception as the slow, complex maturing process of a distinct individual, an autonomous biological reality progressing towards full human stature. Scientists even affirm that this individuality is already perceptible in the fertilized ovum itself, that is, from the time of conception. To be sure, it is difficult to determine the exact moment when we can be certain that the foetus is human. At least in the latter stages of its development there can be no doubt. A mother knows her little one has become her partner in a secret dialogue in already-awakened human love. Mothers are not misled in this basic insight; they know that they bear not merely vegetable or animal life but a human offspring with the right to be recognized as such.

Moreover, for those who think they have good reasons to doubt the human character of the foetus in the early stages of its development, and therefore argue that abortion is legitimate in certain cases, we have a question: Since you too consider human life sacred, can you justify even the risk of taking a human life?

Border-line Cases

The question is sometimes asked: The Church advocates that the unborn be regarded as human and invites man to respect human life in its very origins. In so doing, does not the Church treat too lightly the very serious dangers that sometimes threaten the mother because of the new life within her? The question is asked as if the concern for the human person expressed and fostered by the Church were accompanied by an inability to grasp concrete situations and provide satisfactory answers to them.

We know the anguish felt by mother, husband and doctor when two equally innocent lives are in a mysterious conflict that involves risk of death for the mother, or at least danger of serious or permanent effect on her physical or mental health. When such cases occur, they are always difficult and sometimes tragic. But resort to abortion, because it involves the taking of innocent life, does not render the situation less tragic.

When the mother's life is truly in danger, we understand that there may be a temptation to consider abortion, even direct abortion, as justifiable. Nevertheless, we must point out that this view is contrary to a persistent Judeo-Christian tradition that life is sacred. Likewise, to advocate abortion in order to protect something other than the very life of the mother, even if it be her physical or mental health, is to disregard the sacred right of the foetus to life; also, it is to sacrifice a greater value for a lesser one.

Besides, abortion itself often has harmful effects on the physical, mental and moral well-being of the mother. And it is also relevant that advances in medicine and psychiatry now make it possible to find positive solutions that respect life in many border-line cases.

Medical opinion is virtually unanimous that cases where a direct abortion is necessary to save the mother's life are fortunately so rare these days that their existence is becoming merely theoretical. Less rare, to be sure, is the case where a pregnancy may seriously and permanently endanger the mother's physical or mental health. At any rate, it certainly would be a false approach to think that solution of such border-line cases calls for legislative changes of the kind proposed.

II

ABORTION AND THE LAW

A bill to amend the law on abortion has been presented in the House of Commons. The issue is now something more than the morality of abortion. We must also consider what the state's role in this matter should be and, more precisely still, what one should think of the proposed amendments.

The State, Protector of Life

Effective protection of human life, especially of the weakest, is always a foremost duty of the state. Considering the complexity of modern living and the new and often hidden dangers that threaten life, this protective function of the state is today more important than ever. Through criminal law, police forces, control of public health and drugs, protection for children, social legislation and many other means, the state must strive today, even more than in the past, to fulfill effectively its role as protector of life. We note here, for example, the government's recent praiseworthy measures to assure greater traffic safety and better control over possession and use of firearms.

Everyone speaks of progress, and there is surely no one unwilling to promote it. But do we automatically have to accept as progress every measure made out to be, sometimes in a rather peculiar way, a "liberalization" or a "broadening" of the law. When it is a matter of respect and protection of human life, progress does not lie in laxity but in ever more attentive and effective concern and vigilance. Progress in civilization, we say without hesitation, consists in the increasingly clear recognition of the dignity, sacredness and absolute inviolability of the human person, on both the theoretical and practical levels.

Consequences of the Proposed Amendments

The proposed amendments on abortion are well known. According to the bill, those who procure an abortion would be liable, as in the past, to life imprisonment; but a qualified doctor would be allowed to perform an abortion if pregnancy endangered, or was likely to endanger, the life or health of the mother, provided the abortion was performed in an accredited hospital and a written certificate obtained from the hospital's therapeutic abortion committee. This brings us to the following considerations.

This amendment of the law not only allows the direct and voluntary taking of an innocent life but opens the door to the broadest interpretations. Through the press, radio and television we are already getting expressions of public opinion that show a clear and alarming decline in respect for the life of the unborn. Some, for example, see the amendment proposed in the House of Commons as only the first step towards official recognition of "abortion on demand". Others believe that the amendment, as it stands, already provides the possibility for abortion in a very large number of cases.

Such reactions are not at all reassuring. When we consider also what has happened in countries where similar legislation has been adopted, we can easily foresee what will happen here.

On this point, it should be noted that the parliamentary committee looking into the question acknowledged in its first report last December that there had not been sufficient study and investigation. We must ask, therefore, whether the Canadian people really have before them all the necessary information. Secondly, is it right for Parliament, without measuring through appropriate research the moral, psychological and sociological implications, to venture into new legislation on a problem of such grave consequence for man and for civilization itself?

Illicit Abortions

Many who find the very idea of abortion repugnant still see some merit in the amendment proposed by the government. They think that the new law would significantly reduce the number of illicit abortions and their disastrous consequences.

With regard to illicit abortions, arbitrary unverifiable figures are produced which catch public attention simply by being repeated. To be sure, such abortions are too common; and they do have serious consequences. Every effort must be made to eliminate them. But the real question is what means should be used to bring about the desired result.

There is good evidence that it is only an illusion to expect that the proposed amendment will succeed in reducing the number of illicit abortions. Judging by the experience of countries with laws similar to the one proposed for Canada, we may justly fear the very opposite result. In fact, could it be otherwise? A law that lessens the right of the foetus to life by the exceptions it allows leads to a lax attitude that abortion is no longer a real crime. Lawmakers should never underestimate the educational value of law. Men are all too ready to consider as morally permissible whatever the law itself permits.

True Reform

Progress, especially in human affairs, is rarely achieved by easy solutions. The proposed amendment is just that — a too-simple solution to a serious and complex problem. We have in mind a completely different approach. Respect for human life at all stages of development should be fostered through education and through laws that teach respect for life. A serious study of the frequency of illicit abortions and of means to eliminate them should be undertaken. Medical research should be encouraged. Real efforts should be made to provide mothers in distress with the medical and psychiatric care they need. There should be a more human understanding of unwed mothers and their children and we should provide them with real help. Greater effort must go into the care of those afflicted by mental illness. More adequate social and family policies should be planned and developed with all seriousness and great generosity. The state must devote itself to a program of this kind. For our part, we call on the Catholic people to become active leaders and ardent collaborators in this common undertaking.

This is the way to real social progress and true freedom. For us only one approach is worthy of mankind, of civilization, and of Canada's spiritual mission in the world. That approach calls for creative imagination, not the all-too-easy imitation of other countries. It calls for ever-increasing respect for all human life, including the defenceless and most dependent.

During the recent parliamentary debate on capital punishment, this was said: "We can set an example of our respect for the sanctity of human life to a world that is sorely in need of a higher regard for human life and a higher standard of human conduct". These words, you will agree, touch the heart of the matter. They throw light on the present debate. May they also be its inspiration!

APPENDIX VI

Party standing after the General Election of June 25, 1968:

Liberals	155
Progressive Conservatives	72
New Democratic Party	22
Independent	1
	264

Vote on Clause 18 (containing the proposed abortion amendments) of the so-called Omnibus Bill, Bill C-150. Date: May 9, 1969. Motion 19 proposed to eliminate all references to abortion in Bill C-150. Therefore, those who voted yes, voted against the abortion clauses and against the proposed changes.

YEAS

Messrs:

Alkenbrack, A.D.,   P.C.
  Frontenac-Lennox and Addington

Beaudoin, Léonel,   R.Cr.
  Richmond

Bell, Thomas M.,   P.C.
  Saint John-Lancaster

Bigg, F.J.   P.C.
  Pembina

Burton, John,   N.D.P.
  Regina East

Caouette, Réal,   R.Cr.
  Témiscamingue

Carter, Walter C.   P.C.
  St. John's West

Code, Desmond   P.C.
  Leeds

Comeau, Louis-Roland   P.C.
  South Western Nova

Crouse, Lloyd R.   P.C.
  South Shore

Danforth, H.W.   P.C.
  Kent-Essex

Dinsdale, Hon. W.G.   P.C.
  Brandon-Souris

Dionne, Charles-Eugène   R.Cr.
  Kamouraska

Forrestall, J.M.   P.C.
  Dartmouth-Halifax East

Gundlock, D.R.   P.C.
  Lethbridge

Lambert, Hon. Marcel   P.C.
  Edmonton West

Laprise, Gérard   R.Cr.
  Abitibi

Latulippe, Henri   R.Cr.
  Compton

Lundrigan, John   P.C.
  Gander-Twillingate

MacInnis, Donald   P.C.
  Cape Breton-East Richmond

McGrath, James A.   P.C.
  St.John's East

McQuaid, Melvin   P.C.
  Cardigan

Marshall, Jack   P.C.
  Humber-St. George's-St. Barbe

Matte, René   R.Cr.
  Champlain

Muir, Robert   P.C.
  Cape Breto.1-The Sydneys

Muir, George   P.C.
  Lisgar

Paproski, Steven E.   P.C.
  Edmonton Centre

Peddle, Ambrose Hubert   P.C.
  Grand Falls-White Bay-Labrador

Reid, John M.   Lib.-Lab.
  Kenora-Rainy River

Rodrigue, Romuald   R.Cr.
  Beauce

Rondeau, Gilbert   R.Cr.
  Shefford

Scott, W.C.   P.C.
  Victoria-Haliburton

Southam, R.R.   P.C.
  Qu'Appelle-Moose Mountain

Stewart, Ralph   Lib.
  Cochrane

Woolliams, Eldon M.   P.C.
  Calgary North

Yewchuk, Paul   P.C.
  Athabasca

NAYS

Messrs:

Aiken, G.H.,   P.C.
  Parry Sound-Muskoka

Allmand, Warren,   Lib.
  Notre-Dame-de-Grâce

Anderson, David,   Lib.
  Esquimalt-Saanich

Béchard, Albert,   Lib.
  Bonaventure

Beer, Bruce S.,   Lib.
  Peel-Dufferin-Simcoe

Benjamin, Les,   N.D.P.
  Regina-Lake Centre

Blair, D. Gordon,   Lib.
  Grenville-Carleton

Blouin, Gustave,   Lib.
  Manicouagan

Borrie, Robert,   Lib.
  Prince George-Peace River

Boulanger, Prosper,   Lib.
  Mercier

Breau, Herb,   Lib.
  Gloucester

Brewin, Andrew,   N.D.P.
  Greenwood

Broadbent, J. Edward,   N.D.P.
  Oshawa-Whitby

Caccia, Chas L.,	Lib.	Hopkins, Leonard,	Lib.
Davenport		Renfrew North	
Cadieux, Hon. Léo,	Lib.	Howard, Bruce,	Lib.
Labelle		Okanagan Boundary	
Cantin, Jean-Charles,	Lib.		
Louis-Hébert		Isabelle, Gaston,	Lib.
Clermont, Gaston,	Lib.	Hull	
Gatineau		Jamieson, Hon. Donald C.,	Lib.
Côté, Florian	Lib.	Burin-Burgeo	
Richelieu			
Côté, Hon. Jean-Pierre,	Lib.	Knowles, Stanley,	N.D.P.
Longueuil		Winnipeg North Centre	
Cullen, Jack,	Lib.	Laing, Hon. Arthur,	Lib.
Sarnia		Vancouver South	
Cyr, Alexandre,	Lib.	Lang, Hon. Otto E.,	Lib.
Gaspé		Saskatoon-Humboldt	
Danson, Barney,	Lib.	Laniel, Gérald,	Lib.
York-North		Beauharnois	
Deachman, Grant,	Lib.	Lefebvre, T.,	Lib.
Vancouver Quadra		Pontiac	
Deakon, Walter,	Lib.	Legault, Carl,	Lib.
High Park		Nipissing	
De Bané, Pierre,	Lib.	Lessard, H.-Pit,	Lib.
Matane		LaSalle	
Douglas, T.C.	N.D.P.	Lessard, Marcel,	Lib.
Nanaimo-Cowichan-The Is-		Lac-Saint-Jean	
lands		Lewis, David,	N.D.P.
Drury, Hon C.M.,	Lib.	York South	
Westmount		Loiselle, Gerard,	Lib.
Fairweather, R. Gordon L.,	P.C.	Saint Henri	
Fundy-Royal		MacEachen, Hon Allan J.,	Lib.
Forest, Yves,	Lib.	Cape Breton Highlands-Canso	
Missisquoi		MacGuigan, Mark,	Lib.
Forget, Victor,	Lib.	Windsor-Walkerville	
Saint-Michel		MacInnis, Mrs Grace,	N.D.P.
Gibson, Colin D.,	Lib.	Vancouver-Kingsway	
Hamilton-Wentworth		Macquarrie, Health,	P.C.
Gillespie, Alastair,	Lib.	Hillsborough	
Etobicoke		McCleave, Robert,	P.C.
Gleave, A.P.,	N.D.P.	Halifax-East Hants	
Saskatoon-Biggar		McIlraith, Hon. G. J.,	Lib.
Goode, Tom H.,	Lib.	Ottawa Centre	
Burnaby-Richmond		Mahoney, P.M.,	Lib.
Goyer, Jean-Pierre,	Lib.	Calgary South	
Dollard		Major, Robert B.,	Lib.
Gray, H.E.,	Lib.	Argenteuil	
Windsor West		Marceau, Gilles,	Lib.
Guilbault, Jacques,	Lib.	Lapointe	
Saint-Jacques		Marchand, Hon. Jean,	Lib.
Harkness, Hon. D.S.,	P.C.	Langelier	
Calgary Centre		Marchand, Len,	Lib.
Hellyer, Hon. Paul,	Lib.	Kamloops-Cariboo	
Trinity		Mather, Barry,	N.D.P.
Honey, Russell C.,	Lib.	Surrey	
Northumberland-Durham		Morison, J.B.,	Lib.
		Halton-Wentworth	

Nowlan, J.P., *Annapolis Valley*	P.C.
Nystrom, Lorne, *Yorkton-Melville*	N.D.P.
O'Connell, Martin P., *Scarborough East*	Lib.
Olson, Hon. H.A., *Medicine Hat*	Lib.
Orange, R. J., *Northwest Territories*	Lib.
Orlikow, David, *Winnipeg North*	N.D.P.
Pelletier, Hon. Gérard, *Hochelaga*	Lib.
Pépin, Hon. Jean-Luc, *Drummond*	Lib.
Perrault, Ray, *Burnaby-Seymour*	Lib.
Pilon, Bernard, *Chambly*	Lib.
Portelance, Arthur, *Gamelin*	Lib.
Pringle, Jerry, *Fraser Valley East*	Lib.
Prud'homme, Marcel, *Saint-Denis*	Lib.
Ritchie, Gordon, *Dauphin*	P.C.
Roberts, John, *York-Simcoe*	Lib.
Rochon, Jean L., *Ahuntsic*	Lib.
Rock, Raymond, *Lachine*	Lib.
Rose, Mark, *Fraser Valley West*	N.D.P.
Roy, Jean R., *Timmins*	Lib.
Roy, Marcel, *Laval*	Lib.

Saltsman, Max, *Waterloo*	N.D.P.
Schreyer, Ed, *Selkirk*	N.D.P.
Serré, Gaétan J., *Nickel Belt*	Lib.
Sharp, Hon. Mitchell, *Eglinton*	Lib.
Smith, G.A. Percy, *Northumberland-Miramichi*	Lib.
Smith, Walter, *Saint-Jean*	Lib.
Stafford, H.E., *Elgin*	Lib.
Stewart, Douglas, *Okanagan-Kootenay*	Lib.
St. Pierre, Paul, *Coast Chilcotin*	Lib.
Thomas, Antonio, *Maisonneuve*	Lib.
Trudeau, Right Hon. P.E., *Mount Royal*	Lib.
Trudel, Jacques L., *Bourassa*	Lib.
Turner, Charles, *London East*	Lib.
Turner, Hon. John N., *Ottawa-Carleton*	Lib.
Wahn, Ian, *St.Paul's*	Lib.
Walker, J.E., *York Centre*	Lib.
Watson, Ian, *Laprairie*	Lib.
Weatherhead, David, *Scarborough West*	Lib.
Whiting, R.L., *Halton*	Lib.
Winch, Harold E., *Vancouver East*	N.D.P.

APPENDIX VII

List of members opposed to Bill C-150 at the final vote on the entire bill, May 14, 1969.

Alkenbrack	Danforth
Beaudoin	Diefenbaker
Bigg	Dinsdale
Caouette	Dionne
Coates	Flemming
Code	Forrestall
Crouse	Fortin

Gauthier
Godin
Grills
Gundlock
Hales
Howe
Lambert (Edmonton West)
La Salle
Latulippe
MacEwan
MacInnis (Cape Breton-East Richmond)
McCutcheon
McGrath
McIntosh
McKinley
McQuaid
Marshall
Matte
Mazankowski

Muir (Cape Breton — The Sydneys)
Muir (Lisgar)
Nesbitt
Noble
Paproski
Peddle
Ricard
Rodrigue
Rondeau
Rynard
Schumacher
Scott
Simpson
Southam
Stewart (Marquette)
Tétrault
Thomas (Moncton)
Thompson (Red Deer)
Valade
Yewchuk — 53

APPENDIX VIII

Bishops of Manitoba, October, 1971
Respect of Human Life

A Pastoral Declaration of the Roman Catholic Bishops of Manitoba
on the issue of Abortion

(1) One of the most distressing facts of life today is the increase in the number
of abortions. This destruction of human life shocks and offends many Manito-
bans, who ask what the Bishops of this province are thinking and doing about
it. Has the teaching of the Church changed? What sort of actions do the Bishops
propose? In this Declaration, we want to give a clear indication of our stand.

(2) As teachers of the Lord's word, we think immediately of the Gospel message:
"You shall love your neighbor... you shall not kill."

As pastors, we are anxious that every Christian may be aware of the duty
to respect life and not destroy it.

As fellow citizens, we wish to orient the efforts of Christians toward
collaboration in all enterprises aimed at the common good through service of
life.

A NEW HUMAN LIFE

(3) Most of the facts about abortion are simple enough.

Everyone knows that the sexual union of man and woman may result in
fertilization, when male sperm and female ovum unite. The living single cell zygote
thus produced contains substances from both parents, but is different from any
cell in either parent.

We therefore speak of new human life from this time of conception because
there is abundant scientific knowledge of the developmental process by which
the zygote becomes, in turn, blastocyst, embryo, foetus, and is born, walks, talks,
plays, and comes to live across the street as friend and neighboor.

Because of our prior knowledge of this entire process, we say human life
begins at conception. Pregnancy is a sign that another person is developing within
the woman's body.

Abortion eliminates that developing human life.

(4) We share the Christian conviction expressed in the ancient Letter of Barnabas: "You shall love your neighbor more than your own life. You shall not cause death to the child in its mother's womb. Neither shall you kill the child after its birth." In more modern terms, we say: There should be utmost respect for the marvellous gift of human life.

But, is this respect central in our approach to life? Does our civil law protect life? Or, does present legislation contribute to a deterioration of respect for life?

CIVIL LAW AND LIFE

(5) Let us look at our laws. Since 1969, Canada has had a law that seeks to regulate abortion by forbidding it except when an approved hospital committee agrees that continuation of pregnancy would endanger, or would be likely to endanger, the life or health of the mother.

(6) It is well known that an increasing number of abortions are being performed under this law. Still, there is a massive publicity campaign aimed at again changing the Canadian law, so that it would regulate abortions even less than at present, or not at all.

In the face of this campaign, our convictions are clear: Human life, even unborn, should be protected by civil law.

A law that made abortion easier would represent a reversal of what has become a major concern of legislators. They have been striving to write laws that recognize and defend the value and essential quality of every human life. Even the lives of criminals are respected, as in our laws limiting the use of capital punishment. An easing of restraints on abortions would go counter to this legislative trend. As for complete removal of legal protection of the unborn, this would result in a body of laws that proclaimed, by omission, that some forms of human life need not be respected and safeguarded.

(7) Abortion is thus linked to the nightmarish notion that one can end another's life because the presence of that other is unwelcome for any number of reasons. In face of this, we insist that with regard to abortion true morality and legal sanctions are on two quite different levels. Current laws or customs are not the determinants of the Christian's moral judgment. Gospel insights are. Therefore we said with all the Canadian bishops in a 1970 statement that

"...abortion is primarily a moral question, and never just a matter of civil law or of civil rights. No matter what the civil law may say, to procure an abortion is to be involved in an act that is objectively evil from a moral point of view."

(8) Besides striving to maintain the civil law's protection of the unborn we must all live and work in such a way that more and more people will find abortion less and less acceptable. This we will do more by service and leadership than by protest, necessary as opposition sometimes is.

NEIGHBOR-CENTRED APPROACH

(9) The recourse to easy abortion reflects a philosophy of life that is too common even among Christians: As much comfort as possible with as little effort as possible. This self-centred outlook has to be replaced by a neighbor-centred one, on a much broader front than abortion and its immediate causes, if we are to be credible land effective in the struggle against abortion as well.

(10) Anyone who examines modern society from a truly neighbor-centred viewpoint is struck by the large number of people who live as less than complete self-conscious free human beings. Besides the unborn, one thinks of the retarded, the handicapped, the sick, and many of the aged. One must also think of those whose life chances are limited by poverty, joblessness, discrimination, and lack of full social acceptance.

As your bishops, we cannot encourage you to defend relentlessly the human rights of the unborn without also trying to awaken your sense of respect and compassion for all human life, and especially for those who are weaker and less able to defend and advance their own welfare.

(11) Individual concern and action in these many areas, though imperative, are not enough. Today's Christian must be present, with generosity and skill, in the many social groups and public forums where ideas are shaped and decisions made that either respect life or degrade it. One thinks of Parliament, the provincial legislature, municipal councils, boards and executives of numerous businesses, agencies, organizations, welfare services, hospitals, schools, and communication media.

(12) In these areas, men and women — legislators, business leaders, workers, doctors, lawyers, teachers, counsellors, parents, and all young people — should be seized by a profound sense of their responsibility to love and serve life. Lay Christians have a special mission in this regard, as they are called to seek salvation by engaging in temporal affairs and building them up according to the plan of God. In this way they are the Church in places where they alone are present. Through such involvements, they will come to realize and live, more and more fully, this fact of sharing in the Church's mission in the world. We pastors, in turn, priests and bishops, have our own special responsibilities, to inspire, enable and sustain these very endeavors that increase respect for life and promote its true service.

A CALL FOR INVOLVEMENT BY ALL

(13) After these general considerations, we must mention responsible sexuality, responsible parenthood, and aid to women distressed by pregnancy as three areas of particular urgency at this time.

(14) Major efforts must be made in homes and schools to help young people define and live their sexuality integrally and maturely, learning to acquire a balance of expression and restraint. Parents and teachers cannot remain silent and inactive in a society that screams out a one-sided call to sexual permissiveness. Young people need the views and values of those who can bring forward the insights of authentic life, in an atmosphere of respect and trust. The experiences of Christian love and life have much to offer in this regard.

(15) There is a tendency in many public discussions to include abortion in considerations of responsible family planning. This tendency must be opposed. Abortion may never be accepted as a means of family planning because it involves destruction of life already begun.

The sincerity of Catholics who oppose abortion is often challenged on the ground that they do not seem to be equally concerned about irresponsible parenthood. Indeed, an adequate pedagogy for responsible parenthood has often been neglected in pastoral work. This should be corrected by active programs to develop personnel and other resources relating to responsible parenthood.

(16) Finally, all of us must probe more deeply into the difficulties that bring women to the point of seeking to solve problems by means of abortion. We cannot all be specialists in finding solutions to personal distress, but all of us can in some way help to alleviate suffering.

There are organizations to aid the unwed mother during her pregnancy. There are crisis centres to help women find the assistance and support they need in order to decide against abortion. Such efforts must have the support of all.

(17) We wish to compliment and thank the laity of Manitoba for the initiatives they have already taken in many of these crucial areas of respect for life. They are actually involved in day-to-day affairs, professional and lay, and are often

best placed to discern the ways in which human life is degraded in our society, as well as the ways in which it can be better served. They have provided information and stimulated reflection on the urgency of the abortion problem, so that others have been able to grasp it.

(18) May we all thus live up to the challenge of the Gospel: "You are the light of the world." No one can live in this way by human effort alone. So that our endeavours may accord with God's will and bring it to pass, let us all pray for enlightenment and strength, with a fervor that matches the seriousness of the challenges we face.

This day of November, 1971.

> George Bernard Cardinal Flahiff, C.S.B., Archbishop of Winnipeg
> Maxim Hermaniuk, C.SS.R., Metropolitan Archbishop for the Ukrainians
> Maurice Baudoux, Archbishop of Saint Boniface
> Paul Dumouchel, O.M.I., Archbishop of The Pas
> Omer Robidoux, O.M.I., Bishop of Churchill
> Antoine Hacault, Auxiliary Bishop of Saint Boniface

REFERENCES:

(2)   Lk. 10:27 (cf. Lev. 19:18; Mat. 5:43; Rom. 13:8-10); Mt. 5:21 (cf. Ex. 20:13).

(4)   *Contraception.* History of its treatment by the Catholic Theologians and Canonists, NOONAN, John (1965). Belknap Press, Harvard, p. 87.

(5)   Cf. Criminal Code, art. 237 and the 1968-69 Law modifying the penal code no. 18.

(7)   Bishops' Plenary Assembly, 19.9.70: cf. *ÉGLISE CANADIENNE* (1970), vol. 3, n. 10, p. 327.

(8)   Mt. 5:14.

APPENDIX IX

Abortion in the Christian Tradition

Pre-Christian Law:

Among pre-Christian laws, the Sumerian Code (2000 B.C.), the Code of Hammurabi (1800 B.C.), the Assyrian Code (1500 B.C.), and the Hittite Code (1300 B.C.) all contain penalties for causing abortions. The legislation in the Vendidad of ancient Persia (not older than 600 B.C.) warned a pregnant woman not to terminate a pregnancy. If she did, both she and the infant's father would be charged with murder. Among the Greeks no specific statute against abortion has been found though indirect evidence of the 9th and 6th centuries indicate that it was penalized. The Hippocratic oath, recently changed in Canada to accommodate the new morality, warned against administering abortion-causing drugs. With the advent of Christianity abortion came to be condemned both as a crime and a serious sin.

> "Abortion was classed by the Church as murder, because it effected the death of a human person, albeit unborn. In opposition to Roman

---

* A full exposition may be found in Roger Huser, *The Crime of Abortion in Canon Law,* (Wash., 1942), and in abbreviated version in Paul Harrington, *Linacre Quarterly,* February 1968, pp. 43-61, on whom this survey relies. See also Chapter R of Germain Grisez, *Abortion: the Myths, the Realities and the Arguments,* Corpus Books, 1970.

law position that abortion violated the rights of others (especially of the father), the Church condemned abortion as a violation of the rights of the unborn." (Huser as quoted by Harrington, p. 43)

Early Christian Writers:

The *Didache* (90-100 A.D.) tersely commands "Thou shalt not kill the foetus by an abortion." This same prohibition is found in the *Pseudo-Barnabas Epistle* (before 132 A.D.) and in the *Canones Ecclesiastici S.S. Apostolorum* (C. 300 A.D.). The *Apostolic Constitutions* (C. 400 A.D.), while repeating the previous directives, add that the formed foetus possesses a soul and it would be murder to dispose of it.

In the East, Athenagoras stated about 177 A.D. that Christians believed that women who resorted to abortion were guilty of homicide. In the West, such third century church fathers as Tertullian, Minucius Felix, Cyprian and Hippolytus all considered the intentional killing of the unborn child to be murder.

Church Councils:

The statements of the early Christian Fathers were followed by the condemnations of the Councils of the Fourth Century. In the West the first Council to do so was the Council of Elvira, held in Spain (300 A.D.). The first Eastern Council to consider and legislate penalties for abortion was the Council of Ancyra in 314 A.D. Canon 21 stipulated:

> Women who prostitute themselves, and who kill the children thus begotten, or who try to destroy them when in their wombs, are by ancient law excommunicated to the end of their lives. We, however, have softened their punishment, and condemned them to the various appointed degrees of penance for ten years.

This statute was the basis for most of the subsequent legislation in the Church down to the Middle Ages.

The answers given to canonical questions by St. Basil the Great, (written in 374 and 375 A.D. were considered in the East to have great importance and influence. Canon 2, concerning abortion, states:

> A woman who deliberately destroys a foetus is answerable for murder. And any fine distinction as to its being completely formed or unformed is not admissible amongst us...

In Canon 8, St. Basil observes:

> And so women who give drugs that cause abortion are themselves also murderers as well as those who take the poisons that kill the foetus.

In 524 A.D., the Council of Lerida in Spain, legislated penalties against those who succeeded in killing or who even attempted to kill a child, whether born or unborn. The Synod held at Constantinople in 692 A.D. repeated the reply of St. Basil regarding cooperators in the crime of abortion and explicitly stated that these were subject to the penalties for murder. Although the above-mentioned legislation was adopted at particular or regional Councils, it became the law not only of that region but of the universal Church. It formed the basis for all legislation on the subject of abortion up to the twelfth Century.

In the Greek Church an outstanding canonical collection was made in the year 883 A.D. and recognized as the official law in the Eastern Church in 920 A.D. It continues to enjoy this recognition to the present day. The legislation on abortion, as incorporated in the Collection of Photius and also found in the Pedahon and in the Sacred Canons, is recognized even today by the Greek Orthodox Church as its official law.

The Council statutes of the Eastern Church were introduced into the West by the so-called Italian Canonical Collection. With reference to abortion it quoted Canon 21 of the Council of Ancyra which also appeared in the African, Spanish and Frankish Collections. In 1140 A.D. Gratian collected all existing canonical texts into his famous *Decretum*. He concluded that abortion of an animated foetus is definitely murder and carries the penalties of homicide, while that of a non-animated foetus is not murder. Here one has to remember that throughout the Middle Ages there was acceptance of the distinction between the animated or formed and the non-animated or non-formed foetus. Having no scientific data, Aristotle's theory that life became present after the fortieth day after conception for the male child and on the ninetieth day after conception for the female child was accepted, also because it seemed to be a rough confirmation of when mothers first felt movement in their womb.

Modern science, of course, disproved this distinction by showing that life is present from the very beginning, and that this life is distinct from that of the mother.

Among other penitential and canonical legislation too numerous to mention there are two important constitutions concerning abortion issued within 3 years of each other: in 1588 and 1591. According to the last the penalty for an abortion of an animated foetus was automatic excommunication which could only be lifted by the Bishop. This brings us to the date 1869, which strangely enough, has on various occasions been given as the date of the first condemnation of abortion. In that year Pope Pius IX issued the Constitution *Apostolicae Sedis* which was solely concerned with censures and penalties such as excommunication. Regarding the penalties for abortion he disallowed the distinction between animated and nonanimated fetus and by implication extended the penalty of excommunication to any abortion. As already noted, science today confirms that life begins immediately after conception. Conclusion: Throughout its history, the Christian Church has held that it is a serious sin to destroy the foetus at any stage of its development.

Index

Y